MISSION TO TEACH

MISSION TO TEACH

THE LIFE AND LEGACY OF
A REVOLUTIONARY
EDUCATOR

DIPAK BASU

JBF Books

MISSION TO TEACH

Published by JBF Books,
 an imprint of the Jhumki Basu Foundation
www.jbfbooks.org

Library of Congress Catalog Number: 2013930379

ISBN: 978-0-9888385-0-5

Printed in the United States of America by
Thomson Reuters Book Publishing & Distribution

This book is dedicated to
"Jhumki's kids"

Also by the author

A Flight of Green Parrots

TABLE OF CONTENTS

FOREWORD

This is a powerful, beautifully written book. It is a heart-wrenching testament to a brilliant woman from her father—well, from her parents, for her mother is right there with her husband throughout. How I suffered with them and Jhumki's husband when I heard of her brave battle with cancer that, in the end, was lost. For I too have watched a loved one, my husband Derek, suffer and lose his battle with this horrible disease. But he was over sixty, and Jhumki was only thirty-one, cut off part way through an astonishingly successful career.

I learned about Jhumki's work with marginalized youth when I was invited by the Jhumki Basu Foundation, created in her memory, to give a talk at the second annual Sci-Ed Innovators Expo and Symposium in 2011. There I met her parents, and we had time to sit quietly together and talk about Jhumki and her work before I had to go to the lectern.

Thus during my lecture I was able to say, with conviction, "Jhumki and I would have got on well together." After reading this book, I can assert that with even more confidence that, although our careers took different paths, we shared many interests and passions.

For one thing, as children we both had loving families, and we both showed early interest in—and curiosity about—the natural world. Jhumki was four years old when she asked her father why snow was white and was given her first physics lesson! And I was four when, during a holiday on a farm, I began asking everyone how—and where—an egg got out of a hen. No one was prepared to explain this to me, so I hid in a henhouse and waited there for about four hours until I found the answer for myself. And although my mother had not given me my first lesson in reproductive biology, she did sit down and listen to my

i

story—rather than reprimanding me for making the whole household so concerned about where I was that they called the police!

Jhumki was eighteen when she set off to make the first-ever study on homelessness in post-Soviet Russia, and she was shocked by the poverty and terrible conditions endured by so many people, especially orphans. It was this experience that led to her determination to help disadvantaged children. I was eighteen when I spent six months helping my physiotherapist aunt, who ran the region's clinic for children with physical disabilities. I developed a deep empathy for many of them and was shocked by the discrimination I so often noticed when disabled people were around. And then, when I was twenty-three, I had my first experience of the injustice and cruelty of apartheid in South Africa and, on a less extreme level, in East Africa. And it was these experiences that led to my determination to include disabled and disadvantaged children when I began the environmental and humanitarian program for youth, Jane Goodall's Roots & Shoots.

Jhumki made the most of every day of college life—she actually managed to do a master's degree and a PhD at the same time, while starting her own school and teaching full-time. She was fighting to introduce a revolutionary idea: including students in curriculum development. She wanted to teach science to inner-city youth as she felt it should be taught. She wanted to ensure that students were engaged, listened to, and empowered. Students loved her, and eventually academia listened to her. Through and through, she was a teacher. She learned to know each student by name. She believed in them. She found ways to make them want to learn—in some cases seemingly for the first time. Her innovative methods made it fun for students to learn science and helped them and their teachers to realize that it was not a subject just for privileged children in private schools.

And so I know Jhumki would have appreciated the fact that Roots & Shoots is all about empowering youth in all walks of life. It began in Tanzania and included children in rural primary schools. These children had no electricity, no running water, no hygienic latrines, and sometimes no books. One teacher sometimes had to teach two different "waves" of pupils because there were far more children than the school could hold. Once a R&S group was formed, some of those children began to share their dreams for the future and to discuss ways in which they might move toward seeing dream become reality. When R&S was started in America, two of the areas where it was piloted were poor inner-city primary schools—in South Central Los Angeles and in the Bronx—and a third was an alternative high school in Danbury, Connecticut.

The main message of R&S is that every individual makes a difference, every day—and we have a choice as to what kind of difference we will make. The program's members (all ages from kindergarten through college and university) choose their own projects to help people, animals, and the environment. This provides hands-on learning experience and emphasizes that the members will really benefit only if they have fun when doing their projects.

Yes, Jhumki would have loved Roots & Shoots, just as l love learning about her way of involving youth and teachers alike in hands-on science projects, and hearing about how her enthusiasm and ideas affected students and faculty alike. She knew, as I know, that the energy, commitment, and dedication of young people, once they understand problems and are empowered to take action—that is, once we listen to them—are boundless. It is exciting that thanks to Jhumki's parents, the Jhumki Basu Foundation will be working with R&S on environmental projects at schools in the New York area to make this a better world.

Finally, Jhumki and I would have got on because of our mutual love for animals and the natural world. Of course, it was my chosen career—living with and observing chimpanzees, analysing my findings, and writing books—whereas Jhumki dedicated her life to teaching. But in one of her journals, quoted in this book, we read just how much it meant to her when she spent part of her honeymoon in Botswana's Chobe National Park in a tent deep in the bush. And she loved wildness. In another quotation from her journal, written in Nicaragua, she says, "I hope that there remain only a few paths, meant for walking (not cars) around the periphery of the forest, and that the center remains a secret lagoon, only for the jaguar and not even for the biologist." This is how I feel, except that I want to be part of that secret place, though not as a biologist.

At the same time she writes that she would like to die in the forest, disappear into the loam of the forest floor, so that she could nurture "fresh-smelling tall trees that sustain bromeliads that sustain frogs and so on." And I once wrote a poem in which I declared, passionately, that I wanted to die out in the natural world, to be killed by some great wild beast, to become a part of the cycle of life and death. When I wrote that I was just a child, though the horrors of World War II and the Holocaust had made death seem very real. But for Jhumki death was up close and personal: when she wrote those lines, she was already fighting cancer.

How I would love to have met Jhumki, to have sat and talked with her about the things we both cared about. How electric would have been our meeting, our dialogue, our shared dreams of helping young people to achieve their potential, that they might become good stewards of planet Earth. I wish there were a way I could tell her how her story has inspired me, and to thank her. Perhaps, though, she knows.

The tragedy of her death is a loss to the world. Her passion, her energy, her brilliant mind, and her innovative approach to education are inspirational. Even though her life was cut short so cruelly, she achieved so much. Once she was diagnosed with cancer, it seems she gained additional funds of energy and determination, with the knowledge that she had to achieve her life's goals in a short period of time. We cannot tell what her other achievements might have been, but, as this book illustrates so well, Jhumki's legacy is assured. Sci-Ed Innovators, the movement toward equity in science education for poor urban kids, is a lasting legacy of Jhumki's work and life.

Jane Goodall, PhD, DBE
Founder, The Jane Goodall Institute
UN Messenger of Peace
www.janegoodall.org

A NOTE TO THE READER

Long-haired, reflective, and riveting with his scratchy voice, Billy Green did not allow a traumatic childhood, which included drug-addict parents and homelessness, to quench his abiding desire to improve the lives of disadvantaged young people like himself. After earning an undergraduate degree in chemistry, Billy followed his passion and became a teacher. In 2009 he took a graduate-level science education course at New York University, where he learned about the path breaking work in motivational teaching of a young NYU professor who had died a few months earlier. The following year he became a Sci-Ed Fellow in a yearlong program of the Jhumki Basu Foundation.

Right after completing a Sci-Ed summer workshop in 2010, Billy got caught in gang-related crossfire and was shot in the neck. As he recovered and reflected in a hospital room, he decided to become a science teacher in a setting tougher even than the mean streets he grew up on: the New York City jail at Rikers Island.

Two years later Billy told me a story about how Jhumki's work influenced him to allow students to bring their own experiences into the teaching process and thereby motivate themselves to learn. Faced with an introductory science class of hostile and disinterested inmates with reading levels from first to twelfth grade, Billy drew deeply from his grounding in democratic teaching and asked the class what the fastest thing in the world was.

"A bullet, man!" an inmate replied and everyone agreed.

Then, using the bullet paradigm, the class of convicted drug dealers, rapists, and murderers launched enthusiastically into calculating velocity, momentum, acceleration, and angles involved in escaping the police.

The voice and keyboard of Professor Sreyashi Jhumki Basu are still. To her students Jhumki was a fount of inspiration and compassion, to her colleagues an original researcher and teacher, to her friends a witty and irreverent person. She strove to be the perfect life partner for her husband.

To us, her parents, she was our baby.

In her mission to teach, Jhumki lived and died for her kids, those millions of invisible young men and women of beleaguered urban schools of our great country. Her kids were tough teenage immigrants and minorities, troubled and unguided, often from violent environments, unable to break out of a vicious cycle of neglect and poverty without a helping hand. Jhumki offered a helping hand and a powerful teaching paradigm to the students of New York City's embattled boroughs of Brooklyn, Queens, and the Bronx; of Manhattan's frenetic Harlem neighborhood; of forgotten and impoverished East Palo Alto, East Menlo Park, and Redwood City schools of wealthy Silicon Valley; and of the enormous black township of Soweto, formed from apartheid in South Africa. She showed her students there how to become college-ready through a love of science, and how to bring change to their lives and their communities.

And, as they evolved from school dropouts to college graduates, her students grew to adore a teacher who was not afraid to get close to them. The years passed, and a generation of determined science teachers followed in her footsteps to blaze a new way of teaching that made going to school enjoyable for themselves and for their students.

Jhumki's aura did not fade when the inexorable loom of cancer overwhelmed her defenses at the age of thirty-one. It endures in the impressionable young men and women from poor homes of New York and California. It endures in dedicated science teachers and college researchers whom she inspired. It endures in her movement for a better tomorrow.

Jhumki's story must be told.

My wife Radha and I have marveled and cheered and wept as we watched our indomitable daughter's passage through this world. It is heart-rending, if not impossible, for a parent to maintain objectivity while writing a story such as hers. It is only with Jhumki's own voice guiding me through extensive journal entries, augmented by voices of a multitude of collaborators, that I proudly—and sadly—present her story in these pages.

PROLOGUE

From the Journal of Jhumki Basu

San José, Costa Rica, March 17, 2007

W hen I am gone, I hope these remain—the toucan, the raptor, the hummingbird so small that it seems impossibly alive. I hope that there remain only a few paths, meant for walking (not cars) around the periphery of the forest, and that the center remains a secret lagoon, only for the jaguar and not even for the biologist.

At night I hope we are in terror of no lights and venomous fer-de-lance and colorful amphibians springing and slithering as none of us can. And that in the afternoons the scarlet macaws crunch away on the seeds of almond trees, always in pairs or triads or quartets, not alone and away from their blue sky element instead in cages solitary.

I hope that the capuchin never touches a human hand for bread but remains fiercely wild, recognizing its likeness to us but protecting its difference. And that spider monkeys and lichens— indicators of the health of the jungle—blossom richly instead of disappearing silently in mysterious ways.

If I had children, this is what I would hope for them, a world to recognize the five safe mushrooms, dodge army ants and spot fishing spiders. I know you think my children would be unusual but I think that all kids should learn about how bats are misunderstood.

This is where I would die, hoping to disappear quickly into a sheen netting, like the leaves on the floor sustaining fresh-smelling tall trees that sustain bromeliads that sustain frogs and so on. I would be with the leaf and the mycorrhizae of the fungus without which there would be nothing but plain red clay soil.

On a balmy September evening in 2008, I was walking my daughter to the first fall session of the Teaching Methods course at New York University.

We threaded our way through a welter of undergraduates, out enjoying the late autumn warmth on the way to classes or dinner, blissfully chatting about exams, dinner plans, Rihanna's latest hit, dorm parties, dates, boyfriends and girlfriends. We entered NYU's Silver Center and rode a packed elevator up to the eighth floor and into a classroom.

For this important day, Professor Jhumki Basu wore a black blouse, faded jeans, and a black-and-grey jacket. With the end of chemotherapy, a soft sheen of hair gave her a stylish European look. She was heart-stoppingly thin. Her eyes were cavernous.

I put down her heavy backpack and looked around uncertainly.

"You can stay, Baba," she told me. "Join the class."

I subsided at a table, and soon twenty-eight students filled the room, twenty-nine counting me. All except me were graduate students. All except me were teachers or teachers-to-be.

In spite of her frailty, Jhumki stage-managed the class with complete aplomb. Her bearing was straight. Her voice was strong. Her preparation was immaculate. I watched in disbelief as we sat around tables, drew up semester plans on customized brown-paper bags, and excitedly held group discussions. After a while I relaxed and concentrated on what was being said. Then I surprised myself by suggesting something about training methodology from my work experience at Cisco Systems. Everyone turned to me and paid attention. I felt accepted, talked some more, and was beginning to enjoy myself when it hit me with a shock.

Democratic pedagogy!

Jhumki's teaching model was actually working on *me*. There she was, using my funds of knowledge, to lure me into what she wanted me to learn. The light bulb was still on above my head when our table became a sea of smoke. Dr. Basu had released dry ice to introduce an experiment, and grinned as her students shied away from the fumes. The smoke dissipated. The discussions became debates. The teachers talked about their students and tossed forth teaching suggestions that were deftly captured on pieces of paper and stuffed into the waiting brown-paper bags. No idea was lost. Everyone set goals for the class. Everyone had a good time. On that day I joined Jhumki's band of admirers and wondered, like everyone else: *How does she do it?*

Three months later, on a cold December night, Jhumki was fifteen minutes late for the final session of the same class. Her co-instructor, Dr. Verneda Johnson, had formed the twenty-eight students into teams at five tables when Jhumki and I walked into the classroom.

Just as in the session I had attended earlier with her, energetic discussion was underway at all the tables. Verneda and several students smiled greetings to their professor. Jhumki nodded back without emotion. The conversations did not miss a beat. As I unobtrusively settled into a corner, Verneda told me that the topic of discussion for the day was use of slang in developing relationships.

Jhumki walked over to a table, sat down, and leaned back in her chair. She appeared withdrawn and on the verge of falling asleep. I was concerned but knew her well enough not to intrude unless asked. Then, as I watched, I realized she was listening intently to the conversation at the table and was in complete sync with her students. Knowing how her mind worked, I could imagine the gears clicking in her brain while she analyzed and correlated the circulating ideas. At a break in the conversation she stood up.

"You know, guys," she said, "all this stuff's way cool. But I haven't heard anything about how a teacher can really, and I mean *really,* stimulate students into critical thinking. How can you get into their *culture?"*

The six men and women at her table looked at their professor's ashen face. They were mostly in their twenties, working toward graduate degrees in education, all current or future schoolteachers, all passionate and optimistic about their chosen profession, all dedicated to the difficult task of serving teenagers in marginalized neighborhoods of America. Their faces showed concern for their teacher, whose tall and gaunt figure was visibly frail, whose grey visage and sunken cheeks bore witness to unremitting pain. But there was no pity in their expressions. They knew about the cancer, and they had from the outset, fallen in with their professor's manner of ignoring the disease.

Two months earlier, at a reception celebrating Dr. Basu's tenure and promotion to associate professor at NYU in an unprecedented two years, this class had presented her with a colorful poster that read as follows:

> *Dear Jhumki,*
>
> *If one day we become great teachers, it will be because we followed your lead. You have modeled excellence, resiliency, and compassion to us all. We will always remember you.*
>
> *NYU Methods Students.*

Now, having secured their attention, Jhumki told the students at her table, "Look, I've been reading about teen dynamics. How about we try this? 'Black kids often refer to each other as nigger.'"

There was dead silence. Then a deluge of reaction.

"*What?*" asked an incredulous white student.

"Omigod! We can't use *that* stuff!" burst out a greying

veteran of the New York City school system.

"Of course we can, and we do!" retorted a lanky, dreadlocked Jamaican with a Caribbean accent. "Walk any street in Kingston. You'll see."

After ten minutes of vigorous debate, a new teacher from Detroit schools said, "Man, you know what? You gotta get *real* close to your kids and understand their backgrounds if you want *that* kind of interaction. You gotta be at *their* level in the class."

Throughout the exchange Jhumki had stood stiffly with a straight, almost wooden visage. But a gleam in her eyes—which broke my heart and made me want to go and hug her—betrayed the pleasure of seeing her class duel with creative ideas about student participation in their curriculum development, a mainstay of her teaching philosophy.

"*Good* conclusion, folks!" she said. "Keep going. This is hot stuff!" and went over to another table.

The class ended at 9 p.m., but no one wanted to leave without discussing his or her plans for the next semester with Dr. Basu. Jhumki listened to each student's ideas and aspirations with undivided attention and offered suggestions for his or her career goals. It was 9:45 before the last student departed. Still she would not leave and helped Verneda and me clear the debris of end-of-semester snacks and replace chairs and tables. Walking between us along dark and freezing streets of Greenwich Village, she chatted about lesson plans for the next semester. Before saying good-bye to Verneda, she scheduled a meeting for the following Tuesday.

"We'll discuss learnings from this class at my office, okay? Oh, and we'll try and make some serious improvements . . ." I steered her carefully around a scaffolding support in the middle of the sidewalk ". . . or maybe we'll meet in that hospital in case they want to keep me for some silly reason."

Verneda, a science teacher from the Isaac Newton Middle

School for Math and Science in Harlem, has a big laugh and an even bigger heart. She would have been stunned to know why her colleague had been delayed for class that night.

Radiation treatment for breast cancer that had metastasized to Jhumki's brain had run late. While waiting with her mother for the X-ray machine to be set up in the radiology lab, Jhumki had been utterly determined. Nothing, absolutely nothing, was going to keep her away from her last class of the semester. Even blinding radiation that caused intense nausea had not fazed her after she checked out of New York's Memorial Hospital and her husband Alexander drove us to NYU. She had allowed me to accompany her to class and carry her backpack, heavy with omnipresent laptop, only because dangerously high ammonia levels in her bloodstream caused her to wobble into obstacles.

On the following Tuesday, December 16, Jhumki missed her meeting with Verneda. But she kept another important appointment.

Angela Calabrese Barton, her PhD advisor and mentor, arrived in New York that morning with Edna Tan, Jhumki's close friend and colleague. The two professors had come from Michigan for a pre-arranged meeting with Jhumki and, upon learning that she was in hospital, they went directly from the airport to her bedside. When they arrived, Jhumki's blood pressure was falling and her pulse was thready. She was on partial oxygen, breathing mechanically, sedated against pain, unable to speak or to open her eyes. Horror-struck, Angie and Edna, sitting on either side of Jhumki's bed, held her hands and told her something that meant the world to her. They promised to complete the textbook on democratic science teaching for which Jhumki had conducted and recorded all field research.

Jhumki acknowledged by pressing Angie's hand.

Four hours later she was gone.

PART I

THE FORMATIVE YEARS

"A healthy young lady with fire-soaked eyes, consumed with ideas of changing the world, Jhumki always positioned herself in a place of determination."

Prof David E. Kirkland
At the memorial of Jhumki Basu
New York University
December 18, 2008

"My first hobby in life was to bang dishes together on Sunday mornings."

From "Autobiography"
An essay by Jhumki Basu, age 11
September 1989

1. TO CHANGE A LIFE

"I first met Jhumki when she was a senior at Castilleja School in Palo Alto," said Condoleezza Rice.

"It was 1994. I was the keynote speaker at the school's graduation event, where she was a salutatorian speaker. She was even then a vibrant personality and told me she was going to Stanford. I next saw her when she made her way into my Sophomore College class at Stanford on post-Communist Russia. That's when I really got to know her. What a tremendous intellect she was, and what a draw she was to students around her! She was a natural leader."

Three years after Sophomore College, on a sun-spangled commencement day on the beautiful Stanford campus, Provost Rice presented the Dean's Award for the most distinguished undergraduate thesis in arts and sciences to Jhumki Basu.

More than a decade passed.

In August 2009, Maithreyi Nandakumar, an English BBC radio journalist conducting a series of interviews for this book, arrived with me at the reception desk of the Hoover Institution at Stanford to meet Dr. Rice, who had just returned upon conclusion of her term with the second Bush administration.

Over the years Jhumki had corresponded regularly with her mentor by exchanging notes and keeping Condi informed on her achievements. Jhumki was a staunch liberal Democrat, at the opposite end of the political spectrum from the former Secretary of State. However, Jhumki and Condi managed to keep their political views outside their dialogue, and concentrated on topics of academic success, travel, race relations, family, and teaching.

Condi had readily agreed to meet me when I told her I was writing Jhumki's book. Maithreyi and I came early, expecting

Secret Service checks and escorts, but it was only a friendly secretary who showed us in. Condi rose from her computer with a smile and came around a conference table to shake our hands. Her sincerity and her deep empathy with Jhumki quickly put us at ease.

"Dr. Rice . . . uh, Condi . . . may I call you Condi?" Maithreyi opened nervously.

"Of course. That's my name!"

After telling us about how she had known Jhumki, Condi continued speaking in the compact and assured manner I had watched so often on CNN.

"Can you say what prompted her to join your Sophomore College class?" Maithreyi asked.

"I think she was always looking to draw on other people's experiences, and she liked what I spoke about at Castilleja. Sophomore College was designed to provide very close contact with a faculty member outside of a large classroom. Jhumki was attracted to people she thought she could learn from, and she was a sponge for knowledge. At the time she still thought she might be a medical doctor. But she was getting interested in the policy side, and I had not been too long out of government."

"And how did the process work about what she was going to do in Russia?"

"After we got to know each other in the classroom, I knew she had this very great interest in Russia, and not just Russia but healthcare and health policy. The country was going through a very difficult time, and she was particularly interested in children. She worked for a paper on that for me, and we would talk about it as directed reading. I tried to help her put together all her passions."

"Do you remember what she came back with?"

"Well, she came back even more passionate because she had seen firsthand the kids and parents and people struggling. You

4

know, Russia can be an abstraction if you read about it in the papers, but if you are there you see these great people in terrible conditions. She was especially interested in orphans, and orphans in Russia were always shunted aside. There was never a good system there for taking care of orphans, which is one reason so many Russian kids are adopted into Western families. She was very taken with their plight and their fate and wanted to do something about them."

"We think this experience in Russia shaped who she became," I inserted. "Did you get a sense that it was so important for her?"

"Oh, I think it was incredibly important," Condi replied without hesitation. "She always had an awareness of her own diverse background, about what America meant to immigrant families, and the ability to bridge cultures that are so prevalent in the United States. This was her first real experience outside the country. My own first experience outside the United States was also in the Soviet Union. I felt that somehow Jhumki had connected with Russia and Russia had connected with her. We used to talk about this.

"Like me, she had no Russian blood!" Condi said, laughing. "From then on we shared that passion as well. It transformed what had been a classroom experience, an intellectual experience, into an experience that had deep, passionate, practical roots."

"Do you remember the time of her graduation from Stanford?" Maithreyi asked.

"Of course I remember when she graduated. Jhumki was one of the most extraordinary students that I have ever encountered, and I've been teaching at Stanford since 1981. There are some people you always remember. I felt she was so much like me! Her passion and intellect and caring all coming together in this tremendous radiance that she had, a personal radiance that attracted people to her. And so when she graduated it was a proud moment for me too."

Through Sophomore College, Condi Rice had opened a window for Jhumki into a troubled world, to a scene that offered a worthy challenge to her hyperactive intellect and her thirst for social justice. But Jhumki's personality refused to be satisfied with *just* an intellectual exercise, however fascinating. She wanted to achieve something concrete. The executable aspect of Jhumki's Russian experience came out of her work with Kathleen Morrison, a passionate, well-organized Stanford professor.

Maithreyi and I spoke to Dr. Morrison in a Philadelphia hotel after she kindly traveled the long distance from Richmond to meet us, armed with e-mails and notes.

Jhumki had enrolled in the 1996 spring semester of Kathleen's seminar, titled Urbanization, Poverty, and Children in Latin America. It was unusual for students to be accepted into the seminar if they didn't speak Spanish or had never been to Latin America. Jhumki's application was very compelling, Kathleen recalled. In it, she said, Jhumki had written about her interest in children and provided a worldly perspective unusual for a young woman of eighteen.

"Of course, once she was in the seminar she was the top student!" Dr. Morrison said with a grin.

Kathleen made it clear to her students that even though she taught about street children of Latin America, such children were everywhere. At that time in history, after the collapse of the Soviet Union, it was evident that the numbers of street children in Russia, a country where there had never been street children, were staggering. The contradiction intrigued and even frightened me as we continued talking.

Russian street kids! What had Jhumki gotten herself into? How had she prepared for the unknown?

Ever since I decided to write her biography, a question had been haunting me: where did the spark to teach science to underserved American kids ignite? As I listened to Kathleen, I began to realize that it might have occurred, incredibly, in Russia!

Professor Morrison's 1996 class did a lot of talking about issues of homeless kids and appropriate strategies for interviewing children versus adults. I learned that often in these situations, children say what they think the interviewer wants to hear, rather than what is really going on. Kathleen's class worked on techniques for recognizing when this happened and minimizing its effects.

"At the end of that class Jhumki had ready an exploratory interview protocol for her trip to Russia," Dr. Morrison concluded.

After the fascinating discussion, I was driving mechanically from Philadelphia to New York, my head filled with imagined Soviet scenarios, when the big decision happened. I was now well aware that Russia had made a great impact on Jhumki's life and work. I knew from my own recollections of the time, and from Jhumki's e-mails and journal entries, that Russia had been a vastly taxing experience. But now, new and troubling circumstances were emerging. Right there, on the New Jersey Turnpike, I decided that I had to go to Russia myself, to relive what Jhumki experienced, and to see how it had driven her future.

2. A DIVERSE CHILDHOOD

Baba, why is the snow white?"

Sitting on our New England patio on a winter morning, I explained to our four-year-old girl that unlike grass, which absorbs all colors and gives back only green, snow reflects all the colors of the rainbow.

"What colors?" she wanted to know.

I listed them, and in a minute Jhumki had them down pat: violet, indigo, blue, green, yellow, orange, red.

"Boring old white has all those pretty colors?"

We raided Mommy's crystal cabinet and found a promising pyramid-shaped glass paperweight. We commandeered the flashlight from our blizzard-preparedness kit. We shone light beams through sparkling glass from many angles. We made rainbows to our hearts' content. We plotted and colored refracted rays on sheets of graph paper. We had hours of fun. I am convinced it was on that day that Jhumki became hooked on physics as a simple paradigm shifter in the understanding of science.

Sreyashi Jhumki Basu was born on November 19, 1977, at Torrance Memorial Hospital outside Los Angeles.

She was always called by her middle name, but never liked it when a person introducing her said her name rhymed with "room key."

Jhumki arrived with wide-open black eyes and a thick mop of black hair. As the nurse held our baby out to her mother, Radha anxiously counted her fingers and toes. Standing in cap and gown beside my wife, I watched, awestruck, as our daughter's unblinking eyes sought, found, and focused on her mother's face. The fingers and toes satisfied Radha, and she took Jhumki in her arms. Her obstetrician, big Dr. Christiansen, came in for a closer look. I had a Polaroid camera ready and neatly captured the tiny fist biff him squarely in the mouth. Later they would be friends.

In 1985, seven-year-old Jhumki traveled with her parents to Japan. She enjoyed the sights of Tokyo and visited the international trade fair at the Tsukuba Expo. She took a fancy to the name of one of Japan's Buddhist shrines and startled passersby by announcing to them, "Asakusa Kannon Temple!"

The three of us stayed for two nights in the tranquil, 1200-year-old village of Hakone-machi on the shores of Lake Ashi, whose mirrored surface serenely reflects the volcanic snow cone of Mount Fuji. Everything in Hakone-machi was in Japanese except a book we found in our hotel, *The Hidden Flower* written by Pearl Buck. I love this author's writing and finished the book in one night. The following morning at breakfast, Jhumki wanted to know why Baba was droopy.

Watching the beautiful mountain's image ripple in the breeze, I told her about Buck's World War II story of an aristocratic Japanese girl, Josui Sakai, whose serviceman husband brings her to an intolerant society in the American deep South. Anguished by statutes that forbade marriage between whites and non-whites, Josui, upon becoming pregnant, conceals her condition from her husband, gives the child up for adoption, and never sees it again. As I spoke, Jhumki became increasingly absorbed in the story. When I got to the part about the lost child, she was in tears.

"Mommy, Baba, am *I* a world child?" she wanted to know.

In *The Hidden Flower,* Buck refers to Josui's daughter as a world child. I explained to Jhumki gently that while her mother and I did come from distinct ethnic backgrounds—Tamil and Bengali—we were both Indian in origin, and so, technically, she wasn't a world child. Disappointed, she gazed wistfully at Fuji.

She was very taken by the idea of a world child and mentioned it several times as she grew up.

Two decades later, on one of her visits home, we were pushing pins into a wall map to mark places to which Jhumki had traveled, when she made us jump with a loud *"Ha!"*

She thumped the map and turned to us.

"USA, India, Germany, Russia, Italy, Bermuda, Japan, Hong Kong, Nicaragua, Ecuador!" she said. "I *am* a world child!"

In her thirty-one years, Jhumki lived on three continents, traveled to thirty-seven countries, and spoke seven languages.

Radha's mother, Kalyani, a loving presence in our home during the first five years of Jhumki's life, taught her Tamil. In the late eighties, while we lived in India, Jhumki learned perfect Hindi at her Delhi school. She spent holidays with my parents in Kolkata's Bengali environment and learned that language while enjoying the local seafood and unending varieties of sweets. She learned Latin in high school and her teacher called her Taverna. In Russia she learned the language well enough to read Russian classics in the original. After her marriage she learned Greek to be closer to her in-laws, and even a bit of Hebrew. She was indeed *the* world child.

Jhumki also expressed herself in the language of dance.

At the tender age of three she enrolled at Darlene Wigton's Winchester School of Ballet in Massachusetts and performed as Mother Ginger's littlest bonbon in Tchaikovsky's *Nutcracker Suite*. At the end of her classes it was well-nigh impossible to drag her home. She *had* to watch the "big girls" go through demi-pliés, glissades, *grand jetés,* and *relevés*. For the next twelve years, everywhere—in airports, supermarkets, pediatricians' offices, malls, and lines—Jhumki, oblivious to amused onlookers, practiced pirouettes and arabesques with intense concentration. Her life's ambition was to become a famous ballerina, at which time, she seriously believed, she would use her rich earnings to care for her aging parents.

At age eleven, when we were stationed in India, Jhumki decided to audition for the Royal Ballet, which meant she would have to live in London. I filmed her repertoires for her application, using improvised balance beams in our living room. She was desolate when the Royal Ballet informed her that she was still too young and should train at home a while longer.

Perhaps the little bonbon of Ms. Wigton's class had wished too hard to become a grand ballerina. In early-nineties California, boys in Jhumki's ballet class struggled to lift the sturdy, five-foot-ten girl who guffawed at their heroics. But the writing was on the wall. She had simply grown too tall and Ballerina Basu retired gracefully from the stage at the ripe old age of fifteen.

Jhumki and her fellow creatures were always a potent combination. All through her life she loved watching and being with wildlife, especially primates, just as fervently as she worked as an educator.

When she was three, her mother and I took her to a petting zoo in New Hampshire. She was happily making friends with sheep, goats, rabbits, guinea pigs, and white mice, when a big black goat came over and started to chew on her long hair. There was no scream of "Help, Mommy!" Instead, our intrepid little girl turned, grabbed the offending goat's beard, and held on as the confounded animal reared back. It took all our patience and strength to separate the two.

In 1983, the Basus moved to Germany and Jhumki started school at a U.S. Army Base called Patch Barracks in Stuttgart, where a problem quickly arose. Jhumki had blossomed academically at Lexington Montessori School in Massachusetts. In first grade at

Patch, for every question the teacher asked, she volunteered an enthusiastic *"Me! Me! Me!"* which became an irritant for the class until administrators solved the problem by promoting the still five-year-old to second grade.

After two months in Germany I received an urgent phone call at work one afternoon. It was from the day care center at Patch calling to inform me that Jhumki had not come over as scheduled from the adjoining school.

Thank God for *autobahns!* My little Toyota Tercel tore up the forty kilometers from Zuffenhausen to Vaihingen. I arrived at the base, showed my ID, drove past tank traps, parked, checked at day care, and, with my heart in my mouth, went searching for my daughter on the sprawling military base.

I found her soon enough. She was sitting on a park bench at the edge of a sunny soccer field. With a cool head I would have found a camera and captured the scene for posterity, but my anxiety was changing to anger.

There had been a rehearsal that day of the school's Christmas play. As a key participant, Jhumki was wearing a floor-length, cream-colored gown that glistened in the sun. She had a gold-painted crown on her long hair and shiny white shoes on her feet. When I found her she was waving a magic wand with a star on its end and laughing at the soccer players' antics, some of which were natural, others manufactured for her benefit, especially by her good buddy Ralph.

But Baba was mad. She saw me coming, saw my face, and the laughter disappeared.

"Jhomi!" I admonished, using her nickname. "Are you okay?"

"Yes, Baba, I'm okay. Are *you* okay?"

"No, I'm not okay, Jhomi. What are you doing here?"

"Where? Oh, here? I'm watching the boys, Baba."

Oh, the travails of parenthood!

"But Jhomi, you're supposed to be at day care, not watching boys."

"I know. I'm going to go there. Soon."

"Jhomi, do you know what you've done?"

"No, Baba. What?"

"They got all worried at day care when you didn't come, and they called me at work. I dashed all the way to look for you."

It was only then that Jhumki realized that she had done something wrong, and that I was really, unusually upset with her. I saw the tears beginning and knew it was because she had caused me trouble, not because I had scolded her. I was relieved that she was all right. Plus, she looked as pretty as an angel. She *was* an angel in that getup.

"Jhomi, listen. You must promise never, *ever* to run away from day care. Promise?"

"Promise," she said meekly.

For a very long time after that day, Jhumki sincerely believed the transitional sunglasses I wore, turned dark when I became angry.

Our European sojourn came to an end. After two fulfilling years of windmills, castles, museums, fjords, Wiener schnitzel, spätzle, gelato, and alpine hikes, we moved from Germany to India. A St. Martin's Day lullaby she learned at Patch, rings in farewell to her early childhood:

> *Ich geh mit meiner Laterne*[1]
> *und meine Laterne mit mir.*

---

[1] I go with my lantern/And my lantern goes with me/High up the stars are shining/Below we shine as one/My light is out/We're going back home/*Rabimmel rabammel rabum*

Dort oben leuchten die Sterne
und unten da leuchten wir.
Mein Licht ist aus,
Wir geh'n nach Haus.
Rabimmel, rabammel, rabum.

Notes from this mellifluous nursery song would one day, many years later, spill through grimy canvas walls of a homeless children's shelter on a dirty, crowded street of a teeming Indian city. The words were to be sung in the lilting voices of little girls under the direction of a valiant social worker named Jhumki Basu.

3. A SHAKEN LAND

I n the summer of 1996, Jhumki Basu, age eighteen, registered for the Stanford in Moscow program and left the safe shores of California to embark on her Russian odyssey. As her plane flew over a newly-torn iron curtain, a plethora of conflicting emotions swirled through her pliable heart.

From the journal of Jhumki Basu, Aug 29, 1996

Plane ride east and even further than the square shape of Washington DC. If there is a time for dreaming, the time is now. I know nothing. I can only imagine. Is there really light in Moscow? When will I see the palaces of St. Petersburg? How do Russians feel about the change the Western press has glorified? Are there big lines and porters pushing carts for Western tourists? Will I be reminded of India?

The Kremlin—sinuous domes and walls that hid Yeltsin for weeks.

The Metro—Stalin's legacy and model of efficiency.

What is it to be Russian—to live under communism, Tsarism, unbridled liberalism, to be a mix of East and West, Asia and Europe?

So many questions. Will the thick gold Fodors guide me? Will I ever learn the Cyrillic script? Will Emily's Mix keep me whole? And what will exist when I return to the open hills of Northern California?

There will be a large beige house that my parents are building on land where I only remember sheets of orange flowers. Just one of these days there will be foundations, and then a place where my dog Tiffany can chase the deer of her old-age imagination.

In this aeroplane I could be going anywhere into anytime. I could be meeting Jeff Heys to play him the taped version of "Under the Table and Dreaming." I could be watching butterflies through the eyes of Emily and beside Benny G. Take these chances. Take these possibilities. Is fiddle music part of this journey?

Will there be dancing—folk dancing, ballet? What music awaits us—balalaika tunes, jazz, blues? I will take it all. My hair is short and curled, ready to spring forward. My eyes are clear and far-seeing.

❧

Fourteen years later, having embarked on my own odyssey, I tracked down Maxim Bratersky, head of Stanford's Moscow Center at Jhumki's time, and now professor of economics at Moscow State University. Seated in a comfortable conference room with the April sunshine streaming through the window, Dr. Bratersky told me that Jhumki was one of very few students who came from the United States not just to enjoy the Russian experience, but to actually make a difference.

Jhumki's mission was to interview street children of Russia's two biggest cities about their access to healthcare services. This worried Maxim because, instead of frequenting the usual tourist sites and bars like other American kids, Jhumki wanted to make contact with nonprofit organizations, to visit homeless shelters, and to go to dangerous public places where homeless kids congregated. With Moscow in economic turmoil and mafia-dominated, for safety's sake Maxim accompanied the unusual student to her first exploratory meetings until she got her bearings.

"I would not allow *my* daughters to do something like this," Maxim said to me.

Well, Maxim, I thought, you have touched a raw nerve! In 1996 we would have agreed with you. But Jhumki would have

16

considered your observation a challenge!

It should be noted that at that point in time, our daughter was going through an earnest teenage search for identity. In contrast to earlier and later years, she would not then share her inner thoughts with her parents. And so, to retrace her footsteps back in time to gather material for this book, I found and read old e-mails and navigated her captivating journal entries with growing amazement and horror. As I visited more places in Russia and met more people, those dark winter days of 1996 on the streets of Moscow and St. Petersburg became real, and the dreadfulness of what she had undergone sank in.

The name John Varoli first appears in Jhumki's journal on September 15, 1996, early in her time in Russia. Against his name she writes, *Contact in St. Petersburg with own nonprofit called Off-the-Streets.*

To my delight John was still living in St. Petersburg, and he agreed wholeheartedly to see me. We met at an upscale restaurant that looked out over one of the pretty canals of the majestic city built by Peter the Great on Baltic marshlands. My first impression was surprise at how young he looked. Now a seasoned journalist and writer for Bloomberg Arts and Culture, John went to Russia with the Salvation Army in 1992. Tiring of the organization's inertia, he founded his own nonprofit, Off-the-Streets, and dedicated his work to hands-on provisioning of food and shelter to Russia's homeless children.

E-mail from John Varoli to Jhumki Basu, Sep 24, 1996

I should arrive in Moscow in the third week of October. Will you come to St. Pete before that? How is your research? There's much activity with street children in St. Pete, and I am now convinced the situation here is worse than in Moscow.

I try not to speak bad of anyone, but the issue of street

children in Russia is quite sordid—and not just because of the prostitution and kidnapping. A lot of money is being made on these children by people in humanitarian organizations and in the government who receive grants to help these children. I do not speak idly but have evidence.

Jhumki, impressed with John's on-the-ground knowledge, sprang into action. She took the train to St. Petersburg to meet him and, later the same day, had her first encounter with homeless Russian children in John's company.

From the journal of Jhumki Basu, Nov 10, 1996
Weekend in St. Petersburg with John Varoli:

12 to 15 kids at a campfire by the Turgenevskaya Metro. Aged 7 to 14 or 15. 5 or 6 of them were sniffing glue[2]. The smell of glue was strong, pungent. They smelt it by hiding it in the neck of their jackets and sniffing. One boy, the second oldest, had a high hysterical laugh. The oldest boy stood on the outside of the campfire—dull eyes, no giggling. I think he was less trusting than the younger children.

When John and I approached, they backed away, they were afraid. When he showed them [chewing] gum, they clambered on top of each other to get it. "Daichi mne! Daichi mne!"[3] They would get as close as necessary to get the gum. They were demanding. John bought them bananas and they weren't thankful. They just wanted more gum.

John asked them if they were going to spend their whole lives like this—they said they were "going to build

[2] A prevalent poor man's drug in 1990s Russia. Modern glue is made without the narcotic of that time.
[3] "Give me! Give me!"

themselves a house and fuck each other." There were only 2 or 3 girls; the rest seemed to be boys.

I was afraid when John went to buy bananas, afraid when the child who was high on glue laughed near me with another girl who was someone's older sister. I was afraid of one of the tall thin boys with big grey spacey eyes. What were the kids who didn't talk to me or John thinking? Do they beg, work or steal? How violent are they? Do they carry sexually transmitted diseases? Are they infected with tuberculosis or diphtheria? Do they drink as well as sniff glue?

They PREFER sleeping in the sewers and begging for food, starving, having no family, to living with their parents. John says they might go back when it is freezing cold weather. Then they are forced to go back to a place and people they despise, that they must despise SO MUCH.

As John and I talked in the restaurant, the gravity of the situation in which Jhumki had involved herself, was becoming abundantly clear.

"The Soviet Union had collapsed, but it was still alive in the minds of the apparatus," John told me. "The country was in chaos. The threat of civil war was very real. Salaries were two hundred U.S. dollars a year. So a dollar went a long way, and we could help a lot of people. We were the only folks then actually helping inhabitants of the streets with food, clothing, and medical attention."

How had this situation come to pass?

It was Maxim Bratersky who answered this question rather dramatically.

"During the Soviet era," he said, "unemployment and homelessness were *illegal!*"

It took me a while to absorb the ramifications of this

extraordinary statement. Maxim went on to explain that for all the ills of Russia under Communism, there had been no homeless people between the regimes of Lenin and Yeltsin, an unbroken span of eighty years. When Communism fell, a bizarre process of real-estate privatization occurred. Everyone who occupied a flat or a house became its first-time owner, armed with a sudden marketable commodity. The economy went crazy. Untold thousands of people injudiciously sold property via mafia-wrought deals and landed on the streets with money that went to satisfy alcohol and drug addictions. With laughably meager social services, capitalism's victory thrust forty thousand homeless children onto the cold and uncaring city streets of the former Soviet Union. The kids were a source of embarrassment for Boris Yeltsin as he vied for a second term in an election that was emerging as a virtual referendum on one question: would Russia continue unsteadily under *perestroika,* or would it revert to Communism? This was the uncertain scenario when Jhumki Basu arrived in Russia.

John Varoli looked thoughtfully at ice floes floating down the thawing canal as he continued his story.

"I remember us going to Bolshevik Prospekt, a very rough area targeted for prefab high-rises. You can go there now, but it's all built up and a big shopping mall. Then it was a complex of semi-abandoned construction sites with big pipes with kids living and sleeping in them.

"Jhumki had this voracious desire to learn as much as possible. She wasn't easily scared or frightened. Many people came to volunteer in that unsettled time. They would break and be gone in a matter of weeks. Jhumki stayed. In her there was this rare mix of toughness and compassion."

The Chechen War broke out in 1994 and Russian forces overran Grozny, Chechnya's capital and killed President Dudayev with laser-guided missiles, leading to two years of hostilities. While Russian media vilified the Chechens, Jhumki's long black hair and dark eyes drew the attention of louts in the Moscow subway system. They made threatening gestures and yelled, "Hey, Chechi! Chechi!" at her. In response, she took to covering her head with a scarf when she traveled on underground trains and frigid streets.

Jhumki finished setting up her interviews during the winter months of 1996-97. The following summer, armed with a Strauss scholarship, she went with the intention of conducting them. Arriving in Moscow in July 1997, she called me and made an extraordinary statement.

"Baba, there are no kids on the streets!"

"What do you mean, Jhomi?" I asked in surprise. "There were thousands last winter."

"The tourists are here now. Yeltsin had the kids swept up and sent to the Urals." There was a pause. "Baba, you know what? I'm going to the Urals."

In the silence, a scene or two from *Doctor Zhivago* flashed through my mind before I asked lamely "Jhomi, are you sure that's quite safe?" very aware that our teenager would do exactly the opposite of what I advised.

"Well, the only other places they have these kids are juvenile detention centers."

In the end Jhumki didn't go to the Urals, but she did go to several Moscow detention centers. I tried to visit one in 2010, but the authorities flatly declined permission.

During my trip to Russia I was fortunate to meet some of the country's unsung heroes. None were as colorful or had as much impact on our daughter as did Dr. Aza Rakhmanova.

When I met her at the entrance to St. Petersburg's Mother and Child Center, a well-maintained, lilac-colored, five-story clinic, the seventy-eight-year-old chief medical officer of the city energetically led me up several flights of stairs and through various departments. I was initially intimidated by my steely hostess who glared at the world through big, thick glasses. After the tour, we settled into an empty examination room, surrounded by toys on shelves and children's paintings on the walls. With her staff positioned around her, Aza proudly described the center's services for AIDS-infected mothers and children. She clearly had a highly active mind and was used to running big operations. Her colleagues doted on her.

My nineteen-year-old guide and translator, Sophia Rusakova, had been watching Aza in disbelief. Later she remarked to me, "A Russian grandma who speaks English!"

In the summer of 1997, Jhumki stayed with Aza and her granddaughter, Anna Vinogradova, in their apartment. When I asked Aza why she took Jhumki in, she replied, "Our house is always open to truly committed people."

From the journal of Jhumki Basu, August 3, 1997

I feel at peace here [in Aza's home]—for some reason the lights from the apartment across from me are comforting, not oppressive—maybe because I am higher than the facing building, and I can see the horizon for a change. I have found my family that I love. They are wonderful, giving people. They are dynamic, ambitious women, who manage careers and home with vitality—a line of women with the warmest hearts, strongest intellects and most certain personalities. I will miss the view from Aza's kitchen and the cozy sofa-bed in Aza's house, the yogurt and the fruit, the ants in the bread, all their crazy habits and mannerisms.

Aza Rakhmanova is a respected public figure, a medical and social pioneer from the time when HIV/AIDS first appeared in Russia coincident with Jhumki's visit. One of the first things she told me knocked me over.

The institution we were in, she said, the Mother and Child Center, *was Jhumki's idea!*

While working with street children and studying their access to healthcare, Jhumki had identified cases where the AIDS virus was apparently being transmitted from a mother to her newborn child. She and Aza discussed how this type of transmission could be prevented, and Aza decided to take on the problem as a clinical challenge. And when this aspect of AIDS[4] became a monumental global issue, the Mother and Child Center served thousands of Russian patients. It was hard for me to imagine that Jhumki had forged new methods for AIDS care, of all things, over a decade ago.

Anna Vinogradova, Aza's attractive and self-assured granddaughter, was present at my interview with Aza. A dentist by training, Anna also conducts AIDS research and outreach. When I arrived in St. Petersburg, she had just returned from a conference in New York. She looked me in the eyes through fashionable rimless glasses and, in clear American-accented English, described Jhumki's idealism and dedication to her work. She first met Jhumki when her hired translator had vanished, and Anna had offered to fill that role.

I thought about this for a bit and looked closely at Anna. Then I asked her how old she was. When she told me, I stared at her aghast while a disturbing image formed in my mind: a nineteen-year-old Jhumki with a fifteen-year-old Anna meeting unstable

---

[4] Formally known as PMTCT—prevention of mother-to-child transfer (of the AIDS virus).

homeless children and adults behind metro stations, under bridges, inside sewer pipes, on basement heating ducts, and in abandoned construction sites; being set upon by glue and drug addicts, alcoholics; trying to navigate rampant domestic violence; facing up to mafia desperadoes.

Aza was watching me carefully and could tell I was shocked by what I had heard. Slowly her eyes softened and crinkled as she smiled, and I saw in her face the ocean of empathy that Jhumki had found in "the family I love."

Aza told me that Jhumki was very patient with kids. Many visitors went to her as interns or as volunteers to solve their *own* problems or aspirations. Jhumki's aim, Aza was convinced, was to try to do good for other people. Her support came from the heart. Not many people would offer help to HIV-positive children, but Jhumki's connection with kids at risk manifested itself across culture, language, and status in life. This connection was linked to her personality.

My mind flashed forward to Teacher Jhumki facing off hulking kids in troubled New York City schools in the 2000s. They were bigger—often a good deal bigger—and sometimes even older than she. These students were frisked for weapons before entering school. Yet they loved their Ms. Jhumki and protected her in tough situations. Aza had just answered a question that had been nagging at me: why did Jhumki's American students, famous for lack of discipline, love her unequivocally, and how could she control them without ever raising her voice?

Back at the Mother and Child Center, Aza Rakhmanova cast a final magic spell over me.

"I feel especially close to your wife," she told me through Sophia after we had talked about Jhumki's visit, and I had updated Aza about her later life. While she continued speaking in Russian, I tried to fathom what Aza meant by this comment. She had never met Radha. Was it a Russian nicety?

Sophia began to translate.

"My own daughter, Professor Elena Vinogradova, chief of our AIDS and Hepatology Center, the mother of Anna here, died of cancer at age fifty-two. It was the year just before Jhumki came. So I know how your wife must feel."

I sat back, speechless, and stared at her in wonderment.

Many years after this meeting, Anna, married and living in San Francisco with her Spanish husband, told me about her grandmother's remarkable background. Aza was born an Azerbaijani in Baku in the early 1930s. Her parents were designated "undesirable" by Stalin and the family was transported to a camp in Kazakhstan where her father lost his life in tragic circumstances. Aza's mother, a doctor and a strong woman, somehow kept the family whole before returning to Baku. Aza went to study medicine in St. Petersburg, something very unusual for a woman in the 1950s, and was "rehabilitated" with a formal letter from the government after the death of Stalin. Dedicated to her work in epidemiology, she learned English at age 43, and became a national pioneer in the field of AIDS research. She is writing a book about her family history. I cannot wait to read it.

A month after I returned home, Aza e-mailed me the latest edition of the clinic's newsletter, *Stars against AIDS,* in which she had published a report of my visit:

> *In early April a person came to St. Petersburg from San Francisco, Dipak Basu. We didn't know each other before, but the aim of his visit brought us together—his daughter Jhumki Basu used to work in our Botkin hospital in the mid-90s, and he wanted to know more about his daughter's life and work and people who surrounded her.*
>
> *Jhumki came to Russia in 1996 with a grant given by Stanford University to conduct her bachelor's research on street teenagers' health in St. Petersburg and Moscow. She*

did not restrict herself to a couple of interviews with the orphans—she spent days and weeks in the streets trying to find out more; she set contacts with newly established NGOs working in this sphere. I remember how hard she worked on her research and how compassionate and respectful she was to people who she worked with—little orphans and persons with HIV and AIDS.

In 1996–97 the issue of abandoned children with HIV+ diagnosis was about to become a problem (only 30–40 mothers with HIV gave birth per year then, while a sharp surge in their numbers took place in 2001), but we were prepared to handle it, because Jhumki warned us about the possible developments and initiated a project on social orphanage prevention among kids born to HIV+ mothers.

On returning from Russia Jhumki Basu got a PhD degree and became a professor. In December 2008 she died of cancer at the age of 31.

My mother heart, which has outlived my only daughter Elena Vinogradova, who passed away of the same disease one year before Jhumki came, couldn't help Dipak in his sorrow.

We gave him all the information about Jhumki's work here, and both the project and research information and warm memories of people who used to know her, will become a part of the biography book composed by Dipak.

Throughout her short yet bright life Jhumki helped others and did it with pleasure and devotion. This loss is bereavement for all of us. Her work and deeds will be continued by the Foundation named after her.

On a chilly grey morning in St. Petersburg Sophia and I, muffled against the wind, walked over a bridge spanning the wide, ice-covered Neva. Our destination was City Center for the Family, a homeless shelter where Jhumki had interviewed many children in 1997. The building in which she did her work was still in operation, though it had been renamed Tranzit. Here I met Maxim Bogachev, a social worker who clearly remembered our daughter, who in turn had written glowingly about him in her journal. Jhumki interviewed many of Tranzit's 150 resident kids and developed a rich statistical database. Maxim explained that the kids had understood Jhumki well. She had been shocked by their stories, as well as their propensity to pick up body lice and common illnesses such as tuberculosis.

In 1997 the city had only four shelters like Tranzit for *tens of thousands* of street children. To my horror, Maxim told me Jhumki joined his street militia—an activity forbidden by the government—and had worked until midnight on icy streets to take bereft children to their homes or to shelters. Tranzit processed incoming kids and accepted only those with no criminal record. Here Jhumki interviewed kids of all backgrounds and had scrupulously kept their names and records confidential.

"Jhumki was interested in people, not a good salary," Maxim said. "She was interested in making the government support social workers like me. She tried to learn the life of a social worker. She was a brave and beautiful girl."

From St. Petersburg, I flew south to Moscow on Aeroflot.

According to Jhumki's notes, her visits to the city's No to Alcohol and Narcotics (NAN) center were among the most successful in terms of interviews. Here she met Sapar Kulyanov.

Today Sapar runs a sprawling shelter for abused women called Neznaika, situated near Vnukovo Airport, thirty kilometers from Moscow. When I went there with Sapar, he introduced me to victimized women and children from a bewildering array of places: Somalia, Tajikistan, Congo,

Cameroon, Siberia. Each woman had her own story of horror.

Sapar is a truly extraordinary person. A Turkmen by birth, he attended high school in Uzbekistan near the Aral Sea and was accepted into Moscow State University for scientific studies. He landed a job as a "leading designer with a big salary" but during forays to construction sites and armament factories from Minsk to Vladivostok, he came across multitudes of lost children and broken families. In 1991, with the Soviet Union crumbling, Sapar left his job to serve Russia's street children and was hired as director of NAN.

When Sapar met Jhumki, he told her that Russia's homeless children were everywhere and nowhere. They were invisible to Westerners, invisible to authorities of post-Communist Russia, invisible to Yeltsin. Nobody wanted them. Nobody cared for them except a few die-hard NGOs.

At Neznaika I showed Sapar a video about Jhumki's life using my laptop. Scenes from her work were going by when he suddenly shouted, "*Piristat! Piristat!*" (Stop!).

I paused the video and we stared at an old photo of Jhumki, surrounded by kids and flashing her trademark grin. A big stuffed giraffe and balloons added a festive touch. For years we had taken this image for granted as a sort of generic picture of Jhumki in Russia. Sapar pointed excitedly at the kids. "Ivan!" he exclaimed. "Roman! Aleksi!" Infecting me with his excitement, he said he was still in touch with these kids and promised to try to find them and get them to talk to me. As it turned out I didn't have sufficient time in Moscow, and we agreed to try on my next visit. He assured me the kids were all doing well as truck drivers, factory workers, etc.

Two days later Sapar took me to the Moscow NAN shelter where Jhumki had worked. In a large, brightly painted room he pointed out an empty space where the picture had been taken. The giraffe had passed on. I tried to imagine young Jhumki posing with the kids and celebrating some festive event. Later, I felt an eerie sensation as I sat in the very examination room where, long ago, our little girl had faced a hundred homeless kids and tried to help them. When we parted, Sapar offered to dedicate a room of Neznaika to Jhumki's memory and decorate it with memorabilia from her life.

I left Russia feeling uplifted yet sad. I had gotten to know so much more about our daughter. I now understood where the vital force, that had taken hold of her and propelled her relentlessly, originated. During the trip I had felt her presence by my side as I got to know and admire her friends: Aza, Sapar, John, the two Maxims; Maria Eliseeva, who taught mural painting to orphans; Ludmilla Baranova, founder of Russia's first homeless shelter; and young Masha Yudkevich, with whose family she had stayed in Moscow.

In Russia, I missed Jhumki very much.

The inestimable value of Jhumki's work lay in the volume of data she had collected and in the way she interpreted and presented it. Today experts acknowledge her work as the first systemic study of homelessness in modern Russia.

From Stanford honors thesis of Jhumki Basu, May 28, 1998

"Every child among us has a precious life and holds a precious dream." — Jonathan Kozol in Amazing Grace.

Santa is a Russian street girl. She is 14 years old, and her name is pronounced "Santha." Dirt is packed behind her long, uneven nails. She ties tabs of soda cans around her neck, has pierced her ears in several places with safety pins, and jangles when she walks. She always travels with a thin German Shepherd that is covered with sores.

Since the collapse of communism and disintegration of the Soviet Union in 1991, street children have appeared in

Russia. In urban Russia, an estimated three hundred thousand to one million children live currently on the street (Varoli, "Street Children," 1996).

This study provides some of the first quantified data on the health of Russian street children. The study concludes that Russian children are at heightened risk for physical and mental impairment resulting from heavy and frequent smoking, inhalation of glue, and drug use. Due to frequent exposure to crowded public settings, use of intravenous drugs, poor hygiene habits, and limited knowledge of how to diagnose and respond to disease, street children are also at elevated risk for disease with respiratory, parenteral and/or fecal-oral routes of transmission. In the Russian epidemiological context, these diseases include tuberculosis, diphtheria, HIV, Hepatitis B and C, Hepatitis A, dysentery and cholera.

Though they are high-risk for disease, evidence from this study suggests that street children face obstacles in their access to healthcare and perceive threats to their independence by making contact with institutions.

In an attempt to improve the health conditions of Russian street children and indirectly affect the health of the urban population in Russia, this study outlines programs and public health measures to reduce the number of children on the street and improve support to current street children and children at-risk for life on the street.

UNICEF had partially funded Jhumki's study in 1997 and was impressed with her thesis. Gianni Murzi, head of UNICEF's Russia office, invited Jhumki to present her outreach recommendations to the United Nations in Geneva and offered her a UN job to implement them. Jhumki gave the offer long and hard thought. In the end, the stress, the cold, the crime, the menace of bigots, the entrenched dourness and fatalism, the alcoholism and drug addiction combined to overwhelm her keenness to carry through something she had started. Jhumki reluctantly declined Dr. Murzi's offer.

On October 22, 2011, as part of the twentieth-anniversary celebration of the Russian magazine *AIDS, Sex, and Health*, Jhumki was remembered at a special event in St. Petersburg. The meeting was organized by Aza Rakhmanova, 80, and sponsored by the Jhumki Basu Foundation. At the gathering, consuls-general, leading businessmen, and public health policy makers, paid tribute to a nineteen-year-old girl who had played a visionary role in Russian healthcare and had been instrumental in the creation of the Mother and Child Center, celebrating its fifteenth year. The commemorative issue of the center's magazine carried an in-depth tribute to Jhumki Basu, titled "Stars Never Fade."

4. SHANTI

The white-and-blue Pan American jumbo jet from Frankfurt touched down at Delhi airport on a sizzling May afternoon in 1984. Inside the plane, six-year-old Jhumki pulled on a *Smurf* backpack from which her stuffed and masked Racoonie peered out. She held my hand as we descended movable stairs to molten tarmac, and onto a waiting airline bus where a roaring, turbo-charged air conditioner greeted us with the promise of pneumonia.

For Radha and me, it was a homecoming.

I had left India in 1973 for graduate study at the University of Southern California. A year later I met Radha, then a research engineer at Xerox Corporation, in the decidedly unromantic setting of an electronics conference at UCLA. The first time I saw her, I stared in amazement at the slim, beautiful, and thoroughly Indian woman, clad in a traditional sari, with flowing black hair and large brown eyes, strikingly poised and holding her own in a thoroughly American business setting.

I remember asking myself, *what chance does a penniless foreign student have?*

While our volunteer group organized the conference, Radha, as the group's leader, worked herself into such a state that she had to be hospitalized for exhaustion on the night before the event. The following morning she appeared at the auditorium, pale and weak. I found her a glass of orange juice. She appreciated it deeply. We fell in love.

In the subsequent months we discovered many shared values even though our Indian family backgrounds are markedly different. We decided to get married. In keeping with Radha's heritage, our wedding was held in India's most visited pilgrim town, Tirupati. We prayed for divine brownie points. We got them, and Jhumki appeared two years later.

While appreciative of all the good things America had to offer, the two of us passionately wanted to return to India to give back to the mother country and spend time with our families. We had to wait out an ultra-conservative government that was bent on reverting India to its agrarian roots. Then Indira Gandhi's Congress Party swept back to power, and science and technology were reinstated as priority sectors. Nonresident Indians, a potent brain trust, were courted back. We were excited about times ahead.

After arriving in India we ended up staying for several months with Radha's sister Shanti and her family in a locality of Delhi named Saket. We got along famously with Shanti[5], her husband SNA Chary[6], and their son Ranga, three years older than Jhumki. Their daughter, Sumitra, was away attending college in Chennai. The Charys encased us with love and helped us through the unending problems of setting up a household that depended on corruption-ridden public services. Shanti, a mathematics teacher at Carmel Convent School, was one of most caring people I have ever met. She quickly became a second mother to Jhumki and adopted me as the brother she never had. Her apartment in Saket became our second home.

Radha and I launched into our work in India—she setting up Hewlett-Packard's sales office in Delhi and software development center in Bangalore; I consulting with the Indian government toward establishment of computer networks for the sprawling banking, steel and energy sectors. Throughout the six years we spent in Delhi, SNA, a petroleum engineer by

[5] Her name means "peace" in Sanskrit
[6] His full name is Seevaram Nattu Anantha Chary, but few people know this

profession, was enthusiastic about our work and encouraged us to keep faith while we struggled to make hi-tech change in a change-averse country.

"And so, in Delhi, began perhaps the happiest period in our lives," Radha told me years later after Jhumki was gone. "We always wanted Jhumki to develop in areas where she wanted to the most. We had to give her an environment where she was exposed to lots of people from different walks of life, countries, religions, an environment where she could learn and flourish. I always knew she was very curious.

"My memories of those Delhi years are of so much happiness. Years of just happy-go-lucky existence. Relaxed Sunday-afternoon lunches. Spending time with our extended families. With friends across cultures. I did not have to push her in academics. We lived a simple life, not going after high society. I'm sure we had a lot of problems then. But now I remember it as a flourishing, nourishing environment."

My wife and daughter possessed a very engaged and vigorous relationship in both positive and negative senses. They held strong opinions and expressed themselves passionately.

"Mommy, look, I'm like you," Jhumki would say. "I'm outspoken!"

"Those relationships were often tumultuous, often loving, always complex," Radha said. "In India, I wasn't Jhumki's only mom. I really did like the fact that she had strong and diverse older women in her life—a corporate leader in me, a teacher in Shanti, a homemaker in my other sister Viji, and your mother with her strong social orientation. I did not feel I was the one person who had to bring her up."

On October 31, 1984, Prime Minister Indira Gandhi was gunned down by her Sikh bodyguards and Delhi erupted in ethnic violence.

On that day Radha was away at a HP meeting in Hong Kong and I was attending a telecom conference in Sydney. In Delhi, street gangs systematically sought out and killed Sikhs while police looked the other way. We desperately tried to return, but Delhi airport was closed. Luckily, Jhumki was safe with Shanti. Though our families follow the Hindu religion, we had many Sikh friends in the city and elsewhere. We worried about their safety and, as the troubled days wore on, tried to help them as much as we could. In the unrest the construction crew finishing our new house ran away to their villages, and it wasn't until late December that we finally moved in. For the six months we stayed with them, Shanti, SNA, and Ranga made us feel that our extended occupation of their home was a privilege. Theirs!

Delhi eventually settled down, though memories of those black days still evoke raw emotion. Rajiv Gandhi, Indira's elder son and a commercial pilot, reluctantly took the reins of government. His abiding interest in computers helped our work. Two years later I was honored to demonstrate the emerging technology of electronic funds transfer to the big friendly prime minister.

ॐ

The years passed swiftly.

Jhumki took to Delhi Public School like a duck to water and became head girl in fourth grade. She was so used to being called Jhumki that she had forgotten her "proper" name, Sreyashi. One day at DPS a new teacher asked her to go and find "Shresi," who was apparently missing from class. Poor Jhumki searched the school and returned to report that Shresi was nowhere to be found!

Grandparents, aunts, uncles, and cousins doted on the bright and happy child, who was growing tall and skinny like a weed. She ate like a trooper while we wondered where it all went.

The Charys and Basus went on trips to the Himalayas where the kids enjoyed rides on big shaggy yaks. On pleasant winter weekends we played cricket and visited historic picnic spots around Delhi, and explored remains of millennia-old forts. For *Diwali,* India's famous festival of lights, Kalyani and her three daughters, Viji, Shanti and Radha, awoke at four in the morning to prepare an astonishing variety of sweets and savories. In the evening, the bang and crackle of fireworks in the city merged into a continuous thunder. A visitor unfamiliar with Diwali in Delhi could be excused for thinking the city was under mortar attack.

Jaipal Singh Nirankari, Radha's company driver, became Jhumki's staunch friend. We trusted him with her safety. To report at our house, Jaipal rode his bicycle for two hours each way, through burning summers and freezing winters, not missing a single day's work in our six years in Delhi. Jaipal chauffeured our go-anywhere Ambassador car filled with family and friends all over northern India, with an always-present grin in his big black beard.

Every afternoon Jhumki and Ranga, closer than most siblings, arrived home from school to the Chary apartment. They tucked into a delicious lunch cooked by Shanti and finished their homework as fast as possible. Then it was playtime.

"At that age," Radha reminisced, "she loved to read, write, and play with the boys!"

Ranga—today Dr. Ranga-Ram Chary, a brilliant, gangling astrophysicist at the California Institute of Technology in Pasadena—was one of the boys.

"At that point," Ranga told us, "Jhumki and I already liked animals a lot. And the dog! We were fond of their dog, Tiffany, a black lab. We both liked going on vacations to the same places, so we went to a number of wildlife parks in India. And of course we both liked good food. All the parents used to cook excellent food. We lived very close to each other and went to the same school."

"Did you see Jhumki's love for science developing back then?" I asked.

"I think the love for science happened later," Ranga replied. "At least at that point of time it was all about watching animals. We were fascinated by dinosaurs, which we of course can't see, but loved to go on about them from the encyclopedia. We used to have this chemistry experiment, and that was great for a pyromaniac like Jhumki. We used to create these volcanoes which would blow up."

Pyromania! That aspect of Jhumki's teaching and experimentation was sure to foster excited involvement by her students. She knew kids love things to go bang and smoke to billow.

"What better way to teach science?" she would ask.

Jhumki toughened up during the years in Delhi. Every day she had to hold her own with three boys who were between two and four years older.

"We got into these dire situations!" Ranga said. "We broke windows of our neighbors a few times with cricket balls. Then we would all run like crazy out of the park. There used to be a neighbor whose house was right behind the cricket stumps, and the ball would keep hitting against her wall. That would give her migraines, and she would come and yell at us. So yeah, that's when we got running."

"Shame on you big guys!" Radha rebuked. "Getting the poor little girl into trouble."

Ranga laughed, unabashed.

"I don't think we got her into trouble. We were in enough trouble as it is."

"And did you look out for her because she younger?"

"Nope, we never looked out for her. All of us were in trouble together."

In Delhi, around all the fun, Jhumki began to exhibit many of the qualities of her aunt Shanti: the intense work ethic, the frank and plainspoken manner, the quick and hearty laugh, the absolute belief in family closeness. Shanti was her hero. We could not visit any Delhi restaurant without a young woman coming over with "Hello, Shanti Ma'am. I was in your class in..."

"Immersion in India's history and mythology," Radha said, "and exposure to its myriad conflicts and multiple cultures—Hindu, Muslim, Jain, Sikh, Christian, Buddhist—built tolerance, resilience, and a deep-set value system that later helped Jhumki cope in the tough and diverse public schools of urban America."

As the eighties progressed, Jhumki excelled at Delhi Public School while continuing her artistic pursuits in ballet and piano outside school. Then, in 1989, she hit a wall.

I visited her classroom at the beginning of sixth-grade year. There were seventy boys and girls in the room, three to a bench. Poor Jhumki sat unhappily in the very first row with her bench up tight against the wall. From where she sat, the chalkboard was at such an acute angle that it was impossible to read!

In India there is massive competition for good schools, good universities, and good jobs. When Jhumki rose from fifth to sixth grade, the pressure of schoolwork suddenly became frenetic and all-consuming. Gone was time to learn dance, music, to play, and to travel. Students became machines. Lessons, homework, and tutoring extended into nights and weekends, preparing kids for that *one* competitive exam in engineering or computer science or medicine—still six years away—that would make or break their lives. Or so people believed.

The solution wasn't easy. But it was the only one.

After weeks of soul-searching, Radha and I decided we had to return to the United States. Our professional lives were going well in India, but Jhumki's future was our paramount consideration. We would sorely miss living in India, but we were unified in thinking that Jhumki must keep her career options open at least into college while enjoying a well-rounded and creative childhood.

The Charys were heartbroken. So were we. My father had passed away in 1986. When we broke the news of our impending departure to my mother, Mum masked her distress and told us that if the move was good for us, it was good for her. Radha's mother would come to stay with us in the U.S.

To ease Jhumki's transition, we enrolled her at Delhi's American Embassy School, an institution attended by children of foreign consular staff and expatriates, and run along American public school lines. And at once the situation she had faced back in Patch Barracks in Germany re-manifested itself: Jhumki was too advanced for her American sixth-grade class. And so it came to pass that our daughter was promoted once again, this time from sixth to seventh grade in the middle of the school year. She was just eleven, two years younger than her classmates, but holding her own academically.

At first Jhumki was unhappy at AES, as she felt unable to fit in socially. She wanted to stay on in India, and, Radha recalls, she actually wanted leave the American school and go back to the nurturing but scholastically intense environment at DPS.

At AES in those days, expatriate and Indian kids stayed apart. Being from both communities, Jhumki found herself in a state of limbo. The Indians were suspicious of her because she was "from" the U.S. The white kids, she told us, treated her badly because her color was brown. One day, in front of a group, a white student told her that none of them would drink from the same water fountain as her. Jhumki came home terribly upset. Discouraging my idea of complaining to the school administration, her mother counseled Jhumki to not run away from problems, but to face them head-on. And so back she went to the leader of the expat group and told him, "If you guys don't want to drink from the same fountain as me, that's your problem. You all can go thirsty."

Later this boy became her good buddy and defended her against vindictive older kids. And then, suddenly, things got much better, and Jhumki assumed a position of leadership.

Radha has this story about how it happened.

"On a class trip to Kanha National Park, she was still the underdog. All the kids went by train on the long trip from Delhi in the north to central India. Jhumki was very comfortable in trains and in going to rural places, but most of the foreign kids fell apart on the trip. Girls cried and missed home. Jhumki took charge and became their champion. She helped out one who had lost her money. A girl refused to go to the dirty train washroom, and Jhumki helped her. Appreciating the kids' fear of public places, she organized night watches.

"After the trip," Radha concluded, "kids who were hoity-toity, changed and socialized with her. In October 1989 she was elected head girl of the school."

When at last it was time to go stateside, AES principal David Chojnacki gave Jhumki a stellar sendoff. In a letter of recommendation he wrote:

> As President of the Middle School Student Government, Jhumki Basu has organized a number of successful school dances and parties. She has been remarkably mature, completely honest, reliable and fair, and she has absolutely no trouble maintaining emotional self-control. She is independent in dress, style and thought, and she is confident.
>
> In short, Jhumki is a terrific student, leader, actress and all-round person whom I recommend to you with the greatest of enthusiasm. I will miss her this next year.

5. THE BIG DECISION

After the life-changing experience on the streets of Russia with real people, and graduation from Stanford, Jhumki believed she had found her career goal: to improve healthcare for disadvantaged people, especially children. She made up her mind to focus on her own country, America, where there were people just as needy, just as numerous, and just as invisible as the Russian homeless. In August 1998, flush with optimism, she joined American Practice Management, the largest U.S. healthcare consulting firm, and moved into an airy apartment in San Francisco's Noe Valley with stunning views of the Oakland Bay Bridge.

With their daughter "settled" the elder Basus did a very strange thing: they trekked to base camp of Mount Everest.

I would like to point out that Radha and I are ordinary everyday people. Like good health-conscious California folk, we go on a hike in the woods now and then, try to keep fit, enjoy the outdoors. However, through a series of events we found ourselves in Nepal in November 1998, toiling up lofty Himalayan trails in the company of seasoned trekkers and gentle Sherpas, marveling at Valkyrian vistas of the world's highest peaks. Forgetting the cold and exhaustion, we remember it as a magnificent and immensely satisfying experience.

We returned with our group to Kathmandu's Shangri-La Hotel, and were greeted by a nine-page handwritten fax from San Francisco, a diplomatic *tour de force*.

> *Dear Baba and Mommy,*
> *I've made many decisions in the month and a half that you have been gone. I wanted to write these down so you have a clear idea of what I am doing and so I have a chance*

to put on paper why I made these decisions.

I decided to quit at APM.

My last day is December 18th. I think I am leaving the company having done good work, with a reminder from my boss that the door is open for me to consider coming back, and, most importantly, with their respect.

To summarize why I left: I want to work for a small innovative place where I have substantial responsibility. I don't want to work in information technology; and, most importantly I want to work far more directly with low-income kids. It's what I wake up in the morning wanting to do, and I do it well because I care about this more than anything I have done at APM. I talked to Deep [a family friend]. He says he is not surprised. He remembers many of his Stanford friends felt much as I do when they got out of college, under-challenged and lacking sufficient responsibility.

So the next question is what do I do after I leave APM? Obviously I didn't think in that order: quit first, and then figure out what to do next. When you were leaving for Nepal I was looking for other positions working with kids—I have found several excellent possibilities—if I get any one of them I will be happy. I think.

- *Executive Director of the Stanford Medical Youth Science Program*
- *Program Developer and Coordinator for the Ravenswood (East Palo Alto) School District*
- *Biology and Science Teacher at the Edison Project in East Palo Alto*
- *Teacher at East Side Prep*

Doctors of the World are expanding their programs for street kids in Russia where I would get much responsibility for program development in areas of homelessness and children's health

Since all these potential jobs are through personal contacts I am certain that at least one of them will work out, especially given the need for qualified, educated, energetic people in these fields—teaching and nonprofit healthcare work.

The catch of all this is that I have decided not to start on any of these positions till September. When I get back in mid-May I will start working at Castilleja camp through the summer till I start my next job.

So that's the plan.

I am not the kind of person who sits around and waits—I have never been since I went to Castilleja and Stanford. If there is anything I have learned in the past few years, it is that I am the only person responsible for the quality of my life. I can't expect other people to make my life rewarding or exciting. That said, I plan now and always to be financially independent and responsible—I am paying and will continue to pay for all plane and travel tickets, for my interim health insurance, for rent, for food, for the parking tickets one can't help accumulating in this city.

I've been worried a lot that I make impulsive decisions but while you've been gone I have asked a lot of people for advice. I think in many ways I have had to make these decisions without you here—I have had to look at the world with the feeling that I am financially and emotionally responsible for my future and cannot be an adult if I expect you to take care of me and make decisions for me. Not having you to talk to for a month and a half, given how close we are, has been a coming-of-age for me—a chance for me to realize that I should be and am an independent adult.

Which is not to say I am not scared. Am I going to be

mugged while traveling through Italy? Am I giving up a lucrative, respectable job because I am a hopeless idealist? Am I not making the best of the investment that Stanford was? And Castilleja School?

I have to make these decisions because I have asked myself all these questions and feel that these decisions are the best set of answers for the time being. I want to work with kids and have a large share of independence and responsibility for which I am decently if not lavishly compensated. I have earned some time off by virtue of all that I have done in the past few years and because I am incredibly young not in age but also in maturity for the working world.

I have a strong feeling that you will be concerned by many of these decisions. All I can really say after all this writing is that I am terribly excited about all that seems possible if I frame the world in this way that I have pieced together. And at heart, I haven't made these decisions without you—I have made them with all the skills and abilities and concerns I have collected over the past 21 years—and most of these skills, abilities and concerns come from you. I guess I am saying that it is time to find my place in the world—I am definitely ready and I think, able. Regardless of whether we argue or disagree, I hope you respect how I make decisions and that you continue to be proud of me, but more importantly, have faith in me—faith that I will always try to do the best thing, faith that I will be successful in most, but not all ways that matter to you, faith that I will find stability, love and happiness wherever I decide to spend a piece of my life.

Love,
Jhomi.

၈

With this fax, the blinkers came off our eyes.

Radha and I, conservative Indians at heart, were still worried about Jhumki's future, but we began at last to see that our daughter was talented and free-spirited enough to excel in a "non-traditional" career of her choice. We realized that, as we had just done our own atypical thing on the mountain, so too Jhumki would find her own Everest, and ascend well beyond base camp.

Greg Francis, Jhumki's college friend, has stood by her through many a difficult time. His open mind and global outlook encouraged Jhumki to confide in him during days of her discontent. With help from one of Jhumki's letters, Greg shed light on her resolution to abandon corporate life. In the letter she wrote:

Time passes so quickly. Days, weeks, months go by with people just staring at computer screens and not living.

Jhumki could not go on like this, Greg felt.

"She had the need to make a difference *now*," he said. "To feel people. To teach. To be alive. What came through was her immense drive. Her desire to live life fully. Her impatience to do that which is a good thing. Most people fresh from college would get inured to the situation she faced at APM. But Jhumki quickly realized she had to have concrete plans for actually *doing* what she wanted to do, not waiting for some time in the future."

Later Jhumki told Greg she was thinking of providing healthcare to the East Palo Alto community or entering the field of science education. I made him repeat this point. It was the first evidence of science education in Jhumki's career plans.

But events were conspiring to alter her world harrowingly while Jhumki, woolly-headed after her big decision to leave APM, reflected on life.

From the journal of Jhumki Basu, Dec 19, 1998

I worked my last day at APM yesterday. What makes me most sad is that I won't get a chance to spend time with these smart, bright people anymore and with the Packard Foundation. I miss Stanford. But I have done so much in the past few months: Discover summer camp, ice-skating, yoga, reading Rushdie, became finally financially independent and will continue to be so, bought my own ticket to Europe, decided I was not fit to be a healthcare consultant at this stage in my life, realized that I enjoyed being with the admin staff at work (or at least grew closer to them) than many of the consultants at APM, decided that the silk suits and heels did not qualify me as emotionally mature, rented a house with a view and realized that a cold, empty, well-furnished apartment does not motivate me to cook, to be energetic, to sleep in my own bed.

Walked out to the Embarcadero pier yesterday—end of college, beginning of adulthood, end to the safe beaten path. Two roads diverged in a wood, and I took the one less traveled. And this has made all the difference.

Freedom, footloose, and going one place, just take one or the other path.

Oh, Jhumki!

My eyes moisten.

How could you know after you wrote this journal entry that—as you gazed across beautiful San Francisco Bay, happy and content at long last, as you listened to seagulls and sea lions on the wooden piers of the Embarcadero, as you found yourself free and footloose on the road less traveled—you had four, just four, days of innocence left?

46

6. THE TEENAGER

I n June 1990, we were back in USA, having decided to live in northern California because Hewlett-Packard offered Radha a position in Silicon Valley. After checking out several options, Jhumki decided she would enter ninth grade at Castilleja School, a well-regarded all-girls' institution in Palo Alto.

"What about boys?" I asked her.

"Oh, Baba! Can't you *ever* be serious? It's a good school. Boys aren't important."

She was right on the first item. I have called her a few times on the second!

In San Francisco we were in for sticker shock. House prices in the Bay Area were insane. After looking for several months, we moved into a home we could barely afford. Jhumki settled in at once. She decorated her room and took Tiffany for walks along wide, sparsely traveled streets.

Jhumki dived into Castilleja life from day one, enjoying the social and intellectual challenges of a stimulating and caring institution. Her eight Casti friends were often to be found at our home. They were noisy, happy girls, doing the usual teen thing: hanging out.

Sehba Ali, superintendent of Knowledge Is Power Program (KIPP) schools in Houston today, was Jhumki's very first friend at Casti. A tiny and highly driven young woman, Sehba is blessed with three beautiful children, an authoritative voice, and the knowledge and ability to improve American schools. Two decades after their high school experience, with Jhumki gone, it was comforting to talk to Sehba about those foundational years. In their professional lives, Sehba and Jhumki saw kids grow up too fast, without the amazing elementary and high school experiences they had shared. Many of the children they worked with had to become adults a lot more quickly.

"We had this great opportunity to be just children!" Sehba laughed as she remembered the time I made Jhumki learn to drive a manual-transmission car. Sehba was in the backseat when Jhumki, frustrated and in tears, kept saying, "I can't, I can't!"

"Then she learned," Sehba said. "And later she was quite proud of her ability when everyone else only drove automatics."

The years 1990 to 1994 were all about a group of nine joyful, healthy girls' growing into adolescence. There were parties, sleepovers, proms, and discussions about food, boys, dates, homework, travel, literature, careers, dreams. Along the way nine sets of parents became friends and continued to meet even after the girls went on to college.

Kritika Yegnashankaran, a Harvard PhD and professor at Bard College, has been a constant throughout Jhumki's life.

"We were in a lot of classes together," Kritika said, looking back on the blissful days "Jhumki was very bubbly, laughed a lot, and was very easy to get along with, unintimidating despite her formidable intellect. After going to college I realize that the types of early female friendships we formed were unique. A lot of girls who went to coed high schools grew to think of other women as competitors. That wasn't on the horizon for us."

The two got into the habit of keeping in touch by writing letters while Jhumki traveled during Casti summers. Kritika was struck by one letter that her friend wrote when she was in India for only ten days in 1995. It was from Chennai, where Jhumki wasn't around people her own age and was at a loss about what to do.

"So she volunteered at the Spastics Society," said Kritika in disbelief. "It was so classic that even at age seventeen Jhumki already had that in her. Nonprofit work and social consciousness were already there. She wrote she didn't want too much time to think. She wanted to *do* things."

If Jhumki had a best friend, it was Kritika. Her gentle nature, abiding encouragement for, and wonder about her friend's accomplishments, and her philosophical outlook on life, combined to influence her impulsive friend to confide her deepest feelings. Just before her death, Jhumki requested Kritika to read from a letter she had written for her own memorial ceremony.

At Castilleja, Jhumki's English teacher, Cissy Lewis, triggered a latent brilliance in our daughter: poetry.

Cissy vividly remembers Jhumki, one of her first students, as an alert, engaged, voracious learner, who wanted to discover as much as possible. In her interview for this book, Cissy recalls her student's bright eyes, wonderful intellect, independent-thinking ability, and their pleasure in learning and enjoying one another. Jhumki visited Ms. Lewis the summer before she died and they talked about her teaching, her academic work, her health, and her life with husband Alexander.

In 1993, fifteen-year-old Jhumki eloquently paid tribute to her teacher:

> *Spinning your counsel into a blanket,*
> *you have warmed the world of this child.*
> *Weaving knowledge, experience, and wisdom into literature,*
> *you have endeared English to this child.*
> *Painting the mystery of compassion into everyday,*
> *you have taught soulful living to this child.*
> *These are the arts of a teacher who creates life and love,*
> *which are inextricably linked.*

Over the years Jhumki wrote a multitude of poems in her journal. Some were childish, others dark and soul-searching. Together they are worthy of an anthology.

Every winter Castilleja held a fun event, the Father Daughter Dinner Dance. Jhumki and I would dress up in our finery—hers an evening gown, mine a rented tuxedo. We would bid good-bye to an envious Mommy and head to school. For each Casti year there is a beaming photo record of an attractive girl growing through her middle teens. She has dark waist-length hair. She is tall, fit, and strong from all the ballet and volleyball. The adolescent braces in her teeth make her brilliant smile more touching.

We were clearly mismatched at the dance. Jhumki had started to learn dancing when she was three. I have two left feet. But we managed. I carefully followed the reliable Bengali dance dictum of pushing imaginary lumps of earth forward with alternate feet, and lifting other lumps on my palms from here to there. Try it; you'll like it! I wasn't ol' twinkle-toes, but then, I didn't step on Jhumki's toes either. Most people at the event knew one another, and everyone had a good time. I envied the father who performed "Twist and Shout" with the band at the girls' fervent request each year. He was good, a real showman. Dads and girls joined in to sing the Beatles number at the tops of their voices.

Toward the end of Jhumki's senior year at Casti was the much-awaited Bridal Fundraiser. One evening, in a gaily decorated school gym complete with fashion runway, the girls looked lovely in gorgeous wedding gowns. Dads in tuxedos proudly offered their arms and paraded daughters before assembled guests. There was rapturous applause for every duo.

For the event I wore a traditional Indian tunic. When our turn came I escorted Jhumki along the runway, but who noticed me? Jhumki was resplendent in her mother's salmon-and-midnight-blue wedding sari, complete with gold thread and wedding jewelry. With her flowing hair and shining smile, her gold heels making her over six feet tall, the sixteen-year-old strode confidently down the stage and brought the house down.

After dinner that evening there was an auction of donated items. The *magnum opus* of the night was a magnificent starry quilt on which forty eight-by-eight-inch patches were sown. Each thought-provoking patch was created by a Casti senior using paint, thread, sequins, and beads—an absolute treasure. To our surprise and delight, we won the quilt, which hangs in pride of place at our home. Jhumki's patch is at the bottom right corner. On a pink background she had drawn a sun, a star, and a happy face in gold paint. Above the sun she had lettered a prophetic legend:

Forever effervescent. Forever young.

Jhumki and Kritika were salutatorians upon graduation at Castilleja, the event for which Stanford Provost Condoleezza Rice was keynote speaker. The class was required to wear formal white attire. When the girls proudly trooped in, Jhumki appeared wearing white all right, but a shimmering white silk sari and lace blouse her mother had specially brought from India. Watching her, Radha felt immensely proud.

"She had such passion and looked so distinctive," she remembered. "I told myself that day, 'In a way our job's over. We have a child that is immensely better than we could have expected. She is herself now. Jhumki is now on her own, and she could not be a better person.' I felt a sense of immense satisfaction. She had values that were ingrained in her then. Later we had disagreements on how to execute on the values, but never on the values themselves."

With her slender height and elegant costume, her hair blowing in the California breeze, Jhumki looked stunning as she rose to deliver her speech. While advising her friends against a particular way of living, Jhumki unknowingly foreshadowed the life that was to be hers:

I know for certain that we have discovered the ability to care for each other in the last four years. But I worry that in the process many of us have forgotten ourselves. I speak from experience when I say that we at Castilleja try to be perfect, to be "superwomen." Though this quest for perfection leads us to fulfillment of our dreams, I have seen it lead to self-destruction.

As you move forward into your bright futures, I ask you to take care of yourself as you would take care of others. That is not selfish; it is essential and affects your relationships with, and understanding of, other people. Thomas More says that "care of the soul asks us to open our hearts wider than they have ever been before, softening the judging and moralism that may have characterized our attitudes and behavior." Let us judge ourselves a little more gently and view imperfection as part of personalities. Let us accept ourselves as we are and live in the moment, instead of always striving for a better future, because we do the latter without trying.

It's a wild world. It's hard to get by just upon a smile, girl. So take good care.

"Castilleja was formative for Jhumki in three major ways," Radha explains.

"First, due to the amazingly stimulating environment, she cemented her intense childhood curiosity about learning new scientific principles. Jhumki and Casti built on each other in a positive way.

"Second, she developed a prolific writing ability—to express her inner self, to communicate sorrow about a grievously ill friend, to wonder at the beauty of a rose, to compose a funny observation in chemistry class. Writing every day in her journal was a torrent of feelings, a habit she continued until the very end.

She could not keep her emotions bottled.

"Finally, Casti helped make her confident—in doing science, in teaching, and in assuming her place in the world. It made her a leader."

"At Casti I can do anything," Jhumki told her mother. "Anything is possible."

༄

With her well-rounded skills and excellent grades at Castilleja, Jhumki received undergraduate admission from Stanford, Duke, Princeton, Brown, Berkeley, and Johns Hopkins. Harvard turned her down, which upset our perfectionist terribly. After visiting the campuses she selected Stanford.

Though she often mentioned her "privileged background" in later speeches and teachings, Jhumki funded her educational expenses from senior year at Stanford all the way to her PhD, with grants and scholarships that she secured herself.

Nick Bourke was one of Jhumki's first friends on the Stanford campus. He told me that students there classified themselves as "techies" or "fuzzies." According to Nick, while she seemed a techie, Jhumki defied categorization because she had a good knowledge of poetry. Though intellectually Jhumki was on par with her class, the two-plus-year age deficit placed her in a difficult social situation. Nick adopted her as a younger sister and helped her through a freshman year fraught with adjustments. Many students at Stanford were dating and pairing off into steady relationships. But, according to Nick, Jhumki was "not like that." She was much more about making deep friendships and having interesting conversations. As she evolved and grew, she developed several different types of associations and "tried some things out."

Did she want the serious, stuffy white guy, Nick wondered. Did she want the idealistic, head-in-the-clouds dreamer? How about the brilliant scientist? The worldly businessman? The artist? Like a big brother, Nick was proud when Jhumki began to deliberate in this way. He felt she was awakening and beginning to explore what she wanted out of life. A lot of people might think of her as serious, ambitious, and career driven—and she certainly was. But, Nick felt, she was so much more than that. She valued many things that were not related to work. She valued spending time with friends. She valued good food. She valued travel.

"Jhumki was both a techie *and* a fuzzie," concluded her friend.

Julie Irons was our daughter's freshman year roommate at Stanford. Like most of her dorm-mates, Julie was intrigued by how young Jhumki was. Several of them were comparing driver's licenses one day when, all of a sudden Jhumki didn't want to show hers, even though everyone knew she had a car on campus. They were shocked when they found out she was just sixteen. Jhumki played it down. She said she had moved around, gone to several school systems, and skipped a grade or two between countries.

Julie disagrees with those reasons. She affirmed that Jhumki was simply bright enough to attend Stanford at sixteen. She might have been shy about her accomplishments, but she exhibited a complete lack of shyness about going after new ones.

"Jhumki and I got along just great," said Julie. "She was a poetry writer. In freshman year she took a couple of poetry-writing workshops, and I remember her being very lost in that world when she was writing poetry."

A serious conflict was unfolding in Jhumki's thinking at this time. On one hand, she felt pressure to choose a practical major that would set her up financially such as engineering or pre-med. On the other hand, she was drawn by artistic urges that she satisfied through dance and poetry.

"I can see now why she came up with tying science with teaching as a creative outlet," Nick Bourke reflected.

And around this time Jhumki was toiling with another problem: her parents.

Radha and I have family backgrounds that are characterized by academic proficiency and risk aversion. Tamils and Bengalis make good mathematicians, doctors, professors, lawyers, engineers, scientists, economists, and bureaucrats. They value safe jobs that bring the daily bread home, and are opposed to imperiling life's security on a business or artistic venture. They panic if the safety net disappears.

Basically, Radha and I were middle-of-the-road traditionalists. "Were" I say. Not anymore. Jhumki banished our misconceptions, especially with that fax to Kathmandu.

Through the 1990s our successful high-tech careers put inevitable pressure on our daughter. She believed failure was not an option. To Jhumki, 'A' meant failure when 'A+' was possible. We never had a discussion about "Jhomi, it's okay to fail," because she never failed.

"If there was competitiveness, it was Jhumki trying to compete with her own self," explained Fanta Kamakate, a consulting mechanical engineer from the Ivory Coast who works in San Francisco. It was the summer of 2009 and we were sitting at a picnic table outside Wilbur Hall, where Fanta and Jhumki had roomed together in sophomore year.

"The competitive nature of the premed track," said Fanta, "did weigh on her because there was more emphasis on grades than on learning. She was very interested in *really* learning why and digging in to stuff, versus being able to ace the test. And she got frustrated because the whole track was based on getting good grades so that one could write a good premed application."

Midway through Stanford, Jhumki decided to pursue a human biology major, with the ambition of becoming a great doctor like my father. Her research guide was Dr. William Durham, a popular anthropology professor who shared Jhumki's ardent love of wildlife. In 1996 Prof Durham took her on a memorable alumni cruise to the Galápagos Islands, where she chose a highly original research topic: *Impact of fractals and chaos theory on the growth of coral beds.*

"Did she *want* to do medicine?" Fanta hypothesized. "You know, that's a tricky one. There were two things that were going on. There was her love of teaching and her love for being with kids, which were already there. And there was the pathway of thinking about what she was going to do with her life. Eventually they all merged, and she was able to integrate her love of science with her love of kids.

"In the summer after our freshman year, she worked in in the Discover summer program for little kids from poor homes. You could see how happy she was as a counselor with the experiments she was teaching her kids. I saw a shift in her premed track after she went to Russia. I wasn't surprised about it. But I was surprised by how long it took."

7. THE INSANITY OF LIFE

I t was late November 1998 when we came down from our mountain. The evenings in Delhi were chilly and dark. Inside the cozy Saket apartment, Radha and I excitedly recounted to Shanti and SNA our triumphant journey through the high Himalaya. But even Everest could not mask our concern about what was happening outside.

In the eight years since we had left Delhi, the city had become increasingly unsafe. We were shocked to hear of a recent triple murder in front of a house in Saket, barely one hundred meters from where we sat. SNA was chief of security for their housing association, and we worried about his safety. Around our Himalayan chatter we planned their upcoming U.S. visit for Ranga's graduation with a docotrate in astrophysics at UCLA and Sumitra's engagement in Boston.

"Come as soon as you can!" we urged them.

Radha and I left their apartment on a smoky, wintry night for our flight back to the U.S. As our taxi pulled away, Shanti and SNA, wrapped in blankets against the cold, stood on the pavement and waved good-bye in the dim light of a street lamp.

"Go inside," we signaled urgently from the taxi's rear window. "Go inside quickly."

Three weeks later and two days before Christmas in California, dusk had fallen early when our phone rang. I picked it up in our study. It was Radha's cousin Chakravarthy calling from Delhi. He asked for Radha and I handed her the phone without thinking. She sat down at the desk to take the call. I was walking out of the room when I heard a sound and looked back.

The handset dropped to the desk from my wife's nerveless fingers with a clatter. She reeled back with glazed eyes and would have fallen from the chair had I not caught her.

It is a scene seared into my brain.

Supporting her, I picked up the receiver.

"Hello? Chucks?"

"Dipak?"

"Yes. What's going on?"

"Listen, Dipak. I don't know everything. They have found some bodies near Shanti's house. I am rushing to Saket."

"Chucks! What—?" But Chucks had disconnected.

I didn't have Chucks' phone number to call him back. What in heaven's name was happening? Radha got up and moved away. I instinctively dialed Shanti's number. It rang a few times, and just as I was about to hang up in dismay, there was a click and Shanti's clear voice came on the line.

"Hello?" said Shanti.

A surge of blinding light shot through me. I was about to shout joyfully for Radha when her sister continued speaking in a measured tone.

"Thank you for calling. We are not at home now. Please leave a message at the sound of the tone, and we shall call you back as soon as possible."

'Beep!' went the sound of the tone, and with it went the life we had known.

From *The Tribune*, Dec 25, 1998
No Breakthrough in Couple's Murder

NEW DELHI, Dec 25—The Delhi police is yet to achieve a breakthrough in the murder of an aged couple in Saket in South Delhi on Wednesday night. The police have questioned several suspects, including hawkers who regularly visit the colony. The three security guards of the colony, Hamdar, Bheem Bahadur and Lal Bahadur, were questioned yesterday, the police said.

The bodies of S.N.A. Chary, a retired Deputy General Manager of Engineers India Limited, and his wife, Shanti, a teacher in Carmel Convent School, were found in a park in

Saket. The bodies were found on Thursday morning. They had sustained head injuries from a blunt object. The bodies were noticed by a resident of F Block in Saket, Mr. Deepak Kumar, while he was on his morning walk.

"The couple has a son and a daughter who live in America and are expected to reach here tomorrow," Additional Deputy Commissioner of Police, Vivek Gogia said. He said it seemed that the couple was coming from the market when attacked. A cash receipt found near their bodies confirmed that the couple had purchased some jewelry. The jewelry and a diamond earring of Shanti Chary were found missing. The ADCP said "robbery could be the motive behind the murder of the couple."

After another call with Chucks that confirmed the deaths, it was my unenviable task to break the news to the Chary kids. I still remember every word of those phone conversations, and their horrified incredulity. Then I called Jhumki, who left at once to drive over from her San Francisco apartment. Radha was completely crushed and frantic with grief. Worried that she might hurt herself, Jhumki and I did our best to take care of her while the night wore on. Before the sun rose I was boarding the first flight to Los Angeles to collect Ranga for the long journey to Delhi. Jhumki and Radha flew in the following day, in time for the funeral. A cousin accompanied Sumitra from Boston. Our collective recollections of the subsequent terrible days are jumbled into an amorphous grey. The body bags, the cremation pyre, the hauntingly normal Saket apartment, the frustration with Delhi Police, the memorials at Carmel Convent and at Shanti's home, they were parts of a single numbing ordeal.

Brokenhearted, we turned our backs on the forlorn Saket apartment that had seen so much happiness and returned to our respective lives. It had been established that the motive for the brutality was not robbery. Who would harm the biggest-hearted people anyone had ever known? Was it a case of mistaken identity? A mugging gone horribly wrong? Did SNA see or know something in his role of security chief that caused a murderous assault? We would never know. The perpetrators of the crime were never apprehended.

There is an eerie twist to this agonizing episode.

When I was a kid I used to ask grown-ups this riddle:

Q: What does December have that no other month does?

A: The letter 'D'

Now it has something else. December has become our Ides of March, a trail of fatal tragedies that have invariably occurred in the final month of the year.

In December 1982, Radha's eldest sister Viji's husband was killed in a car accident. KG, as he was known to everyone, was a delightful person who energetically oversaw our wedding arrangements in 1975. On the fateful evening, KG was walking along a Chennai roadside, *en route* to dinner at a friend's place, when a runaway truck hit him from behind. After frantic calls through the night his seventeen-year-old son, Preetham, finally identified his father's body in a police morgue. We were told KG didn't feel anything when he died. It was as simple and final as that. Our first tragedy.

My father was being prepped for cardiac bypass surgery in London's Harley Street Clinic, when he suffered a massive heart attack. My mother, Radha, and I were by his side when Babai passed away forty-eight hours later. That was December in 1986. Mum herself was diagnosed with cancer in December 1993 and left us soon thereafter. Radha's mother suffered a stroke in December 1996 that killed her. My friend and one-time business partner, Prem Shivdasani, collapsed and died on a tennis court in December 1990. We lost Sapna, a close family friend who will soon figure in this story, that same month. Two Decembers earlier, a close cousin of Radha's, along with her nephew, died in a car crash on a Bangalore highway when their driver fell asleep at the wheel. Shanti and SNA were murdered ten years later to the day.

December would continue to stalk us like a curse.

The impact of Shanti's death on Jhumki was devastating. We didn't initially realize how devastating as she seemed mentally and physically strong in Delhi. She took charge of her mother and stayed close to Ranga. But inside she was traumatized as evinced in her journal:

> *Today is Tuesday in Delhi. I don't think I have been alone since last Wednesday night. The whole world seems disconnected from this living room where I am sitting alone with a hot water bottle. I have had no time to think or write or even feel anything but superficial emotions—disgust at the fictitious stories in the newspapers, laughter at immature jokes.*
>
> *Outside, there is so much dirt, pollution filling up one's sinuses and casting a haze over the entire city—my throat is dry and my lungs are filled with dust and grime. I don't remember Delhi like this—literally thousands of short slim men with nothing to do, trees being cut down, people afraid to walk in the parks. I remember playing cricket and field hockey every day where my aunt and uncle were found with their bodies placed neatly, lined up in the dirt—with their heads smashed by iron rods—face down in the dirt all night—a supposedly foggy night when no one in apartments ten feet away could see or hear any part of three or four men with iron rods who attacked an elderly couple and smashed their skulls open. And everyone wants to find the perpetrators, kill them—but no number of trees cut down, police deployed and searches for "the killer(s)" will turn this community away from a world defined by*

bars in every window, suspicious glances between neighbors, fear of walking during the day, not just the night, the paranoia of my dad who is trying to be everyone's parent but cannot face that he is no one's parent—because we have all grown up, especially Ranga who has cremated his mother and father after identifying them as homicide victims in a morgue. I wish I had seen their faces—I wish I had been given the choice—better at least for me, to face the cold realities of truth than forever pretend or imagine—at least facing realities liberates one to fear fewer things. And now we are terrified to be in an apartment that we shared with the people we love in Delhi—paranoid enough to not feel the joy and contentment that used to reside there only a few days ago, not willing to celebrate life, only expressing fear of also being found face down in a pool of blood and dirt. I wish I had seen the bodies—because the story of the crime—murder and the placement of bodies in a park 100 feet away at 7:30 pm in a wide alley next to two well-populated apartment buildings, in an alley where cars pass and the blood was in pools on the ground and no one saw or heard—is quite simply unbelievable.

And I would not cry, or hold anyone here and cry, much as my mom wishes that everyone grieved like her in outbursts and weepy voices. I would rather watch and wait for Ranga, follow his moods and wait for how he chooses to express himself or need people or things. I predict long walks—and many tears hidden through the lens of a telescope and him hanging on to the memory of his father's crumpled forehead and his mother's cheek which crumpled just after the iron rod shattered her diamond earring—shattered so thoroughly that they couldn't find the shards and assumed just one earring was stolen.

Will I come back to Delhi? Only if Ranga asks I think—

because where to walk, how to stand outside someone else's flat that used to be my aunt's window where she cooked and graded papers?

♈

Jhumki had experienced a deeply impressionable time in Russia and had just made a huge, career-changing decision. Along the way she had had a difficult parting with a young man she was seeing. On a lonely night in Moscow she had answered the phone to my voice telling her about the death of her beloved dog, Tiffany. Now she had lost her second mother to insensate violence. Her world was in ruins.

"My predominant memory of Jhumki in college was a lot of silliness, goofiness, laughter," said Kritika. "That changed when her aunt and uncle were killed."

In a letter to her friend, Jhumki wrote that if it had been her parents who had died, people would have understood, but because it had been an aunt and uncle, people had no idea how she could grieve for so long. The inability of others to understand her grieving really bothered her.

"It was a turning point in her life," Kritika went on. "Some amount of her natural lightheartedness was gone because the heartbreak distressed her so intensely. It changed the way she viewed her relationships. For the first time she realized that friends are not just there to have fun and be goofy with, but that it was important for them to be relied on in bad times, when one is not the funniest person to be with.

"Looking back now, there was an urgency with which she pushed herself that hadn't been there before. As hard as Jhumki had driven herself before, it at least doubled after this. We talked about the fact there are no guarantees in life. Things could suddenly, unpredictably, and horribly turn for the worse. It was an awful lesson to have to learn."

Two months later, having resigned from her job, Jhumki decided to travel to Italy alone to get away from aftershocks of the massive tremor that had shaken her world. Her nerves were raw. Her psyche was fragile. She tried to draw inspiration from the glory of Rome, but failed. Radha and I read her e-mails and listened to her on phone calls with growing trepidation. Her mind was disturbed. It was a time when she told us everything and listened to nothing. Radha, submerged under a mountain of gloom herself, recognized that Shanti's death had crushed her daughter's confidence.

"Everything Jhumki took for granted was destroyed during that time," she said in retrospect. "Her view of life was lying in pieces. In an instant she went from a naïve kid to one who had nightmares that her parents might be suddenly gone and she would be all alone. Her faith in God, in religion, in family, in us, was gone.

"'Would you really have come and got me from Europe?' she asked me once. On hearing the affirmative, she exclaimed with childish relief, 'Then it means you are still there for me!'

"It was also the time when her belief in faith and the power of prayer disappeared. She shunned all aspects of religion and of God. It's hard to say if this is true about spirituality—she associated it with other things. It was erratic behavior on her part. I was in no position to be tolerant, as I was grieving so much. We had a big fight when she wouldn't come on a trip to Tibet with all of us. I thought she didn't care to be with the family. She felt that if she didn't grieve the way I wanted her to, it meant she grieved less. She didn't believe in family grief and she was lashing out. I was so hurt that I felt it would have been better if it was I who had died."

And then Jhumki went into free fall.

From the journal of Jhumki Basu, March 1, 1999

If I commit suicide, please read this at a service for me, and let any of my loved ones read this too, and . . .

Please tell Prof Don Barr that if my thesis gets accepted for its first round at the Journal of Public Health I would like him to make revisions they ask for so it can get published. Lots of work went into this thesis. I would hate not to have it published after all this time and effort.

Discover: Dave has all my stuff for Discover and so does Carey. It's all very organized. It should suffice to say that I hope someone can care about this program and more importantly, about the girls who go through this program, as much as I do. If someone has as much energy and love and excitement for this program as I do, I have no worries about where it will go. It's easy to forget that those little girls are the most important thing in the world—they deserve all the love and energy and wisdom they can get.

Besides these two things everything I can think of is transitory. I suppose the list is endless.

I imagine that when I die, people will be sad. But I am fairly certain it will only make them sadder, more frustrated, and more disappointed to watch me try to be all those things I used to be once and no longer have the energy to be. I like the person I used to be—lots of positive energy and excitement and curiosity—and I miss that person perhaps even more. I also have no place to set down my bags though many people have offered their places. What I want is my own place, a place I love coming home to, one that is mine. But I also don't have the energy to make this happen.

I am worried that lots of people will blame themselves for me dying, blame themselves for being bad friends or inadequate support. That is not the case. I have had more love from each of you in my life than a person could ask for, had more opportunity than most people. What I don't have is the will to face my sadness, Ranga's sadness, my parents' sadness. I don't have the will to face myself hurting people who try to help me. I don't have faith in myself—how can I? I cannot imagine a time when the world will be less sad now that my aunt and uncle have died.

To those of you, who have held on to me and listened to me in these darkest of times, thank you. You have created temporary respite and opportunity for me to have moments in space I can call home. Somehow the continuity between these times of peace is lacking and not strong enough to hold me. And that continuity can only come from me believing in myself. All your faith and love cannot substitute for me having faith in myself.

Travel and learn and see a thousand places and love like you have never been hurt and dance like no one is watching. Love each other a lot. Love my parents a lot. Love Ranga a lot. Do the million things I would do in a day, intensely, feel all the feelings I would, see all the places I would discover, and create knowledge and create the strongest bonds with people that you can imagine. I love you, each of you, with all my heart. Safe passage in all your journeys—journeys of distance and journeys of heart.

Take care and much love,
Jhumki.

8. THE VEILED ASSASSIN

Inside the happiness and excitement of our daughter's teenage years, before the heartbreak that was the death of her aunt and uncle, while she was in the company of close friends, of great teachers, and a loving family, there lurked for her a thorn. That thorn portended a pattern that was about to dominate her life: an unending cycle of extreme joy followed by extreme trauma.

Radha describes Sapna Mirchandani, her colleague at Hewlett Packard as "my dear friend."

Sapna and her family were often at our Delhi home in the eighties. A young mother, she was terrified of dogs. When Tiffany came home as a puppy, Sapna would retreat until she ended up standing on the dining table. At other times she would wait at the gate until Tiffany was leashed. In time, though, she and Tiffany became very good friends, and Jhumki was proud that Sapna Aunty got to like her dog.

Soon after we moved back to the United States, Radha received a note from Sapna saying her throat cancer, which had been in remission for six years, had returned.

"You were my guardian and you kept it away," Sapna wrote to her boss. "Now that you are gone it has come back."

Sapna's cancer and subsequent traumatic passing in December 1990 had a lasting impact on Jhumki. It was the first time death had presented itself so starkly, more so because Sapna was young and vivacious and she had played with Sapna's little son.

Jhumki had already had her first experience with the disease when Radha's eldest sister Viji was diagnosed with breast cancer in 1988. Though only ten years old then, Jhumki was quite involved as we rushed Viji to Tata Memorial Hospital in Mumbai and cared for her while she underwent surgery and radiation therapy. Through the grace of God, Viji had no recurrence.

Sapna, as events unfolded, suffered grievously through the last stages of the disease, and Jhumki got to know how rapacious cancer could be. In Sapna, who was so young—she was thirty-three when she died—Jhumki saw the cruelty in the way cancer devastated, deformed, and killed a real and treasured person. When Sapna's news got worse, Radha flew to India to see her and missed Jhumki's thirteenth birthday. Sapna died soon after the visit. During her last days she couldn't hear or see, her face was bloated and she wrote little notes to communicate.

Jhumki drenched her journal with reflections on her friend's rapid decline and death.

Sapna

by Jhumki Basu

from *Mochuelo,* Castilleja's literary magazine, 1992

Somewhere, someplace, you will do
Extraordinary things,
But this is not your time.
The hand you reached out
to whitewash the night sky with your dreams
was cut short by a raging virulent meteor
that neither knew nor cared about the enigma it destroyed.
And that is what you are, an enigma,
A solitary wanderer in a forsaken land.
Even when the tubes spiral through you,
when chemotherapy invades
your private being
and the cancer ruptures chasms in your cheeks
and bones and throat;
Even as the tormenting grasp of fate
has snatched away your ultimate connection,

Your enigmatic flavored voice.
You are the person I first encountered screaming
"Tiffany" to my melancholy-eyed Labrador;
You can take her for walks
when she prances to the Happy Hunting Grounds
in the wake of elusive butterflies.

Our daughter had recurrent nightmares about Sapna as she grew older. In a brooding, psychedelic piece about her friend's last hours, she dramatically illuminates her absorption in Sapna's suffering:

Sapna, blinded and terrified, grabbed on to a cold metal rod. Tossed by the crazed wind, her feet slid upward and met rung after rung of tarnished ladder. She encountered blurred snapshot images of her loved ones spiraling into the chasm. She averted her teary eyes. The rungs were gnarled and uneven now. Her feet absorbed the cancerous coating on the stained metal and the cancer invaded her. Chemotherapy radiation sizzled on the rungs and tubing punctured her fragile body. Blinded by her disease, terrified by her blindness, she crawled on, rung by rung, to the point of light above her. She did not notice the blackness enveloping her. Deaf, she did not hear the air howl, just the wind slicing her with its jagged corners.

At the final rung the light illuminated her perforated gaping face and teary eyes. The wind buffeted her into an ever-tightening spiral and cut into her body, leaving shards of soul in the sunlit air. The shards floated down gently, approaching the chasm. Brushed by sunlight, like crystal they reflected colors and disintegrated to join the hues of the sky.

God must watch over the descent of the tortured.

9. THE LONG ROAD BACK

Paul and Ambika. Carey Davis. Greg Francis. James Monohan. Kritika.

You formed a ring around our daughter, a ring she could not penetrate because she kept faith in you when she had lost faith in herself. You held her away from the abyss. You brought her back. You have our undying love.

In the summer of 1999, two of Jhumki's closest friends, Paul and Ambika Prokop, a newly married couple, were living in Boston. Paul's wit and irreverence, Ambika's warmth and affection, their unshakable dependability, endeared them to our daughter at the lowest point in her life.

In Herculaneum in Italy, solitary, distressed, and frantic, Jhumki suffered a nervous breakdown. In California, Radha and I were sick with anxiety as suicidal vibrations came over long-distance phone conversations. I was getting ready to catch a flight to Rome when Jhumki agreed to return to the States and stay with the Prokops.

Safe in Boston, Jhumki read a lot. She sat in on Paul's classes at Harvard. According to Paul, she could not bear to watch violent movies, which caused her visceral reactions. She had a really hard time understanding what happened, why it happened, and how something like the Delhi calamity could have happened. Ambika and Paul worried because Jhumki talked about hurting herself.

"Hurting, not killing, herself," Paul hastened to point out.

She once told him, "I feel like cutting myself and putting my hands in boiling water to see what it feels like."

Jhumki was exhibiting signs of post-traumatic stress disorder. Perhaps she was numb and wanted to feel something physically, but I think it was deeper than that. In her journal she wrote about wanting to experience the pain that her uncle and aunt had suffered in a dark alley in a violent city. An excerpt from a letter to her friend, James, describes these emotions:

I have been crying a lot. My uncle and aunt's furniture is now at Sumitra's house [also in Boston]. I am sitting at their dining table, writing, and this is the first time since they died that I have been able to spend time alone with their belongings, been able to touch the curves of the wooden chairs, the tassels, and the small rectangular cot that was theirs, being able to touch the towels and pillowcases that belonged to my aunt.

What happens to someone's spirit when the person dies, James? How can all these things still be here, seats on which they sat, fabrics they chose, vases they put flowers into, moments and expressions captured on film, how can these exist in their absence? What happens is that bodies and objects, all those meaningless things, remain, yet the most important things—identity, memory, consciousness, emotions—stop in an instant. All this is so fleeting that it takes one beating, one violent murder to erase, and all other things are far less precious for me.

Two of Jhumki's friends, James and Kritika, were the rocks around which washed Jhumki's turbulent life. She grew up with them. She shared deep experiences—glad and sad—with them, till the end.

James is a rising movie maker working for TV channels in New York. Jhumki once dubbed her skinny, creative, redheaded buddy, "Pixie James." This had something to do with his winning a film-making award that involved pixels. In every celebratory event in Jhumki's life, James was sure to be found behind a camera.

"On the phone to me," James recalled, "describing that incident of her uncle and aunt's murder, was a loss of innocence for her. The deep pain she suffered, the emotional reaction, they affected her for months and months. It resulted in lots of crying, lots of breakdowns, lots of late-night conversations between us in person or on the phone, in which she kept imagining that horrible night when her uncle and aunt were viciously cut down, in which she started extending their death to fears of her own death, or the death of other loved ones."

From a letter from Jhumki Basu to Greg Francis, Mar 8, 1999

I have been crazy lately, Greg—unsettled, unbalanced, irrational, insensitive and impractical. I have been saying things I wouldn't under normal circumstances and irresponsible. I am restless to have something on which to focus my energies.

I get scared about moving back to San Francisco—afraid that I will be overwhelmed with social obligations I do not want, phone calls I don't want to return, and the feeling that I always have something to prove to myself—that I can be alone, can have a thousand friends, can live with minimal sleep or food.

I think one of the hardest parts of the past few months is that I seem to be scared of myself and lack faith in myself— unlike ever before. I am scared of learning new things, of being alone, of not being loved, of failing at work, learning, teaching, friendship, love. This fear makes me not want to start anything because I am afraid of getting hurt or rejected or disappointed.

Today has been a decent day—sent out some resumes, went to yoga, went cross-country skiing for the first time yesterday. I haven't cried yet today which is a first in a while as well. Wrote postcards to my Discover girls!

So that's the scoop, Jhumki.

৯৹

Where, through all of this, were her parents?

Oh, we were around, usually at the receiving end of an emotionally supercharged phone line or a *"So there!"* e-mail. If it hadn't been for our faith in Ambika and Paul, we would have found a way to bring Jhumki home. We knew she was unreasonably angry with us. It was hard, but we admitted that we were part of the problem. She was doing everything—she *was* everything—any parent could ask for. We would have been deliriously happy with much less. But the more she achieved, the more she felt she had to achieve—even when it came to grief. The rebellious feeling was deep-rooted at the time and it accentuated the horrors she was experiencing. With enormous difficulty and against all the instincts of parenthood as she spiraled away, we kept a low profile so as not to antagonize her, watching, waiting, while she fought her way through the murky labyrinth.

৯৹

Soon after Shanti and SNA's deaths, Radha decided to part company with Hewlett-Packard where she had worked for over twenty years. Several hi-tech firms courted her, but Radha held off deciding on her next step until the nightmare showed signs of abating. During the spring and summer of 1999, there were times when I found her sitting on the ground inside a closet in a trancelike state from which it was hard to bring her back. At other times, fiery-eyed, she was determined to go off to India to hunt down her sister's killers. I dissuaded her by mentioning Delhi's unsafe streets and the unholy nexus between crime, politics and law enforcement, which would combine to defeat her quest for justice. And she now had two new children, Sumitra and Ranga, who needed her whole.

In August Radha accepted the position of CEO at a software start-up called Support.com. But before she started, we took Ranga, Sumitra, her fiancé Jonathan, and Viji's son Preetham on another long journey—a pilgrimage this time—to Tibet. Jhumki, busy with summer camp and lesson planning, her faith in family and spirituality destroyed, refused to join us.

Trekking through eastern Nepal to its border with China, we scaled a 15,000-foot pass and descended into Tibet to an immense, blue, and serene body of water, the fabled Mansarovar or "Lake of the Mind." On a crystal-clear afternoon by its shore, Radha chanted a Sanskrit mantra over a sacred fire, while the rest of us prayed that peace be granted to Shanti and SNA's departed souls. We waded into the cold, clean waters and consecrated their ashes which Ranga had brought from Delhi. And at once, all of us felt a sense of closure and a weight lift from our shoulders. We raised our eyes to Mount Kailas, its iconic snow-capped summit gleaming on the azure horizon, and prayed that Lord Shiva, whose abode is the mountain, bestow His blessings and keep the rest of us safe.

In late summer of that year Jhumki hugged Ambika and Paul and boarded a flight back to Europe, determined to try again.

She inaugurated the trip by beginning an exquisitely decorated scrapbook with a quote from physicist Richard Feynman telling his wife Arline:

"It is a time to comfort you as you wish to be comforted, not as I think you should wish to be comforted. It is a time to love you in any way that you wish. Whether it be by not seeing you or by holding your hand or whatever."

Free and footloose once again, she visited historic Bath, Cornwall, and London. From England she went to Ireland and immersed herself in literature. Thence to the Anne Frank House and the Rijksmuseum in Amsterdam, where she devoured the works of Van Gogh, Rembrandt, and Vermeer. In Belgium, while pondering an aboriginal exhibit in Brugge, she tried to understand a tradition that had existed for fifty thousand years and wrote in her journal:

All I can see is a magnificently intricate series of dot patterns. But what the painter is conveying is the story of the creation of the world. Such vivid colors, such a distinctly different use of expression . . . dreaming and singing the world into existence.

At the Hergé Museum, she bought a comic book for me, *Tintin in Tibet,* in Bengali! She put her pack down at the Brussels home of Madhu Anand, Ambika's mother, rested, and wrote extensively about life, dreams and love.

And then, heroically, she returned to Italy.

This time her mind was without fear as she toured the historic places she had abandoned in April. Sitting in the verdant Boboli Gardens of Florence, she pondered science and the great sculptors:

We spend so much technological energy in our efforts to create life. It is ironic that Michelangelo may have come closer than our society has with its genetic innovations. The Four Prisoners and St. Matthew *seem ready to set themselves free and step into life. They are lifting out their heads and lifting their necks, arching out of their rocks, lifting arms and bodies free.*

Jhumki's last day in Europe was spent in the Cinque Terre. There she received an e-mail from Carey Davis, her beloved coach and mentor at Castilleja, which she pasted it into her scrapbook.

jhumki, here are your instructions:

- *keep eating ice cream*
- *don't think about Discover*
- *do think about working at Castilleja*
- *keep sleeping late, or going to bed early, or taking siestas*
- *keep climbing up mountains and steeples and domes*

- *keep telling Ms. Criswell [her Latin teacher] how much you love the Roman Empire*
- *do eat pasta and bread and fresh fruit*
- *do drink red wine*
- *keep writing*

all is well here
love, carey

On that same day, May 5, 1999, Jhumki wrote a bravura proclamation that closed the book on six months of torment.

I call it the Cinque Terre Manifesto.

This is the sound of my voice, the sound of my body, my will, my ability to ponder and struggle and spring back into life, to see detachment and self-discipline, to grow from doing my best and being individually successful to inspiring success, creativity and satisfaction in others so the things I care about are better achieved.

There is a garden to be grown, stories to be told, hands-on activities to be created, a journal to be turned into a scrapbook, coffee to be had with Kritika at Prolific Oven, mountains to climb with Ranga, a coolness and calm and personality to cultivate, an interesting job to be done well, panic to sort through and reduce and overcome, realistic goals to set, an acceptance of sifting through anger and grief and rage and sadness and vulnerability and foolishness and irresponsibility and dependence to be had— to feel these through, accept the reality of these situations and failings, accept that they have happened and how they feel so the light comes.

"Be patient and you will have what you want."

A steely center to move through life, a sense of purpose without reaching immortality or special recognition in the universe.

Sense of purpose in all events and will to pursue that purpose.

Wisdom to rest, retreat, feel and then detach when other people's voices overwhelm.

Then wait for my own voice to speak.

This is the sound of my voice.

PART II

THE TEACHER

Jhumki used to have, on her bedspread, a radial logarithmic map of the universe. We used to lie in bed together and talk. I was nine, so she was nineteen.

From that map she introduced me to astronomy, geometry, physics, planetary motion—virtually every foundational scientific discipline I know today. The woman was extraordinary!

Aman Kumar
January 24, 2009

10. THOSE GENES

"She set high standards for herself!"

James Monohan was speaking animatedly with interviewer Maithreyi on the subject of Jhumki's drive to excel.

"I think a lot of it came from the high standards her parents placed before her. That's my best guess for where these standards came from, because she had some of the highest standards for living that I have ever encountered. For her work, for her social life, her cultural life, and also in terms of physical fitness. I think that was very consistent with how her parents live. They work very hard, they play very hard, they want to do the best they can for other people, for their family members and close friends. They want to achieve to the highest levels of their professions and reach the highest levels of knowledge. So my best guess in terms of where it came from was familial culture."

James was right. Many of Jhumki's abilities and values were inherited and not just from her parents. I thanked him for his kind words and spent the next hour describing to him his friend's family history.

Jhumki's aunt was widowed at seven.

Actually it was her great-great-great-great-aunt, whom we shall call Rupa, as her real name is lost to antiquity. Great-aunt Rupa had an arranged marriage when only five in India of the late nineteenth century, where child brides lived with their parents until they came of age, whereupon they moved into their husbands' homes. Even though child marriage was recognized even then as a social evil, declared illegal by the British Raj, it was, and still is, present in Indian society. When Great-aunt Rupa's husband died, her father, Debendra Ghose, anticipating a lifetime of drudgery that would be a widow's fate, arranged her second wedding when she was thirteen. Indians of the time virulently opposed widow remarriage and a mighty, media-driven battle erupted between the traditionalists and intelligentsia of Kolkata over poor Rupa's second marriage. The furor was heightened because Kolkata was India's capital city at the time, and it was where the country's renaissance was blooming. The Ghose family became ostracized. No one would allow their son to marry Debendra's granddaughter Lila, my grandmother, an educated girl at a time when women were not considered important enough to be taught to read and write. Fortunately for Jhumki and me, Chunilal Basu, a giant of his time, agreed to his son Anil's marriage to Lila in 1910.

And having done so, Chunilal braced himself and stood his ground in the eye of the public storm that arose.

"We are today cutting the legs off our own society," thundered my great-grandfather in a press interview. "On four sides are drawn lines of tradition and negativity. We know but we do not accept what is right and what is wrong. I will *not* hold the coat-tails of narrow-mindedness and preclusion. Chuni Basu never stands on one foot. When he stands, *he stands on both!*"

Chunilal's early life was steeped in poverty. He completed his education but, to his eternal shame, was forced to sell his wife's jewels to fend off starvation. Later he traveled to Burma on a British posting and earned enough

to turn the tide and repay his debts. In time he became a celebrated chemist and raised the family fortunes. His best-selling book, *Food,* published at the dawn of the twentieth century, enlightened Indian readers for the first time about the value of balanced diets. He was a close friend of India's great spiritual leader, Swami Vivekananda, and championed religious tolerance in a country wracked by ethnic strife. Chunilal's hardworking biographer has traced the Basu genealogy twenty-eight generations, through war, disease, famine, invasion, and migration, to five ancient families that journeyed from Kannauj in central India to Bengal in the 1200s.

The brightest luminary in Jhumki's ancestry was my father.

Dr. Ajit Kumar Basu, whom I called Babai, was a true-blue medical pioneer, a heart surgeon, one of India's great sons. Babai performed the country's first open-heart surgery and was applauded internationally for his research in tropical medicine and path-breaking operative techniques in cardio-thoracic surgery. He was a founder of India's iconic All India Institute of Medical Sciences. As I was growing up, Babai would fly off to London every summer to examine fellowship candidates at the Royal College of Surgeons, of which he was a fellow and governor. Or he would visit the United States, the USSR, Iraq, or Israel on lecture tours and conferences. He collaborated closely with another medical pioneer, Michael DeBakey. Babai's research institute in Kolkata conducted exchange programs with Dr. DeBakey's Baylor College of Medicine in Houston. As a teenager I once picked up the phone at home and dropped it in fright. It was the President of India calling for my father.

Babai was equally involved in teaching, research, private practice, and philanthropy. His abundant medals glisten in our living room. He was a big man, six foot three, with a stentorian voice and an imperious manner. During his heyday, residents and nurses quaked in his presence. Bureaucrats, who got in his way, regretted their rashness. His students respected and doted on him. A patient of Babai's once remarked that my father might not remember the names of every person in Kolkata, but he was sure to have done something with their insides. Dr. Basu stories about my father were as rousing as Dr. Basu stories later associated with our daughter.

Babai's last years were among his happiest, spent in India with little Jhumki, the only grandchild he would see.

My mother, Geeta Basu, was an unusually sophisticated and big-hearted person. Having traveled with my father to the U.S. and Europe from the 1940s, and with a diverse friends' society, she filled decorated our home with beautiful souvenirs and entertained with a many-faceted cuisine. At the same time, she was a dedicated social worker. She founded Welfare Society for the Blind in Kolkata and ran it for over thirty years, providing poor, visually-impaired people employment training.

Mum was a friend and an admired role model for our daughter during her formative years.

The Basu lineage gave Jhumki professional impetus. From Radha's side she inherited the mantle of teaching, the dogged determination to achieve, the work-till-you-drop ethic, and the strength to endure misfortune.

In 1926, Radha's grandfather, Srinivasan, a school principal, died in the village of Vangal in southern India and left his family destitute. Like Chunilal Basu in faraway Bengal fifty years earlier, his eldest son, Ramaswami, Radha's father, then sixteen years old, somehow carried the large family on his shoulders, studied hard, worked hard, and climbed the engineering ranks of Indian Railways. He restored family fortunes and moved the family to the city of Chennai.

Jhumki never met Grandfather Ramaswami. While in Los Angeles in 1978, we heard he was seriously ill and packed our six-month-old for the flight to India to be by his side. At the curbside at Mumbai Airport, Shanti gave us the news he had passed away.

Ramaswami's wife Kalyani, all of four foot eleven, always radiated a hummingbird's boundless energy. In the early years of their marriage, she traveled to far-flung parts of British-ruled India and, later, of the newly independent country, to manage a home for her railwayman husband and their three daughters.

One of Ramaswami's assignments was chief engineer responsible for the construction of a frontier railroad in India's remote and disturbed northeast. Kalyani would tell Jhumki, as she grew up, stories of attacks with poisoned arrows in tribal territories on the lawless borders with Burma and China.

From the time of her birth, Jhumki adored Kalyani Paati and included her tiny grandma in all her dreams and triumphs.

In the late 1970s, when Jhumki was a year old, Kalyani came to stay with us in our creaky, 150-year-old house in Andover, Massachusetts. She had never worn shoes in her life, as she preferred sandals or bare feet in the hot climate of Chennai. For the snows of New England we convinced her to wear boots and equally unfamiliar socks.

One winter day, when Radha and I were at work, the sun shone brightly. Our indoor plants, according to Kalyani, looked wilted and in need of fresh air. She hauled on the newfangled footwear, struggled into a parka over her sari, tracked through the snow, and put the plants out in a nice, sunny spot. Later she was reduced to tears when they froze. She could never understand how it could be cold when the sun shone.

We moved to a brand-new home in Burlington in 1979 and spring arrived. The sun shone—warmly this time. It was late evening when I returned home from work one day. I pulled into the driveway and noticed with rising alarm that the house was completely dark. Where were they? Then I made out two small faces peering out from the gloom of an open window. I rushed inside and found to my relief that they were unharmed. Here is what happened. Because the day was nice, Kalyani opened the windows to let in fresh air. Being a big-city lady from the tropics, she didn't know much about springtime in rural New England. Toward dusk, when she turned on the lights, every bee, wasp, fly, moth, yellow jacket, grasshopper, and praying mantis from the neighborhood flew in through our yet-to-be-screened windows. Valiantly defending her granddaughter, Kalyani first took a badminton racket to the intruders and then, deploying Plan B, she bundled themselves against stings and turned the lights off in the hope that the insects would fly out. They did, but it took a week.

Eighteen eventful years passed.

In December 1996, Jhumki arrived from Moscow to Viji's Chennai apartment and her grandmother opened the door. Behind the wan smile Kalyani was suffering from a severe headache and was soon forced to lie down. Jhumki, a strapping nineteen-year-old, settled herself on the bed beside her *paati*, presented her with a white-lace tsarist shawl she had bought in Kiev, and related her experiences at homeless shelters on wintry streets of Russia.

That evening Kalyani suffered a stroke.

Jhumki helped me carry her to a taxi, and to a nearby hospital. There she lingered for a week and passed away with family gathered around her. She was cremated wearing the shawl from Kiev.

To passionately love and protect those who depend on you, to never give up in the face of hardship, to keep on giving when every physical fiber demands rest, these are the traits that Jhumki absorbed from her cherished Kalyani Paati.

11. THREE LITTLE BOYS

While she traveled through Europe on her return trip, Jhumki drew sustenance from memories of carefree childhood days at her aunt Shanti's apartment. She wrote heavily in her journal, and from there emerged a series of short stories collectively titled *Three Little Boys,* adventures inspired by books of her youth in India: children's stories by Enid Blyton, tiger encounters by Jim Corbett, the Billy Bunter series by Frank Richards, and everyone's favorite sport: cricket. The protagonists of *Three Little Boys* are the trio Jhumki played with in Saket parks after school—Ranga, Anish, Bharat—and herself. Cast in a supporting role in *Three Little Boys,* is a mother, modeled on Shanti, calls the players into the house. An uncle, that's me, guest stars now and then, with the boys usually running circles around him.

Each episode has a stirring, sunny narrative and ends with brooding counterpoint on the impermanence of life.

From "Three Little Boys and One Uncle" by Jhumki Basu

Ranga, triumphant child-bowler, looks almost meditative in his role as batsman.

"Ready for a googly[7]?" warns Uncle.

"I will thrash your googly into oblivion, Uncle."

Uncle trots up to the stumps and lets loose the red ball. It whirs in the air, wavers, dances, teases the nervous batsman. Delicious rough-seamed cherry orb, it bounces once and returns to flight, passing Ranga's bat, straining

---

[7] A cleverly disguised delivery by a bowler in cricket.

well past the wicket.

"WIDE!" calls the umpire.

"So wide it must have fallen in the Yamuna river!" Ranga quips.

The boys cannot hold back their giggles. The 7-yr-old girl umpire snorts. And the giggles are so violent the boys begin to hiccup.

"Dipak!" calls a clear voice, softened slightly by the net on the first floor balcony windows. "Dipak, bring the boys. Dinner is ready."

"Mum, you are interrupting play." Ranga is still allowed occasional cheekiness if he flashes his dimpled smile.

"I am interrupting play. You think I am interrupting?"

The voice sounds threatening. They wait, but nothing happens. And when the face behind the net disappears, the boys focus on the game, convinced that impending doom was only threatened.

At the end of her European travels, wounded by the madness of winter and buoyed by the restitution of spring, Jhumki accepted Castilleja's safe offer of a full-time high school science teaching position for the fall semester. She had already spent two summers there as a camp counselor with the Discover program and had done what she loved most and did best: teaching science to deprived kids. Now, as a full-fledged Castilleja faculty member, Jhumki was an introspective and private person.

I asked Doris Mourad, her science teacher in high school and her colleague when Jhumki joined the Casti faculty, about the environment of the school at the time.

"Jhumki taught biology and physics," Doris explained. "She had a bit of a tough time because she wanted to change the world. She had been a student here and realized the strict demand on students. She saw it as stifling.

"At that time in the science department, we were all about book learning and were very tied to our curriculum. We came from the old school, to teach the way we were taught. And, until Jhumki arrived, nobody challenged us to change to a different way. We were essentially going by the textbook, and everything was cut and dry. We were preparing students for college, with the belief that this traditional way is how you prepare them best. In the process we may have some of them lose their spark. Jhumki saw this and wanted to do things differently."

Doris said that Jhumki, as a junior teacher, was teaching biology in parallel with the head of the science department, who was quite set in her ways. Jhumki had set up a lab that she wanted her students to use, thereby creating equivalency between the honors class taught by the department head and her own basic class. This caused problems and Jhumki, being naturally creative, wanted to carry out activities that were quirky and fun, but it did not sit very well with the establishment.

When I asked Doris whether Jhumki achieved her goals at Castilleja, the veteran teacher shook her head sadly. Jhumki was at Casti just two years, not long enough. Doris was sad to see her go but realized Jhumki's dreams were bigger than Casti could accommodate.

The two children of Joelle Mitchell Mourad, Doris's daughter, loved to climb all over Aunt Jhumki. Though Joelle was Jhumki's senior by a year at Castilleja, the two developed a strong bond through mutual experiences as summer camp counselors.

Joelle recognized that her friend wanted to hone her deep love of young people. In 1999 Jhumki asked camp leader, Carey Davis, to launch a science-based summer program. At that point, the camp's programs were focused on the arts, and they were only for fourteen- and fifteen-year-olds from the affluent Castilleja community. Jhumki told Carey, "These girls will do fine in science because someone is going to make sure they do fine." She urged Carey to offer a science program to younger kids who did not have the privilege of attending schools like Casti.

Carey agreed, and Discover was born.

Funds were found, and Jhumki recruited third and fourth graders from poor schools of East Palo Alto, East Menlo Park, and Redwood City. Discover was launched as part of the Peninsula Bridge program.

Involved with little kids and big kids, conceptualizing quirky experiments while jogging along wooded peninsula trails, Jhumki tried to manage the highs and lows of her life and the positive and negative mood swings that pulled her in different directions.

Her journal reads:

My grief counselor is offering me an easy out—a person doesn't feel anything after impact: engineer on the train, don't walk against the river, people die, all life events happen, it is our duty to play the hand of cards we have. So the point of life is to

1) feel good—walk away from difficult feelings and realities so that we don't have to be sad, and

2) not hurt other people—the engineer in the train. I cry for him a river because he couldn't stop the train.

Every day I try to be rational, I try to attach reasons to the feelings I have. I nod my head when people give me advice about how to deal with grief, how to be normal, how to put things in perspective, how to be wise beyond my years. I sit and nod and listen because I don't want people to feel bad because I have already thought about the things they suggest. Tell me something new that doesn't trivialize how I feel, that isn't some philosophical answer to a question about a concrete event or feeling.

ॐ

Remarkably, however saddened though she was, Jhumki did not forget that there was joy in life—and it could always be obtained from annoying a certain scientist cousin. On the same day as the journal entry about her grief counselor, she wrote this e-mail to family and friends:

Ranga's Three Laws—with Modification:

First Law: My body and mind maintain their state of rest unless acted upon by the force of attraction created by some cute athletic European woman.

Second Law: The force of attraction created by this woman is inversely proportional to her mass and directly proportional to her capability of acceleration up slopes of Himalayan peaks.

Third Law: For every silly thing I say and silly joke I tell, there is an equal and opposite (therefore brilliant) response from my delightful cousin.

BTW, last night I realized that Ranga is comparable to Newton in other ways—the inside of his car smells at least as foul as the mercury that Newton inhaled back in his day.

In the summer of 2000, Jhumki secured a grant to spend a month in Nicaragua studying speech patterns of howler monkeys. From deep inside a forest on Ometepe Island, situated on a large lake, she managed to send us this e-mail:

Coming here has been a worthwhile experience. I have learned a little Spanish, seen a small portion of Nicaragua and studied more mantled howler monkeys than I ever care to again!

I have recorded a couple of hours of howler vocalizations, and I have taken a few rolls of photographs. Hopefully, with all these and my notes and research, I will have plenty to take back to my classroom next year. The weather here is reasonably good—lots of sun, and occasional heavy rain. Unfortunately, because the rain breeds bugs, my arms are covered with itchy bug bites. I can't get medicine regularly, because often there is no vehicle, so nothing can be purchased. The place is very poorly set-up for medical emergencies. A girl got bitten by a captive spider monkey, and she missed her rabies shots a couple of days because there was no vehicle to take her to the doctor. A guy scratched the sclera of his eye, and he couldn't get his second check-up because there was no car available.

Jhumki embarked on one more trip that year, this time to India. On the last day of the journey, three years after the heartrending night, she made her pilgrimage to Saket.

From the journal of Jhumki Basu, Aug 19, 2001

This has been a good visit—my time has been under my control, and I have generally stayed with people I like and been treated as an adult.

Though I will continue to visit the Saket flat, the park, the stairway, the gulley, I want to remember it the way it used to be—no gates, just a walkway from the garage to the street, no wall separating our park from the street, no trees or dividers in the park, just open space for cricket and baby trees lining the sides of the park. I picked up a champa *flower—I love the gentle transition from ivory to yellow and its mild but flavorful aroma. The* champa *tree was growing in the park where we played, and where they died—so the flower must have some molecular connection to our past.*

12. NEW YORK, NEW YORK!

"Baba, I'm all right!" came an excited and rather loud voice.

I took the telephone receiver away from my ear and twisted around to look at the digital clock beside the bed. It was 6:10 a.m. Our dear daughter had been in New York for a whole week. Surely she should know by now there is a three-hour time difference between Manhattan and California? With infinite patience I told her I was happy that things were working out for her.

"What?" Jhumki upped the decibels. "Baba, wake *up!*"

I decided to count silently to ten.

"Baba!" she yelled. "You there? Turn on the TV!"

"Why, what's happened?"

"Turn it *on!*"

I fumbled for the remote. Radha stirred on the other side of the bed.

"Is that Jhomi?" she mumbled. "Is she okay?"

"Yes, she's okay. *That* I know. Where's the silly remote?"

I turned on the television set. A tower of the World Trade Center was in flames. We sat up in bed and watched the screen for the next fifteen hours.

From the journal of Jhumki Basu, Sep 11, 2001

What a lousy day. I've been in New York for five days. Four planes hijacked and brought down—pilots, crew, passengers—many probably killed before collision with WTC and Pentagon.

Two people—man and woman holding hands—jump from a floor of the World Trade Center. What is there to say about a man and a woman choosing, in an instant, to hold hands and jump hundreds of feet, knowing that, almost for certain, they are never going to see their loved ones again? What is there to say about being forced to make that choice?

What about kids of Arab origin? Palestinian families? Immigrants from Asia? Will they feel a backlash? Those are the kids I want to be out there for tomorrow—if anyone gets harassed. I want to be one more person who shows that all people are to be tolerated, treated decently and respected.

Goals: Train to be an emergency medical technician and volunteer for the Red Cross.

Fears about Ravi and Srinath. They have apartments in the Financial District.

Three months before 9/11, I had answered a call from a lady in New York who introduced herself as Professor Angela Calabrese Barton. She said she was on the faculty of Teachers College, Columbia University, and wanted to talk to our daughter about her application for their PhD program.

Jhumki was out and I took the message.

In her interview with Maithreyi, Dr. Calabrese Barton said she was excited about Jhumki's application, her strong science background, the fact that she went to Stanford, her teaching experience, and her statement of purpose. They were all of such importance that Angie, as she became known to us, felt she *had* to convince Jhumki that Teachers College was the place she should go. Angie also wanted to convince her that while at TC, Jhumki should work on a specific project funded by the National Science Foundation.

"Jhumki had a lot of questions on our first call," Angie said. "And she wasn't willing to commit to anything. She had to go back and think about it, and, of course, we wanted her to commit right away! I look back over the years and think that's pretty typical Jhumki: asking lots of questions, gathering all the information, and then waiting to make a really powerful decision, not rushing to any quick judgment or decision, especially a decision that impacted her life trajectory."

Angie became Jhumki's master's and doctoral advisor, and her collaborator after Jhumki finished her PhD. Radha and I met Angie at TC soon after Jhumki started at Columbia. Knowing by then about Angie's immense stature in the science education field, I was surprised when Jhumki introduced us to a small, lean woman wearing glasses, sitting jammed into a corner of an office packed with graduate students. As we got to know her through Jhumki's work, I began to appreciate the commitment with which Angie battled injustice in the teaching of students at inner-city schools, and the charisma with which she inspired an almost evangelical corps of researchers, determined to foster change in American pedagogy.

When she spoke, Angie left everyone in her dust. Her speech was a waterfall of ideas and utterly absorbing, provided one kept up. Soon Jhumki began to speak that way too: fast, clear, directed, cogent diction. I learned that Angie was a marathoner and that she and her husband had two little girls.

They didn't make college professors this way in *our* time. Our professors were all male and round and pompous and pedantic and didn't know the spelling of fun.

In September 2001 Sreyashi Jhumki Basu stood upon the watershed of her life. On one side was the sheltered, affluent world of Castilleja, Stanford, APM, Northern California, Silicon Valley, places where knowledge was king and children had every educational resource. On the other side was a diaspora of poor, disturbed, minority, immigrant children of neglected schools in embattled boroughs where parents and teachers were fast losing faith in America's struggling public education system.

Manhattan's 120th Street forms the divide between classy Upper West Side and the colorful district of Harlem, the place to be for African American art, where many-splendored costumes and extraordinary architecture dominate, where soul food, soul music, and jazz fill days and nights. Jhumki's landing at Teachers College on 120th Street was a symbolic watershed.

Extract from Jhumki Basu's Statement of Purpose from her application to Teachers College, Columbia University

After teaching for several years, I would like to start a small school for young women that focuses on science, math and technology and prepares students for four-year college. I know that charter, magnet and innovative public schools have created similar opportunities for students to excel in their education. But very few schools focus on young women from low-income backgrounds, though the values of an all-girls' education and the low numbers of women involved in scientific, quantitative and technological fields are well-documented.

At Columbia, Jhumki started on a teaching project right away. It was NSF funded and was concentrated on urban middle-school youth. Her research was to focus on development of science literacy through after-school learning, and its relationship to issues of culture, power, and equity. Angie gave Jhumki a great deal of freedom in setting up a program to interview kids and assess their work through an out-of-school program that did not look like an everyday in-school science class.

From the program Jhumki developed data for her master's thesis which was published in the *Journal for Science Teaching*. The paper described "funds of knowledge" that kids bring with them to science learning, and providing an open setting that gives them space to bring those personal experiences into the learning process.

Dr. Maria Rivera Maulucci was science curriculum

coordinator and lab director of the school in South Bronx where Jhumki carried out her work.

Jhumki speaks of her as a supermom, but Maria refers to herself as a countermodel. Maria, who is Puerto Rican, already had two children when she met Jhumki and took her to the Bronx. Later she had a third. A PhD from Teachers College herself, Maria is a professor at Barnard College, a women's liberal-arts institution in New York. Maria, with a soft voice brimming with confidence, is a most pleasant and warm-hearted person. How she manages a home in Westchester County, three children, and several high-pressure jobs, I don't know. Oh, I forget; she is supermom!

Jhumki and Loaiza Ortiz, another TC graduate student, were instructors at the after-school science program at public school PS 306, now restructured and renamed Bronx School of Science Inquiry and Investigation.

The first day of the after-school program was very stressful because of the high number of children and difficulty in maintaining discipline. Jhumki and Lo had been expecting a smaller, more intimate group and were overwhelmed by the crowd. On that very first day, Maria remembers, the two brought in machines scavenged from the science lab at TC—old balance beams and typewriters—so that students could take them apart and learn how they worked. The kids loved the activity.

Another member of Angie's Urban Science Education Center at TC, Dr. Tara O'Neill, is the opposite of Maria in appearance. A tiny person bubbling over with humor and energy, Tara has a fascinating, self-deprecating manner of speech that combines irreverence with a well-developed sense of fun, even when it comes to the most mundane of subjects.

"I got to watch Jhumki's interaction with the kids," Tara said, "feeding them space to invent, giving them space to be brilliant. And I was terribly intimidated."

"Intimidated by *Jhumki*?" I asked in surprise. "Why?"

"Well, she ran a different schedule than the rest of us. She took a teaching job in physics, which terrifies me! The rest of us would be in the office together getting all our writing done. She spent her days out in the field and ran this after-school project. I got to be close friends with Lo, and everything I heard about Jhumki through Lo was: she is this compassionate person, such a brilliant person. With our projects we all walked on eggshells. Jhumki didn't! She was like, 'Wake up, you guys, move on with your lives.' With her kids she was very honest, very forthcoming, not scary, with a very strong approach. She did not shy away from questions. She talked to kids as though they were people and not kids."

Since her meltdown in Italy, Jhumki had become self-critical to the extreme in her work and in her relationships. With a fresh start in New York, she turned the self-criticism into a constructive force.

While listening to a lecture, most people note down important conclusions and list action items. Not so, Jhumki. I found she not only filled her notebooks and laptop files with what speakers said, but also jotted down ideas on the fly about ways she could improve her own teaching and research. This was possible only because she wrote and typed at breakneck speed. Abuse of her long-suffering laptop was a well-known facet of her character. A machine gun had nothing on the sound and fury of Ms. Jhumki on the keyboard.

She took a running start on academic life in New York. Angie gave her the license she had yearned for at Castilleja. She threw herself into developing an original science program, albeit an after-school one, in ways she wanted: to test quirkiness, to test innovation, to test fun.

From the journal of Jhumki Basu, November 20, 2001

Plan for approaching life in NY:

1. *Work on developing a friendship base that is strong (quality, depth, few people) and stable (multiple people so that my center of mass is over a support)*

2. *Avoid dating someone till summer of next year (re-eval then)*
3. *Visit Boston, 2nd semester*
4. *Visit Seattle, 2nd semester*
5. *Accept day job at Renaissance Charter School*
6. *Work on thesis*
7. *Make summer plans*
8. *Approach relationships the way I approach work— with a strategy. It's what I'm good at.*

Secure in academia, Jhumki dived into the social scene of the entertainment capital of the world. Always drawn to dance, she scrounged for student discounts for George Balanchine and American Ballet Theatre performances at the Lincoln Center. She went to the Botanical Gardens with Lo. After a Saturday night out, she raved in her journal:

SOBs![8]

Masculine-looking vocalist, congas, saxophone, drums, electric guitar, fine-looking rhythm section, mojito-mint, lime rum, red snapper grilled, yummy and warm chocolate cake, dancing all night—salsa, samba, folk tunes from Brazil, everyone jammin' . . . dancing . . . having fun. Lots of

---

[8] A Brazilian dance and music club in New York's SoHo district.

sparkles, booty-shaking. Laughter. Great lights, great food, people who know how to have fun. Feel free to dance...let that portion of my mind and heart be expressed.

Jhumki was in her element: teaching, dating (despite admonition to herself not to), eating, running, traveling, sleeping, innovating, dancing, cooking, practicing yoga, salsa dancing. She was making new friends, opening up her work to her family, and becoming a joy to all who knew her. Angie shared Jhumki's passion and encouraged her to fly. Her circle of friends applauded her adventuring. And a new love interest had entered her social life.

In California, her parents had gotten a new dog from the animal shelter. Over the telephone Jhumki named her Mishti, meaning "sweet" in Bengali. She looked forward to coming home to get acquainted with Mishti, and fill the void left behind by Tiffany.

13. AND THEN

With the advent of the new millennium, all members of the Basu family grew professionally. Jhumki got her arms around her after-school program and began work on her master's thesis. Just months before the bursting of the dot-com bubble, Radha stewarded Support.com through a successful public offering. I had joined Cisco Systems in 1995, and in 2001, as a Cisco Fellow, I co-founded and took on the running of NetHope, a technology alliance of global humanitarian organizations.

In October, Radha and I decided to take a break from work and indulge in our love of high places. We flew to Peru to hike the Inca Trail. From Cuzco we trekked under snow-clad Andean peaks, toiling up and down dizzy stone steps overhanging the Urubamba River. We admired the Incas' ability to seamlessly integrate architecture and agriculture and, by means of this capability, forge a vast and lofty empire. Our best moment was the entrance through the Sun Gate, Inti Punku, down to the lost city of Machu Picchu, spread gloriously in morning light.

We went on to Bolivia. In La Paz, due to the altitude or a random virus, Radha became ill with flu-like symptoms. While trying to keep warm in a hotel room, she decided to call Jhumki in New York. They chatted a bit before Jhumki told her mother she had recently felt an "indentation" in her breast.

I don't remember how we reacted to this news in the Bolivian hotel room with a grey view from the window. The consequence of what Jhumki had just said was so far outside our ambit of thought, so unimaginably alien, that we did not grasp it at first.

After Viji contracted breast cancer in 1988, Radha had told

Jhumki and Sumitra about the importance of regular self-examinations. On the phone line to La Paz, Jhumki told her mother that this was how she had found the indentation.

Breast cancer, as I understood then, was a disease one worried about when one was older—*much* older. Jhumki was twenty-four. It can't be anything serious, I thought. But remembering her sister, Radha told Jhumki from Bolivia to get a mammogram done right away.

After this, things moved swiftly.

We had just returned to the United States when Jhumki had the breast mammogram done in New York. The results showed "dense tissue in multiple areas." The attending radiologist told her that "something like this was common for young people."

When Jhumki came home to California for the Thanksgiving weekend, Radha managed to get her own doctor to perform an ultrasound scan on a Sunday. The doctor saw "ragged edges" around some tissue and said, while it was probably nothing, she wanted to do a "little biopsy." But Jhumki had to go back to New York and left on a night flight after agreeing to ask her Columbia doctor about the biopsy. She was referred to a specialist and the biopsy date was set for November 30.

All three of us completely believed the biopsy was just precautionary. Still, Radha decided to be with her daughter for the procedure. While her flight was over Illinois, the captain announced that thunderstorms were active in the New York area and all the city's airports were closed. They touched down in Cleveland at 11 p.m. too late for flights anywhere. Radha applied her well-developed powers of persuasion and got a seat on the first flight out the next morning, landed at New York's La Guardia airport, and called Jhumki.

"Hi, Mommy!" came the sunny voice. "Welcome to New York. I gotta go to the hospital now. See you at Beth Israel, okay?"

Radha took a taxi to the hospital and found her daughter berating her laptop in the surgical prep area. Upon seeing her mother, Jhumki jumped up, all smiles, her hair bouncing.

"You didn't have to come, Mommy. But I'm glad you did!"

After she was wheeled into the operating room, Radha e-mailed me:

> *She has just gone in to be prepped. There was a delay due to some preceding surgeries. She is in good spirits but very hungry. The surgeon seems to be caring. I was with her and just came to the waiting area. Say a little prayer for our little Jhomi. Don't worry too much, I am doing enough for both of us. Cell phone does not work here.*

My wife had had a trying night. She settled on a sofa in the waiting area and fell asleep.

I was running a NetHope conference call from the Cisco campus in San Jose when my cell phone buzzed. I left the meeting room to answer it. It was the call that everybody fears and nobody wants. I knew she was in tears before I even heard her say, "It's me."

I held my breath.

"The biopsy was positive."

I couldn't speak. There was a very long silence.

"Can you come?" she asked finally.

"I'll be on the next plane. How is she?"

"She doesn't know yet. Still asleep."

I tried to contemplate the ramifications. I didn't *know* the ramifications. How bad was the cancer? My mother had been diagnosed with gall bladder cancer in December 1993 and had died from it two months later. Viji had survived her bout. Sapna had had throat cancer, a long period of remission, then suffered grievously and died. What would happen to Jhomi? Our Jhomi?

I don't remember the rest of the phone call. I think we were both too shocked to talk much. I asked someone to take over the teleconference, drove home, packed a few things, asked a neighbor to look after the dog, got a seat on a 3 p.m. flight to JFK.

Radha called to give me more details as I was shutting down the house.

The surgeon had woken her up in the waiting room.

"I am so sorry, Mrs. Basu," he had said with a worried look. "I am *so* sorry."

Groggy and confused, Radha had an initial, terrified thought that Jhumki had died in the operating room. Then Dr. Harris told her the biopsy had confirmed breast cancer.

Unable, unwilling to believe what was happening, we talked disjointedly for a few minutes.

"Dr. Harris thinks it is pretty conclusive," Radha said. "The official report will come on Monday. Bring some clothes for me."

I got to San Francisco Airport, checked in for my flight, and was walking down the ramp to the plane when my phone buzzed again.

"Baba?" said a soft voice.

I stopped dead in middle of the ramp.

Passengers irritably skirted around me.

"Love you, Jhomi," I said quietly. "I'll be there very soon."

"Thanks, Baba."

And then she said something I will never forget.

"Don't worry, Baba. It's okay. We'll beat this. We'll fight it together."

I know I was crying on that ramp as I listened to her voice giving *me* courage. She handed the phone to her mother, and, while I stumbled into the aircraft and tried to find my seat, Radha gave me more news.

Dr. Harris had suggested Radha not tell Jhumki the news that night, but Radha had rightly concluded that, given Jhumki's positive mentality, not telling her would be a travesty, and she had disobeyed him. Besides, one look at Radha's face would have given it away.

Jhumki had woken from anesthesia in high spirits.

"I'm feeling fine, Mommy. Shall we go home? Oh, yay, how about ballet tonight?"

Then she noticed her mother's expression.

"What's wrong, Mommy?"

Mommy told her.

"Oh!" Jhumki said. "Oh! Okay." Then she added, "But how can it be? What does it mean?"

Radha hugged her daughter. "I don't know, Jhomi. But we'll find out."

Jhumki went back to asleep. Later she had awoken and called me as I was boarding my flight.

I have no recollection of my thoughts on the transcontinental plane ride. I knew very little then about cancer beyond the fact that cancer cells experience runaway growth and, if not contained, cause death. I remembered a young doctor in Kolkata, at the time of my mother's illness, explaining it rather dramatically.

"A cancer cell is like an insurgent," he told me. "It is a different cell, but grows out of the same population. It forms guerilla cells that take over pockets, then the whole country."

I knew my mother's cancer had spread from gall bladder to other organs before it had been detected, and therefore too late to be curable. We had contained Viji's disease in time. Sapna's had been contained for years but had returned.

It was after midnight when I got to Whittier Hall, Jhumki's dorm. The security guard in the lobby told me the floor and the number of the guest room. I went up the elevator and knocked. Radha opened the door. The small room was dimly lit. We held tightly on to each other for a long moment. She was crying quietly, and put her finger to her lips. I looked over her shoulder to the bed and saw our baby sleeping. I reached out and touched her shoulder gently. She stirred but didn't wake.

"You must be exhausted," Radha whispered, getting back into bed. "We'll talk tomorrow."

I put down my bags, took off my warm things, sat beside my wife, and held her hand under the blanket. After a while her breathing deepened and she drifted away. Jhumki slept soundly on her other side. No one was aware of what had happened. At that moment I felt we were three people alone, suspended in space, in a little darkened box. It was so wrong, the unfairness of it all. Here she was, back on track after climbing out of an abyss.

Now this.

PART III

I DEFY THEE, CANCER

For Jhumki

She forces me unto new ground,
to tread where I have not walked;
She looks at me and asks
if I am anxious or afraid.
How can I tell her "yes, but
I would have it no other way?"
We are both apprehensive of each other,
yet we do not know why.
She is so often beyond my understanding,
a familiar enigma, well-known to me;
She looks at me and asks
why I persist by her side.
To this I hesitate, for words are hard—yet
I would have it no other way.

—from a friend

14. LIFE'S FIRST DAY

What does a young girl, who has just been diagnosed with cancer, say when she wakes to the rest of her life?
A: "Hi, will you come with me to watch the Iron Science Teacher show tonight?"

I slept badly and awoke wondering where I could get on the Internet. Then I turned and saw Radha was silently fighting tears. As I reached out to her, Jhumki stirred and sat up.

"Hi, Baba!" she greeted me cheerfully.

Cheerfully!

As she got out of bed I noticed she was wearing her favorite sea-green T-shirt, the especially ragged one, and plaid pink pajamas, all horribly, engagingly contrasting. She threw up the blinds, let in a weak sun, turned, and studied her parents.

"Look, you guys," she said seriously, "it's Saturday. We'll get the report next week. We can't *do* anything until Monday. So why worry? I've got stuff to do. And I'm *gonna* enjoy the weekend."

With that, she went down to her room to change. We had breakfast with her roommates a little later at her favorite Hungarian pastry shop. I don't remember the rest of day until the evening event.

Bi-Coastal Challenge: Milk Cartons!

Watch as the best teachers on the planet battle it out for the title of Iron Science Teacher. This special edition will pit east coast teachers from Columbia University against teachers from the [San Francisco] Exploratorium's Teacher's Institute. In this zany competition teachers will have ten minutes to create a science activity from a secret ingredient: milk cartons!

Cancer? What cancer? It was quite a show.

The names of the teachers on the teams, linked by transcontinental video, were announced one by one, and they introduced themselves. When her name was called, Jhumki bounced onto the stage and shared high fives with three big guys, her teammates.

"Graduate student, Columbia Teachers College," she proudly told the camera. "Science teacher, PS 306, South Bronx."

Playing her part in the timed competitions with unbridled enthusiasm, Jhumki created fascinating projects out of milk and orange-juice containers. Dramatizing the power of physics, she rubbed a plastic shopping bag vigorously on her team leader's sweater and made it levitate.

We somehow got through the weekend, and then it was Monday. We took a taxi across Central Park to the Upper East Side. As we were descending a steep flight of steps from the street into the offices of Dr. Harris, I had the feeling we were sinking into an abyss.

After a short wait in a tiny waiting room, we were called in.

Surgical Pathology Consultation Report of Sreyashi Basu

Beth Israel Medical Center, November 30, 2001

Final Diagnosis: Left Breast Mass

Multicentric infiltrating ductal carcinoma of high nuclear grade with an extensive intraductal carcinoma in situ components of solid type, comedo with microcalcifications, clear cell features and marked extension to lobules. Focal squamous and spindle celled differentiation (metaplastic carcinoma) present. Inked margins are positive.

Tumor size: Micro invasive to 1.5 cm

Lymphovascular invasion: Not apparent

Nuclear grade: 3/3

Mitotic rate: 3/3

Tubule formation: 3/3

Histologic grade: 9/9
Thus read the document Dr. Harris handed us.
Carcinoma! Invasive! Nuclear!

The terrifying words jumped out like wart-covered goblins. Dr. Harris began to explain the report and I scribbled notes as fast as I could.

Intraductal carcinoma in situ, I learned, is the most common form of noninvasive breast cancer in women. *In situ* or "in place" describes a cancer that has not moved out of the area of the body where it originally developed. There was a silence as we digested this.

"Isn't that promising?" I ventured nervously. "The 'noninvasive' and 'have not moved out' parts?"

"Oh, yes," Dr. Harris replied. "On no account do we want it to move out or for that matter, to invade . . ."

I swallowed, sure there was a "but" coming.

". . . but," said Dr. Harris, "the cancer is the comedo type. Extremely aggressive."

Radha reached for my hand which had suddenly gone very cold. Jhumki sat stonily while the doctor elaborated.

The tumor grading system for breast cancer combines three items: nuclear grade (size and shape of the cancer cell), tubule formation (percent of cancer composed of tube-like structures), and mitotic rate (the speed at which cancer cells divide). Each item is given a score from 1 (best) to 3 (worst). The scores are added to arrive at the histological grade of the cancer. The best score possible is 3; the worst is 9.

Jhumki had scored a perfect 9.

"There is positive news, though," the doctor announced, making us sit up. "She's a T1, that is, the tumor size is two centimeters or less, which means it is really small and has been detected early."

A blessing on Mommy's head for making the girls self-examine.

"It says here, 'No lymphovascular invasion,'" Radha spoke up. "That means it hasn't spread to the lymph nodes, right?"

My wife holds a master's degree in biomedical engineering. She has performed original R and D work in ultrasound imaging in her early years at HP. She knows about human physiology.

"Not exactly, Mrs. Basu. In your daughter's case the term means it is *unlikely* there is spread, but we have to biopsy the lymph nodes to confirm that."

It took fifteen more minutes before we fully grasped the specifics of the report. Jhumki was quiet through it all, intently following every word. She spoke now.

"Okay, Dr. Harris. I have breast cancer. What next?"

How Jhumki!

"Well, you have choices. Breast cancer is curable with today's techniques. Your choices are surgery, chemotherapy, radiation, or a combination."

Dr. Harris paused. He was obviously doing his best in a tough situation, but I hated him, suddenly, irrationally. What he said sounded like vanilla, strawberry, chocolate, or a sundae.

"Your tumor may be small," Dr. Harris went on, "but the biopsy might not have taken out all of it. If any tumor cells remain, they will be microscopic in size. As a result, lumpectomy—surgically removing a lump around the affected tissue and preserving your breast—is likely to fail. I recommend a left mastectomy followed by reconstructive surgery, and chemotherapy."

Mastectomy! Surgical removal of a breast! Just a few days ago Jhumki had been trying to find ways to keep her boyfriends apart. Chemotherapy! Another dreaded word. I saw her face droop and the tears start and put an arm around her. I couldn't take more of this myself.

The room became stifling.

We took a break, walked down the street, and got ourselves coffee at a small corner shop. None of us talked as we studied the foot traffic outside the glass window. Our world had just been turned upside down.

"Why are people so afraid of chemo?" I asked Dr. Harris when we reassembled.

"Well, sometimes it can be toxic."

Yikes! What does that mean? How toxic? Gotta look this up right away, I thought.

"Will my hair fall out?" Jhumki asked.

"I am afraid so. But it will grow back afterward."

Further tests were scheduled. We talked about the surgery and were told it should be performed within two to three weeks, and chemotherapy started soon after that.

In the taxi back to Columbia, Jhumki made a decision.

"Mommy, I'm supposed to be home for Christmas, right?"

"Yes, Jhomi, but what about . . . ?"

"I want to have my surgery in California. Is that possible?"

Radha, holding Jhumki's hand, looked at her uncertainly and took a deep breath. I looked across the girl sitting between us. We both nodded. I took Jhumki's other hand. The lines were drawn. We would face it. We would fight it. We would beat it.

As we got out of the taxi a sudden thought struck me.

It was December.

From the journal of Jhumki Basu, December 8, 2001

Diagnosed with breast cancer.

Most likely will choose mastectomy and chemo-therapy. That means I will lose all my hair. I won't get to go to Hawaii, work the way I like at Renaissance Charter School [where she was to teach soon], take the 20 units I desire to take. I won't do yoga as often and for several weeks. I won't run maybe until the chemotherapy is over. Off dance for a month?

113

"How long till my soul gets it right?"

"Always on the outside looking into other lives. Love will come to you, hoping just because I spoke the word that it's true."

Time to work on playing the piano. Private yoga lessons. Divide weekends and weekdays, esp. post-chemo days between people.

Bronx student: "Are you going to die?"

Ms. Jhumki: "Not right now. Maybe later."

When Jhumki broke the news of her cancer to her students at the after-hours school, Maria Rivera Maulucci was impressed by the way she did it. The school district of South Bronx had the lowest scholastic scores in the country. It was plagued by drugs, crime, unemployment, gang warfare, and governmental neglect. But children there were curious like children everywhere.

"It was pretty amazing," Maria said. "She was very open about her cancer all along, though it surprised me she shared it with the kids. In that district, adults kept things from kids. It was a failing school where adults never had frank conversations with kids. And here was this person for whom those barriers weren't there. Those filters weren't there. I think it was a very courageous thing to do. Some of the kids cried, but she wanted to prepare them for the changes they would see. Her body might change. She was going to lose her hair. She would wear a head scarf. She might lose weight. She wanted them to know it was all part of her medical care. Of course, she was expected to survive. And she encouraged them if they had questions, to ask her. She didn't want this tremendous silence.

"It was a population where if someone in the family has AIDS, it's a big hush-hush. No one talks about it. These were fifth and sixth graders—eleven, twelve, thirteen, that age range. Some kids were very attached to her already and became worried about her. I think it was very brave, very honest, and very refreshing the way she did it. It was the right thing to do."

Angela Calabrese Barton had this to add:

"On the one hand she didn't want to sugarcoat anything and wanted them to understand her experience as it was. On the other hand she thought they might learn some science out of it. A lot of kids thought radiation and chemotherapy were the same thing, that these words were interchangeable. These were sixth graders, and she didn't try to water it down. She spoke at a level they could understand, but she was pretty rigorous with the science involved. Then she let them ask all the questions they had. Most of the questions were more personal. 'How do you feel? What do you think? What does it feel like? Does it hurt? Are you in pain? Is it infectious?'"

With skill and conviction, Jhumki had quickly surrounded the enemy into a science research project, refusing to let it invade her emotions. On December 4, she summarized her preparations for battle through this e-mailed call-to-arms:

> *Hey, I created several folders to sort all the internet information sent to me on breast cancer. So if you send info to me, I'm set-up to process it. It's especially helpful to have an annotation for anything you send me describing content, source of info, and quality of info.*
>
> *J*

15. CHRISTMAS AT STANFORD

Radha and I said muted good-byes to Jhumki and returned home from New York. Mishti gave us a riotous welcome, but we would not be cheered. Our home, our world, our life, were plunged in gloom.

In New York Jhumki had tested negative for BRCA1 and BRCA2. These are genes that, if positive, would have indicated her cancer was of a hereditary nature. I was relieved for the rest of the women in Radha's family.

Roger Sippl, successful Silicon Valley entrepreneur, venture capitalist, and Support.com board member, helped us through a very difficult period. He knew people at the Stanford Comprehensive Cancer Center and worked wonders to find us time at short notice on the calendars of Dr. Robert Carlson, oncologist, and Dr. Fred Dirbas, cancer surgeon.

"We will get her the best care in the world, I promise," Roger wrote in an e-mail to Radha. "She has an illness and there is a scary component to it. But with proper treatment the chances are extremely high she will do well. The treatments aren't even as harsh as they used to be. I think most patients agree it isn't the fear that is so much the problem as the patience required to go through the processes."

We did not realize how portentous Roger's words would be.

The appointment with Dr. Carlson was confirmed for December 7, the day Jhumki's case would go before the Tumor Board, a case review committee of Stanford specialists. The patient, on the other hand, had decided she could not come to California on that day because of teaching responsibilities. One can question her priorities, but Jhumki was, well, Jhumki. Dr.

Carlson considerately agreed to see Radha and me as a special case to answer general queries and to review records. However, since Jhumki was an adult, he could not discuss her case specifics in her absence.

Drs. Carlson and Dirbas answered our long list of questions. We were comforted by their range of knowledge and their compassion for such a young patient. A large part of the discussion was about sentinel lymph node biopsy[9], (SLN), a new and important procedure in breast-cancer treatment. But a disturbing issue emerged when the two doctors could not agree on the value of SLN biopsy. Dr. Carlson felt the procedure could not be relied upon to indicate conclusively whether cancer has spread. He believed that all lymph nodes near the breast should be surgically removed for the best outcome. Dr. Dirbas felt that if SLNs tested negative, further lymph nodes need not be removed.

For Jhumki the matter was of paramount importance. She knew that because many of her aunt's lymph nodes were removed, Viji's right arm had always been sore, often swollen, and incapable of full movement and heavy lifting.

This would be a disaster for Jhumki.

Aside from the unsightly appearance, it would adversely impact yoga and swimming and other sports she enjoyed. And without lymph nodes there were increased chances of infection. For these reasons Jhumki strongly leaned toward SLN biopsy as a diagnostic procedure. Due to the doctors' discord, she agonized

---

[9] "Sentinel Lymph Nodes are the first lymph nodes to which breast cancer is likely to spread from the primary tumor in the breast. In SLN biopsy, the sentinel nodes are removed and examined to determine whether cancer is present. A negative result suggests cancer has not spread to the lymph nodes. A positive result indicates cancer is present in the SLN and may be present in other lymph nodes" *(National Cancer Institute's Q&A for Sentinel Node Biopsy)*.

until the very last moment before surgery, and decided in favor of SLN biopsy just before she went under the gas.

E-mail from Jhumki Basu to friends and family, Dec 20, 2001

So the plan is to proceed with left breast surgery tomorrow and start reconstruction. My surgery is at noon, and I will be out from the recovery room at about 6 pm. The surgery is at the main Stanford hospital in the surgery area.

If you want more details, you can ask my parents. I don't want to talk about lymphodema or blood clots or immunohistochemistry for the rest of the evening. Tomorrow may be another story. After all, the surgeon said, "If you exercise your arm after surgery, and it hurts, push it a little more." So I think I'll be on my feet soon. My brain may take a little longer to recover from anesthesia. Hold your sassy remarks. Thank you for all the things you are doing. I know I'm erratic about responding and being appreciative. But I do read and listen and process all that you do and say.

E-mail from Dipak Basu to friends and family, Dec 21, 2001

Jhumki's surgery was performed successfully today by Dr. Fred Dirbas at Stanford Hospital. All planned procedures were carried out and no problems were encountered. Our day began at 7:30 am. It is late night now. Jhumki is resting under sedation. Radha is spending the night in her hospital room.

Jhomi woke up from anesthesia around 8 pm inside a large elevator while being transported on a gurney. There were several known and unknown persons around her. She opened her eyes and surprised everyone with her first words that were addressed to her cousin:

"Ranga, behave!"

She has been incredibly strong through this enormous ordeal and it is a big relief that the surgical part is over at last. Further medical treatment will be based upon pathological analysis, results of which should be available in a week or so. We expect to bring Jhumki home by Sunday. She should be substantially recovered in a week to ten days.

Stanford Hospital never shuts down—outwardly. Jhumki was moved to a private room where her parents, Ranga, and her friends looked after her. Because of the proximity to Christmas there was barely a nurse around, and Jhumki was one of the very few patients in residence. Do serious illnesses avoid the holiday season? After twenty-four hours of medical disharmony, Jhumki was set—if not fit—to go home. We had been given directions on how to drain her surgical wound. Radha already was draining it when nurses didn't show up on time.

Jhumki sat beside me on the front seat as I drove the ten miles home as carefully as I could. She tried to be strong, but I could sense her wince when an invisible bump made the car jerk. Finally we were home. We kept Mishti from knocking her over. She dragged herself up the stairs to her old room and collapsed on her futon. In another moment she was asleep.

16. ONWARD

During days following Jhumki's surgery, our California home was a concourse of twenty- and thirty-somethings. Facing off the cancer was a house full of merriment, tall tales, and serious consumption of food and wine. Our friend Neela runs a small Sunnyvale restaurant named Panchavati, that offers excellent home-style South Indian cuisine. Jhumki adored Neela Aunty's cooking, and man, could those kids devour it! Large quantities of Neela's *dosa, idli, paruppu usili,* lemon rice, *brinjal* rice, tamarind rice, yogurt rice, coconut rice, *upuma, avial,* pepper *sambar, pongal,* and *paal poli* disappeared at alarming rates.

Mishti is a good antidote for flagging spirits. When we adopted the six-month-old foxhound from the Humane Society a week after 9/11, she was as timid as a mouse and would run for her life at the slightest imagined threat. In two weeks she shook off her timorousness and mutated into a rambunctious, fun-loving, and extremely high-energy dog. She took an exceptional liking to the enthusiastic duo of Jhumki and Ranga. When the three were together, our house was a shambles. Radha called them litter-mates and threw them outdoors when they became impossible.

During this time Jhumki, perforce, had to contend with well-meaning advice givers, not only the ones who said "don't worry, *every*thing will be all right" while she gritted her teeth, but also those who advised her that this was the one occasion when she must be selfish. "Take *all* the love and affection you are due," they would say knowingly. "With chemo your energy level will plummet. You should rest at home, relax, finish chemo, get better, *then* go back to your work in New York." When people said this or a variation thereof, Jhumki was nice and polite and Radha and I tried not to smile. The well-meaning folks didn't know that Jhumki never did anything she should.

Our daughter was pragmatist enough to realize that she would be unable to care for herself during chemo time, when complete rest and special diets would be necessary. She would suffer nausea and her immunity would drop. Simultaneously she worried about being there for her students and her research. She detested the idea of being a full-time patient.

When Radha and I suggested an obvious solution to the conundrum, she did not believe it. She did not believe we would/could come to New York every three weeks for five months to see her through chemo.

Then she believed it and the rest was easy.

E-mail from Dipak Basu to friends and family, Jan 17, 2002

Jhomi went back to work today.

During the day I had appointments to inspect furnished apartments close to TC and, like Glen Campbell's Rhinestone Cowboy, I tramped the dirty sidewalks of Broadway.

At 4 p.m. I pushed an intercom button of a building on Claremont Street in the Upper West Side. Norma turned out to be an Argentine sculptress and painter. I loved her cozy and artistic apartment and the bright living room where she works. It is located on a quiet backwater in the intellectual area between Riverside Drive and Harlem and is, most importantly, four blocks from Columbia.

To close the day I had dinner with three lovely ladies at an Eritrean restaurant, Jhumki and her roommates, Liz and Allison.

Tomorrow, at Beth Israel, we prep the ground for her first chemo session.

Before her cancer was diagnosed, Jhumki had been dating two young men. Simultaneously. Many would struggle with this arrangement in normal life, let alone in a troubled situation like hers. But not our hyper-dynamic girl! In an e-mail on the subject to her friends and family, she wrote:

1. *In case you're confused, I'm dating Tom[10] and not dating Dick.*

2. *Harry (my friend Jane's jewelry-buying husband) refers to them as zucchini-boy and bran-boy. You can take your pick. One of them brushed his teeth with salt water and sand for me. You can figure out which one.*

3. *On Friday night, Dick came over because he was going to stay the night at our temporary apartment so we could leave at 5 a.m. for the breast cancer conference on Saturday.*

4. *Tom was going to meet my housemate Jill. So I told Tom that Dick was coming, and if he wanted to avoid Dick, perhaps he and Jill should meet at his place. But, of course, Tom instead came to meet Jill at my place. Neither boy wanted to meet the other. So Tom stayed in Jill's room with the door shut, and Dick stayed in my room with the door shut for about an hour of Friday night. When I knocked on Jill's door, Tom would sign to me asking me if Dick was here—he didn't want to talk in case Dick heard him. Dick would ask me if the coast was clear for him to get a glass of water. I had to check if Tom was in the kitchen.*

5. *It is like living in a Charlie Chaplin comedy. I think I'm going to date two boys in the same city all the time for the amusement this provides.*

[10] All names in this e-mail message are changed.

Jhumki's beaus, unaware of the hilarity they were providing, took very good care of our daughter, separately, during her recovery from surgery and the difficult time beyond. The two gentlemen played a vital role in restoring and maintaining the spirit of a sensitive, attractive woman at a time when her ability to look and be her best had taken a beating.

Jhumki's friends' circle and irreverent cousins were her precious links to reality, to the laughter and fun she needed to reconnect with life.

 ∾

On January 25, 2002, the Basus walked nervously along a corridor inside Beth Israel hospital, and came to a stop in front of a closed door. A plastic plate on the door announced CHEMOTHERAPY SUITE.

Heaven knew what Jhumki was thinking as she pushed the door open. To our surprise we stumbled into a very large room with pop music playing and sunshine pouring through a wall of glass that overlooked busy Union Square. Jhumki warmed quickly to Diane, her kindhearted nurse, who made her feel comfortable and—most importantly—intelligent. It was a relationship that transformed a dreaded event into a marginally enjoyable experience.

Jhumki's chemo session happened every third Friday. The Thursday before was party time. Even Fridays were fun nights, since the drugs did not take effect for twenty-four hours.

Radha and I arrived in New York on the Thursday before, collected our daughter, and the three of us moved into Norma's apartment. Saturday through Monday was rough. Jhumki was wiped out with exhaustion and nausea. We carefully figured out what she would eat and could keep down. She hated that invalid's food for all seasons, chicken noodle soup—or, for that matter, any soup. Her boyfriends took her for walks in Riverside Park muffled against the cold. By Monday evening she was stronger. By Tuesday she'd had her fill of parental care and Radha and I flew back to California.

Between chemo sessions she was busy as a bee.

Maria recalls with wonder that Jhumki missed only just *one day* of school through cancer diagnosis, biopsy, surgery, and chemo. She had to be ultra-careful, though. Chemotherapy reduces white-cell count and made her acutely susceptible to infection. There could be no crowds, no subway, no sushi, no rock concerts for her during chemo. A few times her white-cell count dropped so low that she had to boost it by injecting herself with Neupogen couriered across town.

The chemo drug combination attacked rapidly reproducing cells in her body, such as nails, hair, and cancer. Determined to forestall the disease at every point, she had shaved her hair before it began to fall out, and made an expedition out of wig-shopping. As she tried out wigs with her friends, everyone collapsed with laughter and took weird pictures of each other. In the end, she did not wear one. Brilliant bandanas and big grin were Jhumki's trademark profile during the first half of 2002 as she became a colorful sight on the Columbia campus and a seamless member of the hip-hop scene in Harlem and the Bronx.

After her last drug infusion we actually had a party in the chemo suite and bid adieu to Diane. Jhumki's cancer had tested estrogen receptor positive, meaning it thrived on hormones produced by her ovaries. As a final action to destroy any surviving cancer cells, her oncologist recommended she take a daily dose of tamoxifen, an estrogen-blocking drug, for five years.

E-mail from Jhumki Basu to friends and family, May 14, 2002

Hooray!

I finished my last chemotherapy session this past Friday, and I'm trying to get back on my feet one more time. I anticipate having silly, annoying side effects for another three weeks. I hope that my hair starts growing back and my energy starts returning to normal soon after. There's still stuff left to do, follow-up surgery, medication to prevent recurrence, but at least the especially toxic portion of the treatment is complete.

Thank you all for being so supportive and for visiting and calling so often. Everyone says that my spirits have been good, and I owe that to all of you. Finally, you should be extra nice to my parents for the next few years. They've spent an immeasurable amount of time listening to me complain about nausea, researching arcane medical facts on the Internet, and sorting through insurance papers. Also, they've been flying a lot and having at least one gall bladder removed [the author's]. *There's no way I could have stayed in New York if they hadn't come here once every three weeks. So whatever strategy you use to make them relax is in high demand right now. That can definitely include teasing them constantly.*

See you soon!

Love, Jhumki.

Heady with the relief of ending the detestable regimen and getting her life back on track, Jhumki e-mailed her friends:

Laugh at me . . .

. . . this time.

I want you to know that in the last 48 hours:

1) I have forgotten three times to send Dr. Glendon the fax # for the referral for my port[11] removal. Of course, this

---

[11] A temporary surgical incision into a vein for administration of intravenous medication. It eliminates the painful probing jabs of hypothermic needles.

is because I forgot to get a referral before I had the port removed.

2) I took the subway all the way to Christopher Street (past 14th) before realizing I had gone downtown from 59th street instead of uptown to 120th. I was reading about sustainable gardening and wasn't paying any attention to the stops.

3) I called Lo and forgot who I was calling by the time she picked up the phone. I must have started doing something else while the phone was ringing.

4) I forgot where the port removal place was located though I've been there three times. I also forgot to look up the address before I left. Therefore, I ended up at 6th and 3rd instead of 16th and 1st. Of course, the former looked unfamiliar because I had never been there.

5) Though I have looked up and told people my cell phone number a thousand times, I still can't remember it. I can memorize piano pieces, dance routines, science pedagogy strategies, and physics equations, but I'm starting to feel like Ranga and/or James, take your pick, about everyday things.

Help! What should I do? Is there medication?

Following chemotherapy, Jhumki's hair quickly grew back into tight, luxuriant coils that gave her a distinct rock-star look. That summer she had an intellectual chat with her cousin.

"I think," Ranga observed a bout of silence, "you're all right."

"Oh, yeah?" Jhumki responded with asperity.

"Yeah. A bird won't build its nest in your hair."

"And why is that, doofus?"

"Well, you know, if it got in, it wouldn't find its way out!"

17. TEACHING AND LEARNING

Youth

by Jhumki Basu

Youth is a pulsar that twinkles through the night
And sinks decadently into warbling dewdrop pools,
Flashing, spitting, chiseling dreams upon the stagnant morning
light.

Yonder the homeless derelict haltingly recites
Memories of fledgling triumphs amidst yarns from archaic
spools

Youth is a pulsar that twinkles through the night.
Lovers from the Knowledge Tree's fruit take luscious bites
Discovering within the core, youth's mysterious tools,
Flashing, spitting, chiseling dreams upon the stagnant morning
light.

To illustrate Jhumki's relationships with her young students, Maria told me the story of Namrita (name changed), an Indian girl who attend Jhumki's after-school program in the Bronx.

"Jhumki took the time to get to know her kids as individuals," Maria explained. "Personalized attention and way-beyond-the-job care for especially needy kids are the hallmarks of a great teacher."

Namrita was from a rural part of India and knew no English. No one in school, not even Jhumki, spoke her language. Early on, Jhumki started trying to figure out what was going on with her because Namrita seemed lost and learning-disabled. She discovered that because she came from such a poor area, she had the equivalent of a third-grade education, but in New York she had been enrolled in a sixth-grade class because of her age! Jhumki started regularly tutoring her after school—actually, *after* after-school—to try to improve her math and reading skills. She also spoke to her family to understand more about her. Eventually, during the after-school program, Namrita's lost look faded, and she eventually integrated into student life.

In 2002 Jhumki began moving forward on another of her dreams. The idea of starting a new school for underprivileged children had been bubbling in her head since she began the Discover program. She sent an invitation to her friends and mentors with a comprehensive plan for a unique institution where students would have a voice in their curriculum, participate in university research, and be conscious about their community's welfare.

From the journal of Jhumki Basu, May 17, 2002
Plan for All-Girls School in Northern California

> *The mission of the school is to help girls:*
> - *develop skills to take advantage of intellectual and career opportunities*
> - *become life-long learners*
> - *become emotionally and economically self-reliant*
> - *be capable of making reflective choices*
> - *be active community participants and innovators*
>
> *The school is committed to:*
> - *preparing girls to attend four-year colleges*
> - *small class size (15 students per class), and a personalized education through advising and counseling*
> - *resolution of problems with student-crafted solutions*
> - *best-practices in teaching and self-assessment*

through university collaborations

- *community improvement, in particular, through service learning and adult education*

Curriculum Goals:

The school will teach a liberal arts, college-preparatory curriculum that focuses on literacy, problem-solving, logical thought, creative expression, and technology as a tool to enhance learning.

Counseling:

The school will have a strong advisory program. Students will stay with one adult for all six years. This advisory system will be the primary method used for monitoring the student's behavior, academic and skill performance, attendance, and life developments.

Character Education and Community Exposure:

Service Learning: All students will conduct monthly community service within and outside school. Service learning will be built into curriculum for all grade levels. Services will include monthly school and neighborhood cleanups, student-managed recycling and composting, cooking meals for kitchen staff and charitable organizations.

Internship: The school will require all students to participate each year in summer internships, research, camps and jobs. The school will help students find positions that help them meet any summer financial expectations from their families.

While she made plans for founding her school, Jhumki's career began to surge forward in two distinct directions.

One: The academic rigor of her work at Columbia intensified as she researched ideas, put them to the test, gathered and analyzed data for her master's thesis.

Two: When the after-school program in South Bronx ended, she took on a full-time science teaching job at the Renaissance Charter School in Queens. Managing and inspiring reluctant kids and solving everyday problems led to a different set of learnings.

Then she applied a masterstroke!

Jhumki saw the benefits of intertwining these two threads so that she could simultaneously live *both* the activities she had grown to love: teaching and research. And by doing so, she set in motion a pathbreaking, data-driven educational research program that was grounded in the reality of teaching.

"Jhumki's approach showed that she was thinking not just how to go about it as a teacher," Angie recounted. "She was relying on data to make deeper sense of what was going on, and what might be the best next steps."

Angie described the evolution of a Jhumki who was experiencing first-hand the deprivation that immigrant urban kids faced. The South Bronx school was located in the state's poorest congressional district, and had been on its failing list for four years in a row. It ended up getting closed down and reconstituted. There were many strikes against it, including poor science instruction. Even though the kids had science four days a week, because the school was so focused on literacy and mathematics, the science class was highly structured and, according to Angie, meaningless.

"Not much authentic science went on there," Angie said. "Except in Jhumki and Lo's after-school class.

For her master's thesis, given this contextual umbrella, Jhumki wanted to understand how unsuccessful kids from this environment could succeed in an after-school science program that was voluntary. The program was not designed as an everyday science class. It required the kids to take ownership for their learning, and cultivate leadership and authoring. Jhumki's research goal was to understand how students could leverage their own cultural knowledge and experience, delegitimized in their normal school setting, in ways that were powerful to them?

"In the research project, Jhumki spent a lot of time documenting the kids' funds of knowledge," Angie said. "Lo tried to understand how kids constructed spaces of authority. Together they showed how and why, in this incredibly disadvantaged environment, kids were nevertheless successful and did some wonderful things."

In that forgotten South Bronx community, Angie, Maria, Lo, and Jhumki were examining withered branches of the American science tree, trying to understand what caused its maladies, trying to resuscitate it.

In the fall of 2002, Jhumki took her research program at Teachers College from the Bronx to a full-time science teaching assignment at the Renaissance Charter School in Queens. There she tried hard to maintain an investigative and creative mind-set in a sea of troubles.

At Renaissance, our mercurial Jhumki was fortunate to find wisdom from an unexpected source.

Richard Doherty is an unusual science teacher. He retired as an engineer in his fifties, entered teaching thinking he knew everything, and (in his words) ended the first day realizing he knew nothing. The grizzled veteran with the gravelly voice guided the impetuous twenty-four-year-old through the bureaucracy of a public school and taught her how to use it in her favor.

"Jhumki came to Renaissance wanting to teach physics," Dick told Maithreyi and me. "I was teaching physics and earth sciences at the time, and so she hung out in my class. I was impressed by her enthusiasm. She was very analytical and would never let go of anything."

An upset Jhumki often came barreling down to Dick's safe haven in the school basement. She trusted him and agreed to talk to him about her problems. She was frustrated with the way she was being directed to approach her teaching. Each of their conversations ended with Dick telling her one of three things: "Choose your battle," or "Is it really worth fighting this one?" or "If you are going to do it, go in with a plan."

"Jhumki was approaching problems head-on," Dick explained. "In a hierarchy of peers you've got to know what you want to get done, and how you're going to get it done. They'll respect you if you've got a plan."

To illustrate this sound logic, Dick launched into his remarkable Botball story. Jhumki introduced Renaissance to a competition in which kids built autonomous robots and learned how to program them. As he watched her lead the program, Dick recognized in his young colleague, a strong exponent of discovery learning, and began to understand the qualities she saw in students.

"She knew when to stand back," he said, "when to quit, when to leave 'em alone. She mediated among them for a bit, but only to show them a pathway. And it's still that way. And it's still going. One of the winning robots entered by Renaissance into the competition this year [2009, the year after Jhumki died] had her name and carried her picture."

Jhumki's calmness in her approach with students contrasted heavily with the severe upset in Dick's basement office. She contained her frustration until she got there, and then she would yell at him.

"Go ahead," Dick would tell her. "Let it out."

What distressed Jhumki most were comments from someone who seemed to have no idea what she was doing. Gradually, she began to get over it. Several times she would arm herself with a plan and go back to a meeting. She found it worked. People listened. And Dick was happy for her.

Jhumki's buddies—as I like to call the brilliant and caring science education researchers trained by Angela Calabrese Barton—are characterized by the fire they bring to their mission to achieve social justice in education.

One of those buddies, Edna Tan, a Singaporean, now a faculty member at the University of North Carolina, started her PhD in Angie's group at TC a year after Jhumki and the two became friends.

At her interview, Edna unveiled an inspirational story that Jhumki had once told her. It was about a boy who picks dying starfish on the beach and puts them back in the water. A man comes by and says, "It doesn't make any difference because you are throwing 0.1% back into the sea, and all the rest are dying." The boy replies, "Well, it makes a difference to the 0.1%!"

"This was the philosophy Jhumki followed," Edna said. "It was wise, and it gave me hope. She was very much a mentor to me in that sense."

Along the way Jhumki told Edna something else that illustrated the realism on which she based her passion for student engagement in science.

"I tell myself that I cannot expect my students to listen and concentrate when they are hungry. I cannot expect them to do things when they are hurting emotionally. Or when they just have things bigger than science in their lives right then. So I will not have that expectation of them, and I will not have the expectation of myself, because it is unrealistic."

Columbia University Teachers College awarded Jhumki her master's diploma on May 22, 2003. Her thesis, titled "How Do Youth Develop a Sustained Interest in Science?" grew out of findings at the South Bronx school and the Renaissance Charter School. In the conclusion to her thesis she wrote:

The findings of this study emphasize the value of connecting students' funds of knowledge to their science experiences if they are to develop a sustained interest in science. The study suggests that connections established between science experiences and funds of knowledge centered on students' career interests, social preferences, personalities, and definitions of science are particularly important in cultivating ongoing interest in science. Also, offering students wide latitude for choice in their science learning environments seems to be a successful method for connecting students' funds of knowledge with their science experiences.

Jhumki's family was on hand to cheer when she received her master's diploma. Ranga arrived from Los Angeles. Sumitra came from Boston. Preetham from San Francisco. Radha flew in from Washington, DC.

I was having a problem.

On a Monday, two days before Jhumki's graduation, I woke up at home with an odd taste in my mouth with trouble swallowing. The base of my neck and my left side hurt.

Radha had already left for DC for a business trip. I called my cardiologist, who advised me to come in right away. After examining me, he wanted an angiogram done at once.

Good grief! I thought. What if the angio comes out positive? And what if I need bypass surgery or something? How horrible would it be for Jhumki if something happened to me at this important moment in her career?

I made an executive decision.

"Dr. Chao," I told my incredulous cardio, "I *have* to go to the East Coast and will be back Friday. Let's do my angio on Friday, okay?"

Dr. Chao thought I was crazy. He agreed under duress but made it clear I was postponing the procedure against his wishes. I did not tell anyone about this development, and soon the pain lessened to discomfort. I arrived at Columbia too late for the award ceremony but in time for the official reception.

I found Jhumki wearing a light-blue Columbia robe and an extra special smile. She looked proud and beautiful. I gave her a hug. A noisy crowd was digging in to hors d'oeuvres and wine. Ranga, never shy about these things, gave me a cheery "Hallo!" and joined the scrimmage at the table. I gave my wife a quick and guilty kiss, but she was too happy to notice my shiftiness. Around midnight, on the New Jersey Turnpike, driving south to a NetHope meeting in Baltimore, I told her. Then I looked carefully at the road and kept quiet. Radha later told me she went through the stages of disbelief, concern, and anger, several times, as we passed Newark making good time. It is a tribute to our love—nay, to *her* love—that she responded with "Well, how are you feeling now?" when I was expecting "You $X!Wo%, how *could* you . . . ?!"

At six in the morning, having already put in an hour of work, Jhumki called my cell phone.

"Baba," she scolded, "how many times have I told you to not be daft about . . ."

On Friday at Stanford Hospital, a cold dye was introduced into my femoral artery while I watched Dr. Chao stare at a display monitor. After some minutes his face lit up in a smile and that was that. I called Jhumki to give her the news. She expressed satisfaction and then became professorial.

"Baba, *listen.*"

"Yes, Jhomi."

"Promise me you'll never do it again."

"Do what, Jhomi?"

"Oh, Baba. You're impossible!"

18. EMASONDOSONDO AND ALL THAT

Jhumki spent the summer of 2003 in Johannesburg, South Africa, on an assignment that had major impact on her future work. It was a joint teaching program of Columbia University and the University of the Witwatersrand, led by Columbia physics professor Jeremy Dodd.

Jeremy, who has since become a dear friend of us all, showed Maithreyi and me a photo from that landmark trip.

"This is a picture I selected from the many I'd taken during a trip to South Africa in 2003," Jeremy said. "It shows Jhumki working with four 'learners' in a high school just outside of Johannesburg. I chose it because it captures her at work in the way that I got to see her that year. She is working with these five students, all looking at a simple electrical circuit. I can see from her face how absolutely involved she is, and how much she is engaging these kids who probably have never seen anything like this experiment before. To me it encapsulates her passion for bringing science to kids who did not have access to it before."

Jeremy told us how one day, out of the blue, Jhumki crossed 120th Street from TC to the Physics department and knocked on his door.

She wanted to be part of the team going to Africa.

Jeremy was surprised and delighted that an educator was actually interested in physics teaching. For some years, he had been leading the South Africa program called Physics *Emasondosondo,* Zulu for Physics On-the move, designed to operate in townships and rural schools of the country as a traveling science show with hands-on experiments for kids. The team worked with local teachers, scientists, doctors, and students to demonstrate that young people of color from a variety of backgrounds could be successful in science. The program staff encouraged kids to think of science as a possible career and, importantly, tried to make it relevant to them.

"Jhumki on these trips, more than anyone else, taught me something very valuable," Jeremy said in the strong, even-timbered voice that now anchors Jhumki's memorial documentary. "I come at science from what might be called an old-school perspective. One of the most valuable things Jhumki taught me early on when she got involved in the program was that one has to make it exciting and relevant for the kids. And the relevance was something that she brought as we worked through *Emasondosondo*. It demonstrated another of Jhumki's ideals: that science should not only be relevant, it should be a lot of fun."

From the journal of Jhumki Basu, July 20, 2003

Well, it's the end of week 1.

Visited Krugersdorp—impala, Hadada ibis with fluorescent wings, four rhinos, several lions and cubs, all sleeping. Kudu, aviary—hundreds of birds, weavers metallic blue, solar panel for waterfall, zebras, baby kudu drinking milk from mother, two bucks fighting, ostrich poking its head into the window.

10K run today ~ seven miles—part of the Jo'burg half-marathon, Madiba's [Nelson Mandel's] 85th birthday. Great energy in a small, rundown city center, all colors, men and women. Got to see the "real city" where I don't get to visit as tourist, because we might get attacked or robbed. So many people of so many backgrounds meeting in downtown Jo'berg, to run for something they all admire—Mandela and what he symbolizes, an united South Africa that can leave its past behind and offer opportunities to all.

Apartheid Museum—lots of history, framing the motivations for apartheid, Afrikaaner poverty, Verwoerd/Melan/Botha. Someone tried to assassinate

Verwoerd twice for his policy of apartheid equals good neighbors, though his idea was a black working force for the white people. Amazing that in the 1990s a country could still believe that white people were so superior that black people could be their slaves. No wonder there is so much crime in Jo'berg—it is the people's attempt to bring social redistribution of all that has been taken away. Will this country be like the US in 40 or 50 years? I suppose the difference will be that this country has a black majority, and so the voices of the country will be black.

Today we went to a school where there was a memorial for a boy who burned to death last week. Some of the people on our team were upset that the school "missed out on the opportunity" of having us teach. Many of the kids will never pursue physics, but, in their minds, the death of their friend will be immortal. Is there a time when people will not oppress others because of skin color? What is our obsession with skin color? Why do we view darker people to be worse than lighter people? How is this opinion so ubiquitous but so irrational? Is it really just an accident of history (who colorized whom?) Or have lighter skinned people somehow evolved this particular attitude?

August 4, 2003

The days are flying, and I rarely know what the date is. The teacher workshop is so tedious, but I always like working with the kids. Wherever we go there is some original question: "If electricity and water don't mix, how can you put water in an iron to press clothes?" "Why do I see in color and dream in black and white?" Several students (called learners here) have talked to me about pursuing careers in science and engineering, studying abroad, doing better in school. I told one girl not to take medicine that some stranger had given her "to make her smarter." One learner told me today that though he wants to be an electrical engineer, he is "The Poet" at school.

I am tired of living in NY; people most other places are so welcoming and friendly. What would be fun? Moving to South Africa for a year—traveling around the country each weekend, camping, hiking, learning Si Zulu and Soto and Afrikaans and Xhosa, leading tours of natural places, training to be a game ranger. I am sick of living in a small room, of not having close friends. Tackle one more year at Renaissance with grace and commitment, but I don't want it to consume my life.

September 1, 2003

School starts tomorrow...

Life and the year start again, and SA will become history, at least the experience in SA. I've learned a lot—about a vibrant country with the opportunity for a new beginning, about open-minded friendly people.

When the news of Jhumki's death reached South Africa in 2008, Dr. Simon Connell, a professor at the University of Witwatersrand and organizer of *Emasondosondo*, sent us this tribute to their visiting scholar:

We remember a warm, vibrant, sensitive, brave, competent friend, vital and alive, with dreams and the capacity to realize them.

19. CROWN HEIGHTS

Jhumki once wrote to us from New York:

I found, in one of the boxes you sent me, the dinosaur pop-up book that I used to read when I was little. I remember each of those pictures clearly. For example, Brontosaurus emerging from the water and Tyrannosaurus fighting Triceratops. I think this is one of the books I would read over and over by flashlight when you tried to make me stop reading and go to sleep. Looking at the book reminded me of why I teach science. I have to say this might be my favorite book in the whole world!

It's been hard to remember lately—school has been very intense, lots of kids with lots of problems that result in fights, conflict, tears and more that I have to handle with infinite patience. I lost it in class yesterday and burst into tears in front of the kids, which I think shocked them a bit. I used to feel this way often when I taught Discover. On one hand committed to developing and enacting a great program. On the other hand, overwhelmed by how much there was to create and how much the kids needed. Carey Davis used to say when I looked sad, "Be yourself!"

The dinosaur book reminded me of what being myself means—finding joy in simple, quirky things, reading for fun (which, given my dissertation, I hardly do anymore), adventurously exploring new places in spirit and body.

In July 2009, Janna Pistiner Ostroff was expecting her first child when she came to interview with Maithreyi. She had taken been a colleague of Jhumki's at Renaissance, and had taken over teaching science when Jhumki moved on.

"We shared an office," Janna said. "She was the biology

teacher and I was teaching chemistry. She was my mentor, my friend, my running buddy, and got me interested in yoga classes. She had a huge influence on my teaching, my philosophy of education, my goals about what to expose students to, and what really engaged them.

"Jhumki had just gotten back from South Africa, and had these amazing materials that she brought back. The first lesson she did on scientific method was research that was done in South Africa about racial differences in intelligence and learning. It really engaged the students. It was awe-inspiring to see how gracefully she introduced this material. It could be very volatile, could be very controversial, but she did it in an expert, professional way, and the kids got it. They latched on to it, and it set the tone for an incredible year.

"We had students from all backgrounds and many different religions and cultures, which are strengths of Jackson Heights and our school. Universally the students adored Jhumki. She wanted to push them to higher levels of achievement. That was continually something she stated at faculty meetings. She would engage with parents on behalf of students to help them reach higher levels of academic success. Her voice was clearly heard. It had a very positive and long-lasting impact and an influence on the environment and ethos of the community. She even arranged for a reluctant student to be escorted physically every day to an internship at Columbia University."

Janna was struck by how Jhumki's students always experimented.

One morning Jhumki had led a fermentation lab in which they actually brewed alcohol. She forgot to un-stopper the flask, and soon there was explosive fermented alcohol and a brewery reek all over the school basement. There was bubbling, foaming, fermented yeast, water, alcohol, and sugar everywhere!

Janna described Jhumki's foray into sexual health

education, basing her sex-education unit around animals. She discussed sexual organs and sexual practices of non-humans, and it really got kids involved. They began to ask questions about things they did not understand about their own bodies—for instance, "do dogs menstruate?" Along the way, students had several epiphanies about animals, humans, physiology, health, and sexual well-being.

"Jhumki was very crafty," Janna concluded with a grin, "at designing bizarre, yet correct and well-aimed lessons."

Perhaps it was the extra closeness with us in Norma's apartment during the period of her chemotherapy, or perhaps she had simply matured and become inclusive in her passion for making change. With the coming of the new millennium, Jhumki began to include her parents more and more into her work life.

On one occasion, when I visited her Renaissance classroom, Jhumki introduced me to a Bangladeshi girl named Ambreen (name changed). In a class universally outfitted in jeans and T-shirts and dreadlocks commonplace, Ambreen stood out in a tinsel-studded south Asian *salwar kameez,* and had very long hair plaited in a braid. Like Namrita, Ambreen did not speak English. I asked Jhumki why, and was appalled when she told me Ambreen's parents believed that if she learned English she would be tempted to marry outside her community. She was only fourteen!

I spoke to the girl in Bengali and encouraged her to learn English by describing the many benefits of doing so. I pointed out that her teacher was as much the daughter of immigrants as she was, and that I would be happy to talk to her parents if necessary. I couldn't be sure if I got through, or if the cultural gulf with mainstream America was just too wide for her. A few weeks later a worried Jhumki called me from New York to say Ambreen was about to be expelled because she had failed to bring in a mandatory tuberculosis certificate. I called her parents and patched Jhumki in.

It took me a full minute to adjust to the parents' turbocharged Sylheti dialect of the Bengali language, and their excitability. We quickly cleared the TB certificate issue when Jhumki assured them it was free. Then they asked me if Ambreen's school was "good." Apparently their friends had said it was "bad" and they were thinking of pulling their daughter out. I hastened to affirm that the school was indeed very good— witness the teacher Jhumki, who looked after their daughter so well. They asked me how old Jhumki was, whether she was married, and since she wasn't, why not. I tried to bring the conversation back to Ambreen, but they were more interested in my opinion on whether America was a better or worse place than Bangladesh. After a while the conversation petered out. Ambreen brought in her TB certificate the next day, but soon got into a fight at school and was expelled.

Jhumki had tried, but she was only human.

At about this time, our daughter was becoming increasingly involved in a start-up project in Brooklyn.

Founding a school had been her dream. She had first discussed it with a friend, Celeste Degeller, during summer-camp days at Castilleja in 1997. While Celeste, several years older than Jhumki, had been keen on joining the venture, she had advocated seriously that Jhumki first get teaching and administrative credentials before starting the venture. Jhumki took this advice to heart. It helped in her decision to leave APM and join the Castilleja science faculty. As her teaching outlook took shape, and as she considered a career in education, Celeste's advice impelled her to enroll for an education doctorate at TC, and to take special courses at Baruch College in Brooklyn to obtain administrative credentials.

While teaching at Renaissance, Jhumki began to associate with a determined group of educators bidding on a grant from the Bill and Melinda Gates Foundation. Their objective was to carve out a new, progressive school from a large and poorly performing one in the Crown Heights area of Brooklyn.

E-mail from Jhumki Basu to friends and family, Jan 11, 2004

Our team received 196 out of 200 on the combination of our proposal, presentation, team capacity, team leadership and partner capacity. It was the highest score of all the school proposals this year and possibly ever. We lost a few points 'cause we (not just I!) were not dressed formally enough. That's pretty funny—you can see why I fit in. (One team presented in black suits and white slacks and carnations. What dorks!) I'm telling you our score because you're the only people to whom I can admit that I like beating everybody else in the field :)

We present to Gates on Feb 26th.

At that critical presentation Jhumki made an impassioned appeal for the creation of a school that was based on the evolving technique of student inclusion in their own learning or, as it was getting to be known, democratic pedagogy.

From Jhumki Basu's presentation to the Bill and Melinda Gates Foundation

Teacher Perspective:

Let me say, first off, that the school will offer an academically-rigorous curriculum. But why will students embrace this type of curriculum? Kids in school normally do work because they are supposed to, or do the minimal. In either case they don't understand why they are required to have an education. This means that they are often pushed, pulled, cajoled and forced into learning. The school actually offers kids a reason to go to school. The philosophy of the school is that education allows a person to transform his/her society for the better, not in the future, but starting in the here and now. Having this purpose of education for change provides a reason for every member of the school community to be committed to every kid getting the highest standards of education.

The efforts of Jhumki and her team were successful, and the School for Democracy and Leadership was born.

Press Release

School for Democracy and Leadership Opens Doors to Next Generation of Community Leaders

Brooklyn, NY, Sept 15, 2004: The newly formed School for Democracy and Leadership today announced its opening this week to serve the needs of students in grades 6–12 who aspire to make a difference in their lives and their communities. 150 sixth and ninth graders from Brooklyn took their seats for the first time in a learning environment that uniquely links student choice, community participation and the realization of personal potential.

Formed in association with New York Urban League, New School University's Center for Urban Education, and the Sadie Nash Leadership Project, SDL is rooted in the belief that democracy and education are inextricably linked. The School's teachers were handpicked based not only for their outstanding academic credentials, but their passion for helping students transform their individual worlds by an active participation in their own education leading to college. Each of them has demonstrated leadership ability in his or her own right, with backgrounds ranging from participation in the NASA Educator Astronaut program to management responsibility within the Caribbean Disaster Information Network, and from internationally recognized magazine illustration to community development in rural Thailand. All of them share a commitment to sharing their leadership skills inside and outside of academia to make a difference in their students' personal growth.

"SDL fulfills a long held personal belief that empowerment is the foundation of democracy. An educational process that lacks real student engagement and a connectedness with their teachers leaves them unfulfilled and disconnected from the democratic process," said Nancy Gannon, principal. "In the words of Paulo Freire, an internationally acclaimed author and educational thought-leader, our goal is to create a 'pedagogy of hope' and, in the eyes of our students, create a learning environment where staying after school is seen as a reward not a punishment."

Jhumki (left) at last NYU Science Methods class, Dec 9, 2008

Anna Vinogradova and
Aza Rakhmanova in St. Petersburg

Receiving Dean's Award from Dr. Rice

Castilleja Bridal Show

In Delhi: With Ranga watching *Star Trek* (left), with Shanti (right)

Friends: Kritika (left) and James

Family:
Chunilal Bose (L)
Ajit Kumar Basu (R)
Kalyani Ramaswami
and Geeta Basu
(Below L)
Parents and Mishti
(Below R)

Nancy Gannon

Paul Prokop

Angela Calabrese Barton

Maria Rivera Maulucci

Christopher Emdin

Helen Dole, running for Jhumki at the New York Marathon

With Students of South Bronx School

Receiving Doctorate from Columbia University Teachers College

20. DEMOCRATIC PEDAGOGY

Nancy Gannon was the founding principal of the School for Democracy and Leadership. In view of their close personal and working relationship, in this chapter I will let Nancy tell you in her own words about a critical period of Jhumki's life.

◆

At Columbia Teachers College, Jhumki was a student of my close friend Britt, who knew I was starting a school.

"I know you are interested in teaching physics," Britt told Jhumki. "Are you interested also in thinking about starting a school and/or being involved?"

"No," replied Jhumki!

It was understandable.

At the time she was overwhelmed with the things she was already doing. She had her hands in about a thousand things. But she was interested in maybe coming to a meeting and just listening. And after a meeting or two she decided she was in. Then she went from just being an observer to being very actively involved and taking on leadership roles in the planning team. There were about fourteen of us doing the planning, including parents, students, teachers, community members. She took on the role of mapping the science piece for the school.

Jhumki and I talked a lot about the Physics First movement that was going on in different places in the country. It is a program where students start in ninth grade with physics rather than the traditional science or biology. Jhumki was interested in that. One of the program's arguments is that physics is a foundational science more than other sciences. The program allowed black and Hispanic kids to take physics because, if it is in the senior year—which physics traditionally is—often minority students don't take it. So whatever our ideas were for the school we agreed every kid would take physics as a foundational science.

It was a very intense time.

We met Tuesday and Friday nights and all day Sunday every week. We were working at full-time jobs so everyone was trying to cram it in. It involved a lot of talking, presenting ideas, writing, and researching.

Ours would not be a charter school. It would be a public school. There was a request for proposal that was put out by New Visions for Public Schools, a small nonprofit educational organization in New York City. New Visions had received about eighty million dollars in grants from Gates, Carnegie, and Soros Foundations. The RFP was for people interested in school reform. The idea was to shut down large and ineffective high schools, and replace them with small high schools that were intimate, personal, supportive, and college preparatory. We had to follow decrees of the Department of Education of New York City and we would be evaluated by them.

There were a few things politically that were happening.

In May 2003, Mayor Bloomberg was elected. He said education was his platform and he was interested in shutting down large schools and starting small ones. Another important thing that happened at the same time was the Autonomy Zone, brainchild of Eric Nadelstern of the United States Department of Education. The Autonomy Zone was a program you could apply to be in as a school. If you were in the Zone you were freed from many regulations of the DoE. We were part of the original Autonomy Zone, which is now called Empowerment Schools. We were one of the thirty-two schools that signed a waiver saying that in return for relaxed regulations, if our school did not work out, we agree to be fired. We believed that if *we could just run the school the way we believed, it would do well. We didn't want to be hindered by all those rules and regulations.*

There was still planning left.

We had to observe the United Federation of Teachers' contract. We had to observe state mandates. Being in the Zone, it allowed us to teach physics in ninth grade. It allowed us to change the order of the curriculum and use curriculum we were interested in, and change the schedule. We had a very non-traditional course sequence.

Jhumki mapped the science department completely. After we agreed we were interested in physics first, she mapped the physics curriculum. She and I talked about how to incorporate hands-on experiential learning because it was important to both of us. I came with a real interest in democratic pedagogy and she avidly shared that interest and we talked a lot about how to incorporate it.

Democratic pedagogy is making sure that the students' voices are integral to our work. It is the idea that a student is not a vessel into which you pour knowledge, but a living human being who brings his or her own knowledge and understanding of the world and many things to share. It is the idea that education is more about building on each other's strengths, sharing with each other how we understand the world, rather than one person being the giver and another person the receiver.

Democratic pedagogy is definitely something many new schools across the country are interested in. However, other new schools follow the traditional model. Democratic pedagogy is something schools strive for and often don't attain. If you walk through the School for Democracy and Leadership, which we founded, fifty percent of the classrooms would not be conducting democratic pedagogy, though it is aspirational.

It was intense. Amazing. Really exciting. Really hard.

For some of the ideas we had needed inordinate support. One of the big challenges was that we had very young teachers. They were still struggling with how to decorate their desks while we wanted them to do something really challenging. Setting up a democratic classroom was very difficult.

In retrospect, I realize it required a real sense of self-confidence in our teachers, so that they did not have to control what students were doing. That it can be a shared experience of teacher and student. This is very hard to do in a classroom for a 21-year-old teacher, especially with a population of students that is used to tight reins and dictatorial ways. Kids would come to Jhumki, assistant principal at SDL, and say, "Miss, you've got to talk to that teacher. She is letting the kids talk too much or letting the kids do what they want in the classroom!"

Teachers struggled with finding an in-between place, just letting kids do what they want, which is not democratic practice, and letting students have an important voice in the classroom, which is.

We started with about seventy-five sixth graders and seventy-five ninth graders, eleven teachers including Jhumki, me as principal, and a secretary. We started with a camping trip for ninth graders and a three-day orientation at the school for sixth graders. The camping trip was super fun. The kids had a great time. During the trip the students' personalities became clear quickly. We had students who were excited about the opportunity to engage and to have a voice when they hadn't before. There were others who were very uncomfortable with it.

I remember Jordan Franklin, who became an important person to Jhumki and vice versa. Jordan was miserable at the beginning. She was uncomfortable with herself and excruciatingly shy. She connected with Jhumki early on. She was rude to Jhumki, yet Jhumki always came back with pleasantries and corrected her when she was wrong, and when she had stepped too far. She was there for Jordan consistently. By the end of two years at SDL, Jordan had changed so much. She was confident and funny and beautiful, had tons of friends, and everybody loved her. At the high school graduation, she sang a song, and people cheered. At a different kind of school she would have gone through four years of fostering that self-hatred.

There was one kid, Peter, who was at SDL for two days when I got a call from the school district office asking if he was at our school. I said, "Yeah, he's in math class right now." They said he was not supposed to be there. He was suspended. He had attacked his last principal with a golf club. He was not allowed in school right then.

Another kid hated our school. Hated it every day. He told us how much he hated it. He told us his mom was dying of cancer, and he was really struggling. We simply couldn't get in there. We couldn't get past how much he hated all of us. He finally transferred to some other school. A week later he was arrested for murder.

There were really dramatic things going on inside and outside our school. Peter, the kid with the golf club, had a fight once with Gedison, another tough kid who was close to Jhumki. Gedison and Peter entered the school at the same time and had a little pecking-order problem. Peter was a very smart student from a very rough part of Jamaica. Lots of gold teeth, a real gangster kind of attitude. I saw him change a lot.

How did a twenty-six-year-old Jhumki handle these difficult kids?

I believe to work with children like these, one works the same way as with anybody. Jhumki was being herself. Kids recognized and respected that. She was a very honest person. By that I don't mean not telling lies. She was who she was.

When a student was wrong, she would tell the person that he or she was wrong. She was respectful of others. She was contemplative and thoughtful and kids respect that. There isn't anything different about these kids except they don't get respect from most people. There were teachers in the school who were clearly afraid of them or intimidated. Jhumki wasn't. She was very real. It was just Jhumki's nature. That's the way she treated people.

One of Jhumki's most important characteristics was her intense energy. A thing almost inhuman. I don't know anybody else in the world that could do a master's and a PhD together while trying to start her own school and teach full-time. Jhumki not only did it but she thought it to be normal.

Jhumki would never sound a false note. She would not make a remark that later she couldn't stand by. It's really hard to live one's life like that. She had a very strong sense of right and wrong, and of justice. That people are obligated to give back. She has this humility and authenticity in the way she lived her life that was remarkable.

PART IV

INTO HIGH GEAR

"I am in the business of collecting treasure for my spirit and mind."

Sreyashi Jhumki Basu
Quito, Ecuador, 1997

21. THE GREEK SCIENTIST

Sreyashi Jhumki Basu was rumored to maintain a spreadsheet that listed the pros and cons of the young men she met and liked. I have not seen this infamous document. No one else has, as far as I know.

George and Susan Remsberg have been our friends from the time Radha and Sue worked together in the early days of Support.com. Jhumki built a unique relationship of her own with Sue. On bi-coastal phone calls they discussed topics such as clothes, rebelling against doctors' orders, and boys.

"The men in her life who genuinely cared for her," said Sue, "really *got* it. They understood her. And, of course, that infamous spreadsheet! We were once talking about boyfriends, and she said, 'I've built this spreadsheet, and it has all these data points.' And I said, 'Oh my God, you cannot pick a mate based on a spreadsheet! That's just so unromantic. But it's so *like* you.'" Sue laughed heartily. "This conversation took place around the time she met Alexander. And as she started talking to me about him I asked her, 'Well, have you put *him* on the spreadsheet?' and she gasped and said, 'Omigosh, I forgot!'"

Ted Diament lives in New York. Reticent yet warm, with a low-key demeanor, Ted makes light of multiple successful careers in software, law, and finance. He is a friend and former roommate of a tall, straight-backed, good-looking computer scientist from Greece.

Ted first met Jhumki when Alexander brought her to a restaurant on 100th Street and Amsterdam in New York's Upper West Side.

"At the dinner I definitely had the impression she liked him," Ted told Maithreyi as we sat on benches in Battery Park with microphone and voice-recorder, while buses and delivery vans rumbled around us.

"At that juncture Alexander was clearly very interested in Jhumki, though she was still checking him out. And ostensibly there was some boyfriend in the wings. I didn't think that was going to be much of an obstacle based on what I had seen. It may just have been posturing on her part to buy time.

"I think they were very sweet together. I have not met many of Alexander's girlfriends, but one could tell there was something special going on here. Alexander's official story is that Jhumki and he 'somehow' bumped into each other at the Silver Moon Bakery on Broadway. But I knew Alexander had targeted Jhumki because I was at the yoga class where he pointed her out and said that he was interested. So it was not quite accidental. I wouldn't say he was *stalking* her, but that he had his eye on her. Maybe under enough pressure we can extract a confession from Alexander, but I think this is pretty solid."

After Jhumki left the restaurant that night, Alexander told Ted he was helping to move her things to a new apartment, and that he did believe the boyfriend was an obstacle. Ted, on the other hand, thought a beautiful woman like Jhumki *should* have a boyfriend.

"They hit it off very quickly," Ted continued. "I clearly remember a few dinners early in their relationship, again with me and Alexander. Once she ate a whole fish with her fingers, which struck me as unusual and interesting, and I liked it. I think Alexander liked to see someone dig in, tuck into food."

"What was so funny," Kritika adds to the story, "is when Jhumki first mentions Alexander to me, it is in a letter and she mentions him so casually! She doesn't even mention him by name. She is on her way out of town and writes, 'I've started seeing this other guy, and who knows what'll happen.' When she first spoke about Alexander, it wasn't 'Oh, he's going to be the one!' or 'He's the one who is going to win my heart over.' However, by the time I met him, I had heard about Alexander a lot. He seemed quite mature. But it was only when I hung out with the two of them that I realized they were extremely serious and extremely silly!"

From the journal of Jhumki Basu, August 1, 2004

> *so many firsts*
> *new job at SDL*
> *SDL = new school*
> *Master's dissertation done*
> *new apartment*
> *new neighborhood to live in, Brooklyn, after 3 years*
>
> *I looked out across the Reservoir today. It's been a gift to live in this part of Manhattan. It's close to the hub of the world. From 42nd Street/Times Square you can go anywhere!*
>
> *new love interest potentially*
> *fear of Δ's in routine!*
> *Alex?*
>
> *Well, only time will tell. So far, he surprises me each time I see him. I'm sure problems will arise with Alexander. But I think I will go with what he said recently, "I have no vision of how things will be." What do I like about him? Feeds me, direct about his thoughts and feelings, affectionate, has smart fun friends, has a full life, smart and intelligent, has a sense of style in areas I have not—truly I did not understand any of what he said about his work project—clothes and living situation, independent, speaks Greek and Hebrew, has lived not in the US which is a plus, athletic, yoga, competitive swimming, biking. What's not so good? Relationship might be too intense for me. I might be too busy. I might not be able to afford his lifestyle.*

Radha and I were introduced to Alexander late in 2004.

From the way Jhumki had spoken to us about him—

appreciatively, incredulously ("Mommy, is he for real?")—we knew it was going to be an important meeting. Radha and I were anxious, wanting everything to turn out well. We didn't think of it then, but the stress on Alexander must have been more severe.

We were the first to arrive at Cafe Lalo, our daughter's favorite patisserie, a place awash with fragrant aromas and jammed with happy people. We secured a table, sat shoulder-to-shoulder with animated patrons, and strove mightily to hold on to two empty seats against the surging crowd.

Jhumki joined us.

A minute or two later, the three of us watched through tall glass windows as Alexander walked toward us along 83rd Street with confident strides. He entered the cafe and looked around through clear, rimless glasses. He saw us, nodded, smiled, pushed his way through the crush, shook our hands, and greeted us in a soft voice that had a pleasing Mediterranean accent. The pressure dissipated, and the talk became natural. Radha and I were awed by his fascinating Greek/Israeli heritage. We talked about his research project, Radha's start-up company, my nonprofit work. We discussed disaster management and self-healing computer networks while Jhumki watched us with a dreamy, satisfied smile, not saying a word, contentedly tuned out of the technical jargon. She was delighted that her beau and parents were getting along. And, while we talked, she worked her way steadily through leek and potato soup, eggs Benedict, a pile of éclairs, and a caramel latte.

A few weeks later Alexander came to California to see us. After the visit he wrote:

> Dear Radha and Dipak,
> I'd like to thank you for welcoming me to your beautiful home. I really enjoyed spending more time with you. It was a treat to be pampered with great food and company! The pictures of spring in the Santa Cruz hills are certain to stay

with me for a long time.

Over time I've grown to appreciate the different aspects of Jhumki that add up to a unique and lovely personality. One of the first things I noticed about Jhumki was her confidence in herself. I now know that it is built on the strong foundation of your family, and rooted in a rich old tradition.

Thank you for all that you have done for Jhumki. I'll do my best to take care of her while she's away in New York!

Not long after this, Jhumki told us that she and Alexander wanted to go away over spring break and spend time together.

Things were getting serious!

We liked Alexander very much and wanted the two to have a good time. Alexander was surprised that Jhumki didn't want to go to Cancún or Palm Beach like many college kids on spring break from the cold Northeast. Instead, Jhumki wanted to be in the wild with animals. This time though, in consideration of her less backwoodsy boyfriend, she asked me to recommend a "nice place off the beaten track."

I sympathized with Alexander. The idyllic European was about to discover the intrepid explorer. After several phone exchanges they agreed to go to Belize, where Radha and I had spent an enjoyable vacation two years earlier. Belize is a tiny English-speaking country on the Yucatán Peninsula, in actuality not very far from Cancún. Considering its size, it has an immense variety of attractions—barrier reef for divers, rain forest for explorers, Mayan ruins for lovers. Jhumki felt it would be a good trial for them without going overboard. Upon their return, she wrote to her parents:

When we were in Belize, I think, for the first time in a while, I ate as much as I wanted whenever I was hungry (which is a little bit all day). I also slept enough every night.

159

Coming back, I think was a bit of a shock to my system—it's also a lot colder here in New York. I had a really big headache last night and had to go to sleep around 8 pm. So, this morning, though it took an extra five minutes, I went to Starbucks instead of the bagel place where I normally go (bagels aren't much nourishment) and spent $17 on a rich hot chocolate (I think I need to be eating more carbohydrate and fat for how much exercise I get and how much I'm on my feet), an Odwalla orange juice, an egg salad sandwich and a Mediterranean salad plate. So, I should have enough food to eat and drink all day, especially given my class is till 8:30 pm.

I know you tell me this all the time, but I think the contrast between how I felt in Belize and how I feel now really stood out to me yesterday. Alexander is great and often packs me lunch, but I need to make a point to prioritize having enough food over finishing that extra ten minutes of lesson planning, no matter how much pressure there is to teach better and do more so that students do better in school.

Ideally, of course, I wouldn't spend $17 on lunch, so I need to get my act together this weekend and do some grocery shopping for peanut butter, power bars, fruits for a shake, eggs, bread, and some other things I rely on!

22. PARENTS, FRIENDS, AND NASA

"She was like an open book."

It was September 2011. We were on a Skype video link between California and Kolkata and Radha was reminiscing on her stormy relationship with her daughter.

"She would tell me what she felt right away. That's why we got into fights, because she could never keep her feelings in. She *had* to say, 'Mommy, why did (or didn't) you do this?' It would come out, boom, like that. The great thing about her was one never needed to second-guess her. One never had to say, 'Is she thinking something else?' She was an open book—with all the faults. One day after we had fought and I was feeling really down, Jhumki sent me this song:

> *If I had a spell of magic*
> *I would make this enchantment for you*
> *A burgundy heart shaped medallion*
> *With a window that you could look through*
> *So that when all the mirrors are angry*
> *With your faults and all you must do*
> *You could peek through that heart shaped medallion*
> *And see you from my point of view[12]"*

Radha paused for a while after reading the song to me. I was wondering whether the Skype connection had gone down when

---

[12] From "Burgundy Heart Shaped Medallion," lyrics by David Wilcox, Hal Leonard Corp. Reproduced with permission.

she continued.

"You know, we fought a lot."

"Yes, you did," I agreed. "But in the end you both saw the wisdom of each other's views."

"We disagreed mostly over four things," she went on. "First, it was about her clothes, because she really thought I had no idea of dress for her. Did she *have* to wear T-shirts and jeans with lots of holes? Did her clothes *ever* match? She was so different in her everyday dress habits. Then she would surprise me by going and buying a stunning office suit or a glamorous evening gown!

"We argued about her doing crazy stuff. She was so stubborn about things like running the triathlon while going through chemo, or going alone to a detention center far away from Moscow. At those times she would put her chin on my head and say, 'And Short Stuff, what about when you were just twenty, came to the U.S. with only eight dollars, and no one that you knew?'"

The third thing mother and daughter clashed about was Jhumki's medication. That was the hardest, because it happened late in her illness when she was going through an extremely difficult health situation.

"I really felt," Radha said, "that having more and more medication in her system was going to cause her liver damage, which actually happened. I felt that she should look at alternative cancer medicines. But she wouldn't. She wanted scientific evidence and based her regimen on Dr. Hudis, whom she trusted completely. If he said, 'Malarkey!' then it was malarkey. 'Prove it otherwise!' she would tell me. I think in the end it hurt her." She sighed and added, "But who can say?"

The final item of discord was about boys.

"Jhumki liked some people and didn't think of the consequences," Radha said. "I thought a lot about the consequences."

I laughed.

""Ah yes," I told her. "All those boys! Jhumki was very scientifically oriented about medicines, just like you said. But when it came to men, she let her heart rule her head, which is not the usual Jhumki. *You* are very much like that too. You got *me*! See?"

"Yes I did, didn't I?"

We sighed over cyberspace.

"Jhumki was the kind," I continued wistfully, "when somebody took an interest in her and liked her, she didn't worry about his background or his intent or his personality."

"I completely agree," Radha said. "She went very much from not just the heart, but whether somebody made her laugh. The humor could be very shallow, but she went with it. She never thought about the actual person inside. Invariably she liked nice, good-looking guys, but didn't go for the high achievers, like, you know, the ones really successful, well-to-do, earning a great salary. Someone was nice to her and made her laugh, and she fell for him!"

"All this, of course, was before Alexander," I pointed out.

But Radha stuck to her point.

"In that way, Jhumki had a flaw. That's the thing about her. She was very real and very alive. She wasn't a perfect person. The flaw was she made quick judgments about people, both positive and negative, and then it was hard to change her mind."

After a moment's pause she continued.

"The Burgundy Heart Shaped Medallion reflected our relationship because we could be angry with each other and we could see through to the other side to each other's faults. We were both very stubborn. We were able to feel very deeply. We had very strong personalities. We could see each other's faults so much that, as she grew older, she became my companion, my friend, more than my daughter. We became equals. And the heart-shaped medallion was the love. We figured out each other's points of view and that's what our relationship became.

"Even when, on the second-last day of her life, she knew she was nearing the end and I wouldn't face it, she said, 'Mommy, you are so stupid. You are so silly. Why can't you see this is *it?*' She was angry with me, and yet it was Mommy who was next to her. It was Mommy's hand she held and pressed when she couldn't talk anymore. That was the absolute reality and how alive our relationship was. It was so honest. I know I don't have this relationship with any other human being in this world. The most real, alive, honest connection, and it had every element of life. It was magic."

Unlike with her mother, Jhumki's relationship with me was practical, non-mushy, and non-confrontational. We left the difficult things for Mommy to clear up. We shared lists of things to do for each other, animal and geographic trivia, etc. She depended on me to handle boring stuff like clearing up old bills and making on-line purchases. When she wanted something done, she came to me. When she was struggling with a problem, Mommy got the call. And so I was really surprised when I received this e-mail on Valentine's Day in 2005:

Re: Baba's Day

Baba, you're an inspiration for me—the breadth of your interests is the reason I do so many things!

Love, Jhomi

Wow! Jhomi, where did *that* come from? I love you too, Jhomi! Dearly.

Reading that message after many years created for me a mental image of rainbow arches through which we had walked hand-in-hand. The arches made the unrelenting inclines of the road of life bearable.

On a roll, Jhomi sent around another rainbow arch message to a wide distribution of friends and family.

> *My Baba is likely to know all of the following: the capital of Burundi, the independence date of Ecuador from the Spanish, the range of the Inca, Olmec, and Mayan civilizations in Central and South America, the highest landmass in Greenland, the path hominids took out Africa, the population of Luxembourg, and what Phoebe wore and ate in Episode #37 of Friends.*
>
> *Recently, I have been trying to find the results of an ovarian ultrasound that I took last year. Baba sent what he thought was a copy of the ultrasound/sonogram to my doctor. I asked repeatedly that he check that it was not a breast sonogram. But Mommy says that what he showed her was indeed imaging of a breast, not an ovary.*
>
> *Dear, Baba! Go back to school and take some reproductive health classes.*

Jhumki's burden of work at this point in her life—assistant principal, new teacher mentor, science department head, physics teacher at SDL, coupled with completing her PhD at Columbia and securing administrative credentials at Baruch—was an unrelenting incline.

No one better understood the strain on her than did her fellow science teacher and running partner, Helen Dole.

Helen, tall, blond and statuesque, is a serious marathoner, and one of our daughter's colleagues actually younger than her. Helen would happily run all day if she didn't have to stand still and teach for a living. I am convinced that endurance running and dedicated teaching go hand in hand. Both activities require much of the same qualities.

Helen was a fresh college graduate when she came to teach sixth-grade science at SDL. In 2009, she described her trial by fire rather theatrically: "In my first year I barely survived teaching. In my second year I added in sleeping. In my third year I added in running. And in my fourth year I had friends and was running, sleeping, and teaching!"

Helen described Jhumki in that first year at SDL as a sort of dean of the school. Kids were always in her advisory office. Her laptop and the school computer would both be going. Students would be lined up inside and outside. Helen and other young teachers would come to her in tears.

"When Jhumki was working with you, it was all on you," Helen said. "She might be doing a lot of things, but she had this amazing way of making you feel front and center if you were talking to her."

To this day, Helen is convinced Jhumki is the reason she still teaches.

"I'm kind of a stubborn person. I don't like to fail at things. I believe that if you work at it, it will ultimately get better. This may lead one to being very unhappy or feel successful and proud about making a difference. I think the successful part and making a difference and mattering is largely attributable to the way Jhumki mentored me in different ways, constantly making me better."

Helen said she is motivated every day by Jhumki's undying belief that teaching is a noble calling that deserves high esteem, a philosophy that is especially helpful at low moments.

"I once found myself sitting in a subway train holding a canister of liquid nitrogen that Jhumki asked me to pick up at NYU for a class at SDL. It was an empty one, but I was worried I could end up in the police department because they thought I was going to explode the subway. But the kids loved the experiment. Or, here's a good one, I just wanted to teach a class about the atmosphere, but Jhumki was pretty sure I should have the students write a story about what would happen if they go up in the atmosphere without a spacesuit on. She had great ideas about space. I know because I had to write her a recommendation about being an astronaut."

෨

In June 2003 Jhumki had applied for the position of NASA Educator Astronaut, motivated by the Educator Astronauts' success in developing interest in science among inner-city children. Among her heroes was teacher Christa McAuliffe, who had been selected from 11,500 Educator Astronaut applicants. As is well known, space shuttle *Challenger* broke apart after blastoff in 1986 with Christa aboard, while millions of horrified schoolchildren watched on TV. Another hero was Barbara Morgan, who replaced Christa, went to space, and spoke to students while on an *Endeavour* mission.

Jhumki's determination to be selected for this role is evident in her petitions against the bureaucracies that impeded her candidacy after she was selected as a finalist.

From a petition by Jhumki Basu to Renaissance Charter School, June 2, 2004

I recently asked to receive teacher release days for professional development, from June 15th to 18th, during Regents week, because I was chosen to be a founding teacher in NASA's Educator Astronaut program. The school does not have to spend money on this professional development. NASA will cover my plane ticket and housing and I do not need a substitute. I am very excited to go. The participants sound amazing. I will be learning from them and developing curriculum.

But the school has decided that investing in me is not worthwhile, given the possibility I may not return next year. I will attend the NASA conference, regardless of whether money is deducted from my paycheck if I return to Renaissance. I work hard for the school, as do many other teachers. Much of this work is done in good faith, with the assumption that students, families and administrators appreciate all that is being accomplished. Teachers do not receive end-year bonuses for high-levels of commitment and competence, as they would at a business. So, in the future, I suggest to the school that it view professional development as an experience that rewards good teachers for their contributions to the success of the school.

From a petition by Jhumki Basu to NASA Medical Review Board, July 26, 2005

In early 2003, I applied to the Educator Astronaut Program in hopes of pursuing my dual passion for practicing and teaching science. I felt that I could contribute, through the Educator Astronaut program, to our society's understanding of the universe while simultaneously engaging youth in the mysteries of space science, inspiring them to pursue careers in this field. However, I was eliminated from the astronaut selection process—specifically because I once had breast cancer— despite the fact that I was then, and continue to be now, cancer-free.

Since my initial petition regarding my disqualification, I have exchanged letters with you and your office several times. In your most recent letter, you suggested that NASA was likely to revise the medical standards it was using at that time. I am writing to ask you if any changes have been made that are relevant to cancer survivors.

I am in complete remission!

I am completing my PhD in science education at Teachers College, Columbia University while employed as a full-time physics teacher and assistant principal at a brand-new inner-city public school. I am 27 years old and run, swim and practice yoga each week. My doctors continue to be supportive of me pursuing my interest in applying to NASA and do not believe that the training, or space flight, will cause me medical problems.

Discovery just took off today! It looks as if NASA's manned space program is back on its feet. I would like to apply again to be an astronaut with the hope that this time I can be considered based on my knowledge and skills. I believe I have many of the qualities you seek in a candidate, and in particular the kind of perseverance and energy that comes from my experience as a young cancer survivor.

If changes have not been made, I am curious as to the reasons that a person with my history of recovery from cancer is judged to be unfit to apply for a position as an astronaut. I look forward to hearing from you and hope that our dialogue results in qualified cancer survivors having a fair and full chance of applying to be astronauts.

Sue Remsberg bore the brunt of Jhumki's frustration at this highly contentious time.

"The affair with NASA was one of her major disappointments after the cancer diagnosis," she remembers sadly. "We talked a lot about it. We wrote letters to NASA. We researched any way we could to get her there. I was a little surprised that this could so deeply affect her. She wasn't going to let their rejection stop her from being all that she could be. This was hugely instinctive in her. And then she was really furious at NASA for implying it—*that she was going to die.* This was the point in time when she was genuinely angry that *they* said she couldn't be all that she could be, because she had every intention of doing it. She felt she was being cheated. If she thought she could be strong, why couldn't they follow suit?"

Jhumki received final word that NASA would not let her appeal their decision to disqualify her because of cancer, and that the decision would hold as long as current medical rules held. The chief flight surgeon noted that the rules might change one day, but would not mention a time frame.

Jhumki realized this was a battle she was unlikely to win and reluctantly moved on.

Meanwhile, a *Glamour* magazine article rumbled about the unseen world of cancer.

Jhumki met Stephanie Williams, a writer, at Beth Israel hospital when Jhumki was undergoing reconstructive surgery following her mastectomy. Stephanie's article in the September 2004 issue of *Glamour* was titled "Saying Goodbye to My Life" and published after she died. It evoked a flood of sentiment in chat rooms and cancer support sites. Jhumki wrote about it in her journal:

> *Reading about Stephanie in* Glamour *was a shocker. I will have to purchase her novel. She died four months ago. She was in the process of dying as I was reclaiming my life, so boldly and arrogantly. She had to let go of the love of her life, whom she met four months before she was diagnosed with cancer. Who let her get a sonogram a month later??! With a large lump that caused her pain? I remember her coming in to talk to me about the tissue reconstruction she had done with Dr. Mark Smith, my surgeon. I remember thinking how crazy she was to wait so long, to wait when she had a lump the size of a golf ball in her breast. And what she wrote was right on. You want the best for other people, you want them to live rich, fulfilling lives, you want them to find love, but you want it to be a life with you in it. You want to be a source of the rich fulfillment and to experience with the person. You want to be the person with whom love happens. Like me, Stephanie was an ambitious career woman, driven, focused, always on the move,*

accomplishing things. And she found peace with someone who moved to a slower pace, found joy in smaller things like reading the newspaper, listening to NPR and drinking coffee on a Saturday morning. She lived her life the way she wanted, once she knew she didn't have much of it left to live—she moved to an apartment in the right neighborhood and decorated it in the colors and styles she wanted. She got a dog and was left wondering when he would figure out that she would someday never come home.

No heroic measures.

And that's what I think too. No stupid feeding tubes and things that keep your body alive but destroy and violate your spirit. It's made me feel humble to read about Stephanie because I've had such optimism and confidence about recovering from cancer. I've acted as if it was never in question that the road forward was positive. Stephanie's story gives me pause. I am reminded that missing tamoxifen is no joke.

People die of breast cancer. I am lucky to have caught the lump early, to have survived.

Adding to Jhumki's aggravation was her worry about the health of her mentor, Carey Davis, whose own cancer was progressing rapidly. December came and the person who had shown Jhumki much of the way left her. Carey's personality, wisdom, guidance, illness, death, and celebratory funeral had enormous collective impact on Jhumki's psyche.

"Carey's influence on Jhumki cannot be overstated," Joelle Mourad said to me. "She was very much an inspirational, motivating kind of person."

At the Discover summer camp back in California, Joelle and Jhumki had admired Carey to the point of hero worship. Carey, they felt, was amazing and dynamic. The two young counselors wondered how Carey could do so many things so easily—especially things that would inspire self-doubt in them.

"The way Carey operated," Joelle said, "was a big part of Jhumki's and my development in terms of feeling okay about working with young people. We had an adult we really admired, one who inspired us to feel, 'Yes, this is good work. This is important work and we have the tools to do it.' Carey was very good at instilling confidence and making us feel, 'Wow, this person thinks I can do it.'"

From the journal of Jhumki Basu, Dec 1, 2005
Things from Carey I want to keep:
- *her e-mails and notes*
- *"It's about the kids"*
- *"Be yourself"*
- *Music*
- *Style of doing things:*
- *energy*
- *no bureaucracy*
- *fun while learning*
- *all-girls' programs*
- *opportunity to create your own classes and programs*

Build a community of teachers and friends with a Carey philosophy of doing things. Still have things to learn from her, would rather that she embody and enliven these ideals than me having to hold onto them without her. Energy of her last e-mail v. her not being around anymore.

23. THE PILLARS OF TEACHING

I n January 2009, a month after Jhumki died, while sorting through her office at New York University, I noticed a tiny, innocuous, sticky-note on the outside of a drawer. About to crumple and throw it away, I glanced at it a second time. Then I looked up and looked at Radha incredulously.

"What?" she exclaimed, seeing my expression. "What's on the paper?"

I handed it to her, and we stared at it for a long time. Then I carefully copied and formatted its contents into my laptop. On that three-by-three-inch piece of curled and faded canary-yellow paper was Jhumki's teaching philosophy, her everyday work goal.

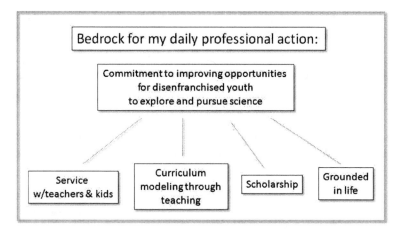

"That Post-it was Jhumki, and Jhumki was our Post-it," Helen Dole told me proudly when I showed it to her. "Whenever we were working with Jhumki, she would send an influx of that message to us, to remind us to keep striving for that attitude."

჻

Dr. Christopher Emdin is a forceful, mile-a-minute professor of physics education at Columbia Teachers College and a sought-after public speaker on socio-economic topics related to urban youth of color. Chris, a Board Member of the Jhumki Basu Foundation, is even today unable to refer to his friend in the past tense.

As Jhumki was a co-founder of SDL in Brooklyn, so is Chris a co-author of the proposal that created Marie Curie School for Medicine, Nursing, and Health Professions in the Bronx. Their careers progressed a year apart with much in common. Chris's innovative book, *Urban Science Education for the Hip-hop Generation,* was released to great reviews in 2010.

"It was kind of odd to find somebody else who had the same passions and did the same kind of stuff as I did," Chris said.

The two fierce educators first met in 2006 at a National Association for Research in Science Teaching (NARST) conference in San Francisco, where Chris was in the audience when Jhumki presented a paper. He remembers staring in wonderment at the high school students on stage with her.

"And I, like, lost it!" he exclaimed. "Oh, man, we do all this work in kids' education, but nobody ever actually brings their students to an academic conference."

He was amazed Jhumki had brought the kids—her coauthors and the subjects of her paper—all the way from New York.

"It took a while," Chris said, "but when we finally met after the initial context of e-mails, our relationship really sparked. I like to think that I got the best of Jhumki, because it was when she was getting really comfortable and excelling at her job. She had this air about her that said, 'I know what I'm doing. I know what I'm about.' So I got to know her when she was, you know, in her prime, and in her *zone!*"

ॐ

Jhumki was definitely in her zone.

In the fall and winter semesters of 2005, she ramped up writing papers for publication. Her PhD direction solidified through research data from a study of four SDL students who were subjects of her teaching framework and who joined her on the San Francisco platform.

Donya Locke was one of those students.

Donya and Jhumki's relationship reminds me of Jhumki's bond with Carey Davis. Radha and I have watched the soft-spoken, undemonstrative, always-smiling Brooklyn girl evolve from a happy-go-lucky high school kid to a committed young woman, admired by her friends and family. Donya came to the United States from Jamaica as an eleven-year-old, and her speech has traces of a Caribbean lilt. Her mannerisms are characterized by spontaneity and humor.

"I met Ms. Jhumki at the Brooklyn high school fair, and we got closer at the camping trip which was the orientation," said Donya during her interview. "We were taken to this fair to look at the different schools we would like to attend. When I went to the SDL table, Jhumki was there with a warm smile. She was really friendly and told me everything about the school and why I needed to come there because of what I wanted to do with my life. She *won* me. And I went to that school the following year.

"Later, at the camping trip, Jhumki was the one barbecuing. She was the one trying to get everyone to actually participate in activities, trying to get the communication going because everyone didn't know anyone, and to talk to each other. She was really jolly, and everybody felt comfortable and warm with her. That's how it started.

"At school Ms. Jhumki had so many roles! She was assistant principal, she was class teacher, she was advisory teacher. She fulfilled all these roles, and everybody kept complaining, 'Why is

Ms. Jhumki doing all these things?' She did them because she was so good at them. It was great because I was in her advisory in the first year of the school. At the end of the year no one wanted to leave her advisory, so she had to keep all the same people because no one wanted to switch, and add others. Everyone was like, 'I want to stay with Ms. Jhumki,' so the principal agreed that we could stay with her. I was in her advisory for two years. We were really close. We did so many great things. We fund-raised. We went on field trips. All the other guys were really jealous of us, and it was just great. She helped us with many different things that she didn't really have to. She just did it out of the kindness of her heart. That's why we loved her."

Donya described how Jhumki got her interested in science.

"At the beginning, I was never big on science. I wanted to be a lawyer. And Ms. Jhumki was the one who got me into science. I wasn't doing very well in science, and she took me to her office. We spoke for a really long time, and she said, 'I have to find a way to incorporate what you are passionate about into science, because you have to do well in school.' So we planned this lesson and I had to *teach!* I was not aware of that at the beginning. I had to go into the class and give this lesson on black holes[13].

"Ms. Jhumki said, 'Since you will be a lawyer, we will structure it in a courtroom debate. So this is the science class. Your law is incorporated into it, and we structure the classroom into a courtroom!'

"We created a debate question saying that 'If anything gets sucked into a black hole, can it come out?' We had a side that

---

[13] Inspired by a guest lecture at SDL by none other than Jhumki's cousin, Dr. Ranga-Ram Chary of Caltech.

said no. We had a side that said yes. The whole class participated. I was the leader. The teacher. I assigned a judge. I assigned lawyers. I was the person who watched over everything."

Donya had just brilliantly described in anecdotal terms one of the pillars of Jhumki's teaching: democratic pedagogy, the involvement of students' own interests in their classroom learning.

"Initially I didn't know what Ms. Jhumki was trying to accomplish," Donya continued. "But then after we did the research and went to California, I realized what she was trying to do: to show that it is good for teachers to get their students involved in lesson plans, in actually teaching a class. I really understood what she was trying to do, and it made a lot of sense. When I saw how my peers were reacting to me actually teaching the class, I understood what she was trying to do. I had a completely different impression of science after meeting Ms. Jhumki. Because I didn't fail!"

Donya got really into science. In the following year she took two extra science classes and did well in them. For the NARST conference in San Francisco, Jhumki helped prepare her four accompanying students' note cards. Then they had to practice for days to get comfortable with what they were going to say in front of the rarified audience. Finally, at the conference, they went onstage one at a time before the academic community to talk about how they participated in her research.

In 2012, eight years after she entered Jhumki's high school class as a freshman, Donya Locke graduated from Lehman College, a liberal arts institution in the Bronx, and headed to Columbia University for a master's degree in social work.

During her Lehman days she interned at the East Side House Settlement, a nonprofit community-resource center providing education services to the young and the elderly in South Bronx.

177

"At East Side House," Donya said, "I worked with senior citizens and children—people who have lost someone, children who have lost someone, people with general depression, kids with anger issues."

Later Donya told Chris Emdin, who was present at her interview, that she was working with an autistic child and helped her learn.

"Is there anything of Jhumki that you bring to your work?" Chris asked her after getting over the fact that this poised young woman was one of the "kids running around" at the NARST event.

"There is a picture of Ms. Jhumki sitting at a table that I carry in my mind," Donya replied. "It shows me how she worked with kids." This, as we found out, was the same picture that Jeremy Dodd showed us from South Africa. Donya continued, "Jhumki taught me how to speak to people, how to look at their faces to understand how they are feeling, how best to interact with them. All of this helps me now."

Did Jhumki's brainwave—coupling black holes with an abiding interest in law—develop in Donya the skill of critical inquiry through science, Jhumki's other teaching pillar? And did it help Donya think analytically years later? Listening to the confident person recount with pride her work and her well-thought-through aspirations, I was convinced that it did.

"After Columbia I want to go into the legal aspects of social work and advocacy," Donya ended. "I want to go to court on behalf of my clients."

Jhumki's very last e-mail, sent from her hospital bed a few days before she died, was to a student, another of the four subjects of her NARST paper. In it she had typed laboriously:

Neil—we are not willing to be your legal guardians given that you have able-bodied parents. Is your stepfather

coming to the appointment at the Door? Did you schedule
the appointment? You need to take some responsibility and
go to the Door with your stepfather and get a lawyer.

Even at that late stage in her illness, Jhumki was trying to get Neil's stepfather to regularize his immigration status through the pro bono legal firm she had found for him. One of the last things she did before she died was to ask her mother and me to take care of Neil.

Neil Clairmont can be considered Jhumki's poster child. He personified the impact of Jhumki's teaching and how it could turn a completely lost child into a responsible and caring person.

In Neil's early childhood, his parents emigrated from the island of St. Lucia leaving him behind with an uncle and aunt. Neil described himself in St. Lucia as a "bad, bad, bad, bad boy, always getting into trouble." He claimed to have been a terrible student there, always scoring failing grades in tests.

At the age of fourteen, Neil came to stay with his mother and stepfather in Brooklyn. He was still a "bad boy" in the eighth grade—in trouble with the police, getting into fights, even spending time in juvenile detention. His parents provided no guidance and his teachers were unable to help. Like many other black adolescents like him, Neil was on trajectory toward a life of crime, violence, and drugs. Jhumki used to mention Neil as one of the myriad problems she struggled with in the early days of SDL. To me Neil sounded like a lost cause. Jhumki did not believe in the term.

"I had never studied science before joining SDL in ninth grade," Neil told me in 2009. "But Ms. Jhumki made me love science."

"How?" I asked.

"One day she came and said to me, 'Do you want to do robotics?' 'No,' I told her. 'I don't like robots. What am I? A machine?' I had no idea of robots then. Ms. Jhumki told me a bit about robotics and left me with the suggestion, 'Think about it.' I thought about it, and after three weeks I agreed."

Neil and two other boys formed a team that went to NYU Polytechnic Institute to build robots and to participate in the citywide Botball competition. Jhumki and Alexander helped them program the robots, which moved objects around on a game board and placed them in a corner. Jhumki often stayed late to help Neil operate his robots because she saw he was really interested. Later, he addressed his peers in class about his project and its possibilities.

"Tell me, what can I do to make you learn better?" Jhumki often asked him.

"More hands-on activities," Neil answered on one occasion. At other times he suggested she "make the people work in groups" and "keep the class moving."

Today Neil's mind is still immersed in robotics, a subject closely associated with his career plans.

"Out of all the things possible," I asked him, "why did Ms. Jhumki get you into robotics?"

"She talked to my dad and found that *he* was into robotics."

So there she was, digging into something, *anything,* from a "lost" student's background to get him interested in science.

In fall 2006, Jhumki left SDL but kept in close contact with kids like Donya, Neil, and others. Always available, always sympathetic, she helped them with scholastic and personal problems.

Neil surprised even himself by graduating from SDL in 2008 and receiving admission to a computer-science program at Borough of Manhattan Community College. Then a great obstacle blocked his path. He was now eighteen, an adult, with no resident status in the United States. Through no fault of his he was, in Uncle Sam's parlance, an illegal alien. Without a green card he could not apply for financial aid and his education would come to an end. Jhumki tried to get Neil's stepfather, a U.S. citizen, to sponsor him for immigration. He refused.

After Jhumki passed away I continued to meet the young fellow who was growing big and burly. I went to his Brooklyn home and appealed to his mother. I found a lawyer prepared to swing into action at a moment's notice if anyone agreed to sponsor him. We kept trying. At times Neil became panicky as we talked and broke down in tears right on the street. At times he was thrown out of his house and slept in strange places. My heart bled for the boy. He worked odd jobs to make ends meet and to save money to pay for intermittent computer-science courses at BMCC.

Then one day in 2010, Neil called to say that his stepfather had finally agreed to sponsor him. True to her word, the lawyer moved swiftly and filed a petition in court, and a few months later Neil became an official resident of the United States. Proudly, he showed Radha his green card.

After receiving his BMCC diploma, Neil set his sights on getting a mechanical engineering degree in—you guessed it—robotics.

"And," he added, "if there's financial help, I'll go all the way to a master's."

"What is your long-term goal?" I asked.

"I want to be a robotics inventor and an expert. I still have a proposal for a robot which Ms. Jhumki helped me write. I want to build that robot for the military. It will detect IEDs [improvised explosive devices] in places like Iraq and Afghanistan and save the lives of men and women in uniform who protect our country."

I asked what his lasting memory of Jhumki was.

"Ms. Jhumki said, 'Education is the key to power' and 'You have to push yourself to be where you want to be.' I took this into consideration and matured. She changed the way I saw things. I was bad in school. I used to be a pest. But after meeting Jhumki I knew I had to stop. She was my role model. There was nobody else like her. There were so many doors she opened through the knowledge she gave me."

Jhumki's life had become a runaway train. She strove mightily just to get through each day. This journal entry goes deep into her internal struggles and exhortations to will herself on. In a journal entry titled "Will I last?" she wrote:

March 22, 2005

One of the biggest challenges of my job is to remind myself that I am successful. There is never a moment to sit back and accept things for where they are. I wonder if at some point Nancy Gannon will say, "Okay, this is good. Take a break from all this intensive professional development." In the final shakedown, are the teachers at the school feeling more committed to the school because of the ways in which they are growing, or are they saying, "This is the right thing to do, but it's just too much!"

The kids can say hurtful things and act in profoundly disrespectful and rude ways. Do I have to work with that to an infinite degree? At what point can I say, "I will not accept this anymore"?

Back-pay still hasn't been fixed. I have to deal with all this and not even be paid the right amount! Four years and then out. No recruitment fair this weekend. I have other priorities, and I need to sleep at least on Saturday.

We have developed a strong foundation for our school—kids are known, generally, systems are working for grades, referrals to a counselor, professional development, after-school programs, support for failing kids, challenge to our strong students. At least, we've put a foot forward in all these areas, as well as with Change Projects, and are raising money.

In terms of my teaching, I have made a stab at having kids pursue complex problems and have built more direct instruction into my classroom. It has been a challenge tying all our labs to a large complex issue. The connections between calculating speed and acceleration and how black holes suck people in, are not obvious.

The most important issue I am facing is that I don't know how to balance my teaching commitments (being a lead teacher, developing a strong curriculum, engaging recalcitrant students) with my administrative duties (transcripts, mentoring teachers, leading the 9th grade team, being a dean for students, ordering, etc.). Also, there is the additional pressure of having to present the right "face" at school: to be excited and energetic when I am not, to show buy-in with projects when I am feeling overwhelmed. I have a difficult time with this . . . it's not generally my nature to feel one thing and show another.

I wish we had started with more "content" focused ideas at the beginning of the year, jumped right into measurement, instead of spending a lot of time on "If I Were a Physicist"—something to redo next year.

Do my students feel they are "agents of change"? Does this idea have to be built into every physics unit? Or can it be the focus of just a modern physics and science fair unit? How can I use my dissertation and journal to organize my teaching portfolio? It would be a good opportunity to think about "critical science agency"—what I have achieved and where I want to go. Maybe this can be the structure of my teacher portfolio: vision of "critical science agency"— knowledge, skills, understanding, engagement, agency, reality. Plus what I think needs to happen in each of these areas to get my students where I want to go this spring, so some element of problem-solving lesson planning for the two units that interested me, plus electricity.

Does Nancy [Gannon] think I'm good in the classroom? I need to continue working on my attitude at school. It's important to be cheerful. It's also important to set clear boundaries for kids and teachers and with Nancy.

I'm tired of being paid $50K to do a job that's worth at least double that. I'm tired of my commute and trains not running. I'm tired of my stuff being stolen. Is it my personality to wake up each morning and not really want to go to work? What if I collected my data and just quit!?

I grow more confident as time passes. But to truly connect the curriculum in the way that I desire, I need design questions that are deeper than asking kids how what they are seeing connects to their lives. I need to create opportunities for them to act—internships, mentorships, community projects, while still teaching them with rigor, the kind of content we are emphasizing now. The science fair will be a step in that direction, I hope.

The research questions and pressure to collect data around the questions I have chosen, definitely drive me to create better curriculum around what I value.

Democratic Pedagogy was the first pillar of Jhumki's teaching. The second pillar, as she states in the "Will I last?" journal entry was Critical Science Agency.

I, a lay person, understand this phrase to mean people's ability to think critically, to exhibit curiosity, to ask questions about science. And at once my mind goes flashing back to Massachusetts, when a four-year-old asked me why the snow was white, and I created homemade experiments that captivated her.

Professor Angela Calabrese Barton explains critical science agency in rigorous terms as conceived by Jhumki:

- *Students develop a deeper understanding of science in a more authentic way than set up in formal school science*
- *They construct identities of themselves as capable science people*
- *They use science to leverage their own identities to make meaningful changes in their lives*

According to Angie, the challenge to fostering critical science agency is in understanding the process of identity development through science, and then using the process to help students better leverage the range of resources available in a science class. In critical science agency, traditional resources such as science knowledge, information from textbooks, and relationships with teachers, are combined with non-scholastic funds of knowledge, such as a student's experiences through his or her father's job, or a particular interest or passion.

This was the theory.

How did Jhumki actually implement the concept of critical science agency in her students, especially the difficult ones?

Gedison Ashby is a case study in point.

A big and strong young man, Gedison brings his twinkling eyes and spontaneous guffaw from the island of Trinidad. As I read about his background and temperament in Jhumki's notes, it became clear to me as never before, how thorny were the issues she faced when attempting to develop critical inquiry through science in kids like Gedison. And I was amazed by the unbelievable amount of extra work she did for him. Here is an extract from her class notes, titled "Portrait of Gedison."

January 13, 2006

Gedison's father, a strong, consistent presence in his life, was a truck driver for a company in Manhattan. Gedison described his family as "happy, we can always talk when we needed help with school and with work."

Gedison was arrested and sent through youth criminal proceedings for a charge of grand larceny. He was on parole with a probation officer while these interviews were taking place. Choosing not to participate in a group involved in robbery was a recurrent theme in Gedison's discussion of wise and poor choices that a youth might make in response to peer pressure.

Foundations for Critical Science Agency:

Transforming Class and Curriculum:

Gedison felt that one important way of judging the success of building projects was to see if they were creative, if the product shows feelings. Associating the success of products with their emotional content and creativity differentiated Gedison from other students who referred more to meeting the expectations of a teacher, the assignment or a rubric or receiving a high grade.

Gedison was a loud, emotional, volatile, outgoing student. I think he saw an opportunity to express himself through the building he could create.

Career Aspirations and Interests:

Gedison expressed his interest in becoming a mechanical engineer. He designed a brown-bag lunch talk to motivate himself to learn more about mechanical engineering and earn himself some credit in science and math. Polytechnic University, a field trip for Gedison with several other boys interested in a technical education, clearly impressed him with its resources and opportunities. The trip opened doors that he envisioned pursuing towards his career.

Transforming the Larger World:

Gedison's dream, as a mechanical engineer, was to create a high-tech, efficient building in which people could take care of all their needs such as "welfare, housing and paying bills," instead of going to multiple locations around the city. This project, in his mind, makes learning content about electricity and measurement useful and worthwhile.

There is a great deal more of detail in those case notes.

When Maithreyi and I sat across from Gedison to interview him for this book, the first thing he told us was he missed Ms. Jhumki a lot.

"It was kind of awkward, because she was so sweet," he said with a big smile. "She was very helpful on my first day at SDL and showed me around. She helped me with all my classes. And from there"—he laughed heartily—"it went out to the sky! She was always on top of what I did. Called my dad, telling him I did this well in class. She was complimentary, and yet she criticized a lot. She was always making sure I did the right thing. Checked how I was doing in my classes. If I needed help, she was there to help me. If I needed extra work to make up, she'd always find it. I don't know how! She always found something to keep my time occupied."

While at SDL, Gedison, like his classmate Neil, built robots and participated in robotics competitions at NYU Polytechnic Institute. It was fun and a new learning experience. Through science, Jhumki kept him out of trouble with the police.

"Jhumki would say to me, 'Keep busy, read a book, make it work, stay active, and your mind won't want to go and do the wrong thing.' That's what I was thankful from her. When Jhumki wasn't there to protect me I was always getting into trouble."

It always intrigued me the way Jhumki guided her big and rambunctious students without yelling at them or scolding them. I asked Gedison about this.

"'Get your work done!'" he replied without hesitation. "Jhumki's class was always fun. She wouldn't come in and get to work right away. She would come in, relax, and say 'Okay, you guys ready to get started?' and then went about the lesson. I remember when we were dissecting a cow eye. She went out and bought the eyes and brought them to school. For the *guys* it was fun. For the girls she'd go like, 'Stop being scared!'"

Gedison laughed at the memory.

"Did she get upset in class?" I wanted to know.

"It took a lot to get Ms. Jhumki upset. A lot, a lot, a lot. She was very patient. She wasn't always looking over your back. She gave you the space. As long as you got your work done, there was no problem with her."

He paused and added, "When she's upset she usually cries!"

This triggered a memory in memory in me of a teenaged girl in tempestuous standoffs with her mother and me. Those arguments would climax with her jumping to her feet, saying a few nasty things, bursting into tears, storming out of the house, slamming the front door. Later I would track her down and bring her home.

Gedison watched me as I thought about this.

"When she's upset, she cries. She never yells," he said. "I remember when she cried. I don't remember about what, but she did cry in front of the class. It was shocking 'cause no one ever saw her cry before. She was really upset at that point."

"Did you help Ms. Jhumki keep order in the class?" I asked.

"Yeah!" he said enthusiastically. "I'd get up and tell the kids, '*Hey!* Ms. Jhumki's talking. Keep quiet!' and they'd listen. I really enjoyed that."

In late 2011, when I last spoke to him, Gedison was resolving his own immigration problems, working with his father on the floor of a retail warehouse, staying out of trouble, and looking forward to going to college.

24. A SPLENDID YEAR

"**B**aba! You shall not do *anything*!"

Our thirtieth wedding anniversary was on December 14, 2005. Jhumki, her cousin Preetham, and his wife Vardhini decided to organize a party to commemorate the day. When I tried to get involved in the planning or '"interfered" in any other way, Jhumki laid down the law in no uncertain terms. As we were always at the center of family events, it was a strange feeling for Radha and me to have others do things for us. But we soon got used to it—and grew to like it.

The festivities kicked off on a Saturday evening at the Cupertino Community Center in Silicon Valley with our favorite daughter holding sway as mistress of ceremonies. The decorations were tasteful and understated. About seventy guests arrived and were seated according to a chart.

Then Ms. Jhumki got going with her new "class." She eschewed science for just once and focused on class engagement through creativity and fun. Lots of fun.

"Okay, folks, I hope you're settled in," she announced over the PA system. "'Cause now you have to work for your dinner!"

Our friends looked at one another worriedly. Work? They had already scratched their heads about the strange table names: Oruro, Ngorongoro, Namche, Tikal, Elbert, Tuolumne, Jungfrau, Hemkund, Urubamba, Manasarovar, Ocho Rios. Upon being told these were places her parents holidayed, they grumbled, "Your folks are crazy, Jhumki. Why don't they go to London and Paris and Bali like normal people?"

This of course was music to Jhumki's ears.

Then she told her audience ominously, "Guys, you're going to have to sing in groups. Okay? Songs that you will compose together."

People sat up and studied her face carefully. Was the girl serious? Was her tongue in her cheek? No, not at all. They actually had to sing. In public!

And so it happened.

Strangers were formed into teams. They were given instructions, guidelines, props, themes, ideas, time limits. They were encouraged to drink wine. The guests became animated. Creative. Competitive. Lyrics and melodies were original—and hilarious. Closet actors emerged jubilantly. Jhumki bounced from group to group, a coach on springs.

Why is she so unusually animated? I wondered. And it wasn't long before I figured it out. There happened to be a certain person in the crowd. Everyone studied him curiously, but Jhumki would not introduce him; and ignored him as if he weren't there. Finally I couldn't stand it.

"Hi, good evening!" I told a group. "Everyone, this is Alexander, Jhumki's friend from New York."

Everyone looked at Alexander. What *sort* of friend, they didn't ask. And all through the evening Jhumki didn't tell.

Guests from the night's excesses were invited to brunch at our home the next morning. Alexander was the self-appointed chef, Jhumki his *sous-chef*.

Two days before, I happened to open the fridge, and rounded objects—eggplants, cabbages, oranges, cucumbers—cascaded out and rolled away in different directions like ping-pong balls on *Candid Camera*, with Mishti in hot pursuit. When cooking operations began, Radha and I watched from a safe distance. Kitchen counters filled and overflowed. Woks bubbled mysteriously. Pots formed tall piles in the sink. Intriguing aromas wafted. Internet connections hummed. A hotline to Greece crackled.

Now and then we were noticed when we got too close.

"Baba, can you go somewhere?" our daughter remonstrated.

"Like, away?"

To the thirty brunch guests the mystery person of the previous night revealed himself through a magnificent Hellenic feast—vegetarian in deference to his girlfriend's mom—created from hallowed recipes of his mother, grandmother, and aunts, who had anxiously played supporting roles offstage. The kids had cooked all day and all night. There had been frantic midnight calls to Greece and emergency dashes to Safeway.

When everyone was assembled and awestruck, Alexander enlightened them on the repast with precision and style. He pointed out *mujadera, patates dophinios,* spanakopita, tahini, *shakshuka,* hummus, *tzatziki, fasolakia, keftedes, galaktoboureko, manitaria gemista, maroulosalata, melinznes se ksidi*—four appetizers, four salads, eight entrées, and four desserts. Each dish delicious, distinct, and integrated.

Someone dug me in the ribs and whispered, "He *is* a computer scientist, isn't he?"

Our little girl, true to character, stayed silent as a mouse, while sporting a Cheshire cat grin. It is my duty to record that Jhumki's special someone made a memorable first impression on our circle of friends. We were proud of them both.

A few months before this extravaganza, while thinking about to how to surprise my wife for our thirtieth anniversary, I let my mind expand. Where could we go that was outside the realm of possibility? How could one top Mount Everest? I thought and I thought. Then my mind actually expanded and a bizarre idea came to me!

Which Bengali boy or Tamil girl has up and gone to *Antarctica?* In that venerable temple of knowledge, Kolkata's *Coffee House* on College Street—where I have spent many a youthful timeless evening in company of good friends—upon hearing we were going to the seventh continent, great thinkers would lapse into the vernacular. Their wit would be biting.

"*Pagol?*" they would say. "*Na matha kharap[14]?*"

Well, with or without my head messed up, I took my wife to the bottom of the globe.

Antarctica turned out to be not all snow and ice as I had naïvely imagined. The dramatic scenery, the teeming marine and avian wildlife, the enthralling geography, and the celebrated guest speakers on board our ship were all beyond compare, as our journey followed the route taken by my boyhood hero, Sir Ernest Shackleton, a leading figure of the Heroic Age of Exploration. His ship, *Endurance,* was crushed by polar ice in 1913, and, after an epic journey, Shackleton and two of his officers staggered into Strømness whaling station on South Georgia Island more than two years later. Shackleton fought ice and storms to go back to Elephant Island on the Antarctic Peninsula to rescue every one of his soldiers, marooned for almost five months. Theirs is one of the greatest stories of survival and leadership.

My overriding memory from that trip though, does not involve Shackleton, animals, birds, big waves, or famous people. It involves Jhumki.

Radha and I decided to take a satellite phone with us just in case and had set up a schedule to call our daughter even though she thought it was completely unnecessary.

"What's going to happen to me?" she wanted to know.

The prearranged time came on a dark and blustery evening, when our doughty icebreaker, *MV Bremen,* was threading her way through small islands and large icebergs of the Antarctic

---

[14] Crazy? Or head messed up?

Peninsula. To get a clear line to a satellite, I perforce had to climb an assortment of ladders to the ship's bare topmost deck. A freezing wind and contrary current made *Bremen* swing uncertainly in an arc and I had to hold on tightly to railings and roll with the side-to-side motion. My mind dwelled briefly on whether anyone would hear me call if I happened to slip and go overboard with the icebergs. I put that thought away and concentrated on making the satphone work.

Imagine a globe. Most communication satellites orbit Earth high above the equator. *Bremen* was close to the South Pole. Consequently, to make contact with a satellite, I had to point the satphone antenna *downward* from the top deck while holding it high above my head. In this contorted position, while holding on for dear life with one gloved hand, the other glove in my teeth, I tapped in a complex set of numbers with fast-freezing fingers of my other hand.

"Hello?" said a voice as I watched the inky water far below me.

I had gotten through in one try. Amazing!

"Hi, Jhomi," I said brightly, and added, "oops!" as the glove in my teeth dropped and disappeared into the Weddell Sea. Recovering quickly I said, "Whatcha doin'?"

"Baba!" The squeal of surprise indicated she had completely forgotten our schedule. "It's my dad," she told someone in the background.

"Where are you?" she asked me. "How's Mommy? What's all that background roaring?"

"Oh, just the wind."

With some bravura I depicted where and how I was situated, while not omitting the leopard seals and the killer whales we had encountered of late. Through it all, a *"Man!"* a *"Daft!"* and several *"Oof!"*s came down from the faraway satellite.

"Baba, can you do me a favor?" she asked after I ran down.

"Of course, Jhomi. What?"

"Can you please disconnect and go down to where it's safe?"

I had to agree it was an excellent suggestion.

"Okay, Jhomi. Mommy sends her love. Ciao."

"Bye, Baba . . ." and then, ". . . he's calling to find out if *I'm* okay!" I heard her say to the mystery person before I pressed the OFF button.

E-mail from Radha Basu to friends and family, April 20, 2006

This afternoon Jhumki's PhD thesis committee unanimously approved her PhD dissertation titled "How Urban Youth Express Critical Agency in a 9th Grade Conceptual Physics Classroom."

We were thrilled to be present at Teachers College with Alexander when she passionately articulated her thesis and findings to the committee. We were called back into the room after the committee reached a decision. Dr. Basu will receive her degree at Columbia's graduation ceremonies on May 17.

On May 15, 2006, we flew to New York.

The sun shone brightly from a cloudless sky. The city was pleasantly warm without the usual summer humidity. A holiday atmosphere prevailed on the Upper West Side. Large numbers of Columbia students with parents and siblings and balloons thronged Broadway. It was the day before the university's commencement.

Alexander had invited us to his apartment on 73rd Street. We arrived and looked around for our daughter.

"Where's Jhomi?" Radha asked.

"Don't worry," Alexander said. "She'll be here shortly."

He looked preoccupied, and I wondered if something was wrong.

"Why don't we sit down?" He indicated the sofa.

When Radha and I settled, he pulled up a hard-backed chair and sat facing us. In the ensuing silence I began to worry. Then Alexander looked straight at me and smiled.

"Dipak, I would like to ask for your daughter's hand in marriage."

These are words every father lives to hear. Many don't hear them these days, as an impending marriage is usually presented to parents as a *fait accompli*. I was speechless as my mind grappled with the proper and traditional thing to say to the proper and traditional gentleman sitting across from me. I was just thinking what a great guy he was when I was distracted by noises and looked around.

Radha was on her feet and hugging Alexander and going *"Yayyyyy!"*

Then there was another silence, and I found the two of them looking fixedly at me. It was only then that I realized Alexander was actually waiting for me to say yes.

Or no!

For the record, I said yes, and warmly embraced my son-in-law-to-be.

Jhumki arrived on cue accompanied by a supercharged grin, and we excitedly hugged her. The queen of understatements in our family surveyed the situation and said, "So Alexander told you, huh?"

We poured champagne and toasted them. Sumitra, Ranga, and Preetham arrived. We poured more champagne and had a fine celebratory dinner.

What I still had not grasped was that Alexander was following the rule book to the core. To his thinking, he was required to get my approval *in advance* of his proposal to Jhumki. So Jhumki's wasn't an understatement at all. Later she wrote to her family about this.

Alexander proposed to me today with a beautiful engagement ring, and I said, "Yes." I know he was worried. We've never discussed marriage before, and people say that in this new era, the girl shouldn't be surprised because most people talk about marriage before the fellow proposes. But Alexander and I are pretty traditional as you know.

I promised him I wouldn't stand him up at the altar and that I would alert him if I was allergic to my engagement ring. It happens sometimes, then you have to go to the allergist, who sometimes tells women they're having psychosomatic problems. I heard this from a friend.

To which, of course, cousin Ranga had to send in a trademark repartee:

:) This could be a Seinfeld episode running backwards! So, maybe I should say snoitalutargnoc (almost sounds Welsh) instead of congratulations.

I am pleased to hear that Alexander's knees didn't buckle. Do we get a jpeg of the ring? I want to examine it closely to ensure it is worthy of SJB.

Columbia University has a stunning campus. Surrounded on all sides by America's premier city, the famous university has a Roman setting: a giant amphitheater encircled by imposing buildings, a green lawn with fountains, endless wide stone steps leading to Ionian columns of the monumental Low Memorial Library.

On May 17 the massive, sun-drenched arena in front of Low was awash in blue and black. Thousands of young men and women were graduating, a small proportion with doctorates. For the main event Jhumki sat lost in a surging crowd of mortarboards several hundred yards away from us. Yet, to my astonishment, from the seat next to me, Alexander clicked a perfect picture of his fiancée with a new camera and super-duper zoom lens he had purchased just for the occasion.

Later in the day, doctoral candidates were accorded a special hooding ceremony at St. Paul's Chapel.

At the call of "Sreyashi Jhumki Basu!" in she bounced, head high and a toned-down professional smile. She accepted her degree, shook hands with the provost, posed for the official photographer, turned and strode/skipped down the dais steps. She unbound the smile and waved cheerily to her groupies in the balcony. Alexander, naturally, videotaped the triumphal moment.

After Jhumki died, in a tribute edition of *Cultural Studies of Science Education,* Angela Calabrese Barton and other colleagues published several articles on the significance of Jhumki's doctoral research.

Angie's contribution reads:

> *Jhumki's research focused on access and equity in science for urban minority youth. Her dissertation examined student learning in a classroom geared towards developing "critical physics agency" and "democratic practice." Her work was grounded in a rigorous approach to deep understandings in physics while at the same time it focused on how youth gain voice in and through science. Jhumki's dissertation was ground-breaking in the meaningful connections it made between cognitive studies of student learning in science and socio-cultural studies of the learning context.*

25. IN ANCIENT LANDS

In July 2006, Radha and I traveled to two countries we had long dreamed of visiting, Israel and Greece. Alexander met us at Tel Aviv's Ben Gurion Airport at midnight and took us to our hotel. The next day was a landmark event for the two families meeting for the first time. Alexander's parents, Vasilis and Ilana, and his sisters, Ariadne and Anna, came to our hotel. The chemistry was excellent! The spontaneous warmth of the Greek family drew us in.

Vasilis was everything you can imagine in an archetypal, free-spirited, gruff Greek elder. The first thing he did after packing us into his big green BMW was to drive through a stop sign. Ilana scolded him at once.

"Vasili, what are you doing?"

"It's okay, Ilana. Relax," Vasilis said to his wife gently. "It's Sunday. I can go through a stop sign on Sunday!"

The rest of us couldn't stop laughing.

One of the first things Vasilis did was to introduce me to the very Greek social medium of ouzo. I formed a deep attachment to the strong, anise-flavored aperitif that turns cloudy upon coming into contact with ice. The two fathers-in-law-in-waiting hit it off and had a great time together.

Ilana was the quintessential mother, bringing the best from her Jewish heritage. She was a loving and hardworking lady and the keystone of Alexander's family. Vasilis and Ilana fell in love in the 1960s at the University of Jerusalem, where Vasilis, an archaeology graduate student, was engaged in excavating Herod's Steps below the Temple Mount.

We had come for Ariadne's wedding to an Israeli. Jhumki arrived a few days before us, and we saw at once how much she was already a part of their family. She and Alexander's sisters closed ranks to tease the big brother. We could see that Ilana and

Gia-gia, Vasilis's mother, genuinely liked her. Jhumki had learned some Greek and could actually converse with the elegant and caring Gia-gia, who reminded me a great deal of Jhumki's Kalyani Paati. We found Ariadne to be a charming young woman who treated us with warmth and affection. At the time of her wedding she was studying for a PhD in religious mythology at the university where her parents had met. Later I discovered she was a runaway expert in memory games.

We loved the open-air setting of the Hebrew wedding with incantations from the *Torah* with strong involvement of the families.

The rest of the day was reserved for partying.

Wearing a simple flowered frock, Jhumki blended in beautifully. In fact, no one present wore anything formal or severe. She danced with Gia-gia. She danced with the men. She danced with the women. She danced in arm-linked groups of thirty, twirling slowly to evocative music. Family and friends, Israelis and Greeks alike, went out of their way to make Radha and me feel at home and special. When it was time to leave, we were teary-eyed about our daughter entering such a warmhearted and loving family.

We continued to Greece and took in the famous sights of Athens for a couple of days. But our minds and hearts were in northern Greece, where Alexander's family had their home.

On July 12, 2006, Jhumki and Alexander were officially engaged in a simple ceremony on a large, shaded balcony that wrapped around Vasilis and Ilana's high airy apartment. In proactively trying to study her future daughter-in-law's culture, poor Ilana had made the mistake of searching the Internet to learn about Hindu customs. For her trouble she was drenched by a fire hose of confusing Vedic rites and myths!

On the day of the engagement, the Alexander's family wore traditional Indian garments that Radha had brought with her to

Greece. Preetham and Vardhini had arrived from California to add moral support. The assembled guests were entranced by the bright colors and Sanskrit hymns. Greek food, augmented by *payasam*—ceremonial rice pudding made by the mother of the bride-to-be—was excellent and endless. So too were ouzo and Metaxa.

Jhumki and Alexander's impending wedding was "announced" in five languages as part of the ceremony. Drawing from Vasilis' stock of antique parchment and handmade inks, we wrote the following epistle in English, Greek, Hebrew, Tamil, and Bengali. J&A later framed the announcement on a wall in their apartment.

By the grace of God—
On this auspicious 12th day of July 2006, it is announced that
Sreyashi Jhumki, daughter of Dipak and Radha, shall be
married to Alexander, son of Vasilis and Ilana, with blessings of
family and friends.

In the evening everyone piled into cars and drove to City Hall, where Alexander and Jhumki were married in a civil ceremony. The traditional weddings would come later. Since it was likely that Gia-gia, age eighty-six, would be unable to travel overseas, Jhumki and Alexander had decided on a wedding in her city.

Most of those that attended the events of the day were exhausted after weeks of travel and merrymaking. Leaving them to rest, Radha and I said our good-byes and drove south leisurely in a rented car. On the way we stopped to climb Mt. Olympus, and gazed awestruck at the Eastern Orthodox monasteries of Meteora, floating high in the sky on impossible freestanding rock pillars, reminiscent of scenes from the movie *Avatar*.

26. MESSENGERS OF YOUTH

I t was 2003 when I first visited a remarkable place called the Sundarbans. Located on the common delta of two mighty rivers, the Ganges and the Brahmaputra, and spanning two countries, India and Bangladesh, the Sundarbans is an enormous green-and-brown mosaic of mangrove islands, around which flow a network of silt-laden rivers and creeks. The Sundarbans is a UNESCO World Heritage Site where the Royal Bengal Tiger has made its last stand. It is also home to 5.5 million desperately poor farmers and fisherfolk, who eke out survival and are often pushed beyond it by cyclones that roar up the Bay of Bengal.

Sitting on the porch of a mud-walled, thatch-roofed hut beside an emerald rice paddy, I made a promise to assembled village elders that one day soon I would do something to help them in a significant way.

In April 2006, after eleven years with a great company, I took early retirement from Cisco Systems with the trepidation of a career-paycheck-earner, to devote myself to nonprofit work. A month later Radha stepped down as CEO of Support.com to join forces with me. Our goal was—and still is—to fulfill my promise to those villagers and to empower impoverished people of India to secure livelihoods in the country's burgeoning economy.

To do this we set up Anudip Foundation.

Jhumki told her kids, "Find your passion and follow it." Late though it was in our lives, Radha and I had just found ours.

After the joyous stay in Israel and Greece, Jhumki traveled to Kolkata and attended the inauguration ceremony for a new rural training center that Anudip was opening.

Here was a totally different girl!

Not the teacher lady. Not the madly-in-love romantic. Not the witty, pretty, party woman. Not the dancer. In the bucolic

Bengal countryside, in poor villages, in the crushing slums of Kolkata, natural and self-assured in simple Indian garb, here was a fearless social worker.

At the Anudip center in Dara village, Jhumki spoke in broken Bengali with barefoot children who clustered around the tall *didi* (elder sister). During the inauguration ceremony she listened to speeches of local bigwigs extolling the importance of computers in rural development. She leaned over and asked me to translate if she did not understand a word or a phrase. Then she strolled with community workers along footpaths between rice paddies submerged by huge swaths of water from monsoon rains. She picked up a tiny baby goat and laughed happily when she saw seven ducklings swimming in a straight line behind their mother. Watching her, I was reminded of little Jhumki in New England.

Back at Dara village, while her parents worried about germs, Jhumki dug into rice, fish and vegetable curries, and sweets prepared by the wives and daughters-in-law of our hosts. She clearly enjoyed it all tremendously. Our foundation staff watched and wondered where she put it all away.

That same evening, ActionAid, a human-rights nonprofit and a NetHope member, scheduled a visit for us to an activity center for street children in Kolkata.

It was 9 p.m. when Jhumki and I drove with ActionAid staff along the city's dimly-lit and congested streets. From Beliaghata Main Road our car turned into a narrow lane that ran between a filth-choked canal and the fifteen-foot wall of a factory. Clinging to the wall were minuscule, plastic-roofed, burlap-walled shacks. These flimsy little boxes were homes to whole families. Men sat together or slept on dirty sidewalks on both sides of the road. Children and dogs romped around them. The scene was lit by ghostly, mist-shrouded, street lamps. Women squatted and cooked in the shacks with hanging curtains thrown open.

I had been this way before.

I had seen these people before. I had not looked *at* the poverty then; I had looked *through* it. I had looked *away* from the disease-ridden and the disabled. That night, with Jhumki beside me, everything stood out in unadorned detail.

Our car came to a stop in the very midst of the pavement dwellers. I was considering having to actually exit our "safe" vehicle when our guide, Mr. Poddar, got out and walked over to one of the lean-tos. And then, goodness gracious me, Jhumki opened her door, got out of the car, and without a moment's hesitation, followed Mr. Poddar into the grimy shack and disappeared.

Hurriedly I stumbled after them, pushed aside a sackcloth curtain, and looked in. The interior was pitch-dark. Absolutely black. I took a couple of steps and stood still in confusion. Then my eyes adjusted to the glimmer of a single kerosene lamp, and I moved next to Jhumki, ready to protect her from I knew not what.

And then, out of the darkness, in ones and twos, came the children. Their eyes gleamed in the lamplight. Their teeth shone astonishingly white when they recognized Mr. Poddar and smiled at him. It was only then that I recalled we were visiting a children's activity center. I had imagined a clean, well-lit room with books and toys and welcoming teachers. This was it! I began to relax while more children appeared, all dressed in clean clothes. They were all girls. Their long black hair was braided down to their waists. They bunched together and, from a safe distance, stared up at the tall young woman by my side. Jhumki sank down on to some sort of tarp on the floor. The girls came closer.

"Hello! *Ki koro tomra?*" (What do you do?) Jhumki asked and the girls needed no further invitation. They brought out coloring books and compositions and crowded around Jhumki.

Happy voices filled the "room."

"Didi, look, see mine!"

"Didi, see Jeel and Jack!"

"Didi, I wrote poem!"

After a while the singing began. The children sang several Bengali nursery rhymes. Here is one that I have translated:

> *Our little fellow goes,*
> *Wearing bright red shoes;*
> *Older sisters peep and stare,*
> *But baby doesn't care.*

The kids clamored for their new *didi* to teach them something. Jhumki consulted with me, and we remembered the nursery rhyme from Patch Barracks, and before long Canal Road South rocked with children's delighted voices chanting, *"Rabimmel, rabammel, rabum!"*

I took a look outside.

A crowd had gathered drawn perhaps by sounds in a strange language. Then a lady in a printed sari pushed aside the curtain, entered our crowded space, and greeted us with joined palms and a *"Namaste."* She introduced herself as the kids' music teacher. Turning to Jhumki, she asked her to join the group which was learning a new song. Jhumki agreed and to my surprise, the Tagore song the teacher chose was one I knew from when I was a child.

Time passed quickly, and at last we reluctantly said our farewells.

"Didi, abar esho kintu!" (But you must come again, *Didi!*), the girls said.

The people assembled outside turned out to be parents of the girls. They smiled and bade us *"Salaam"* or *"Namaste."* They told us how happy they were because we had come. As we left, Jhumki was humming the tune of the song she had learned from the teacher. In the car she asked me to explain the lyrics. And so, while we drove through the darkened city, I translated on the fly:

We are messengers of new youth
We are restless!
We are unique!
We are messengers of new youth
We break bounds,
We bloom in bright moods,
We shatter storm shackles,
We are lightning!
We are messengers of new youth

At times we blunder,
Diving in depthless water
We struggle to find land

Wherever a call comes,
When life and death are poised,
We are prepared!
We are messengers of new youth

After I finished, Jhumki sat silently for a long time. When the car pulled up in front of my aunt's home, I gave her a nudge.

"Hey, kiddo, why so quiet?"

Jhumki sighed wistfully and stretched.

"Nothing, Baba. Just stuff. Life."

That night she wrote in her journal:

If one does not look at something distasteful like poverty, if one looks through something distasteful like a homeless person, if one looks away from something distasteful like a crippled beggar, then these things don't register in their mind. And the day isn't de-harmonized. It's like living in an artificial self-made cocoon.

PART V

TEACHER TO
RESEARCHER

"I wish I were ambidextrous.
I could do so much more in the same amount of time."

Sreyashi Jhumki Basu, 2001

27. NYU

With the advent of Alexander, Jhumki began to take Sundays off, go out for entertainment, and sleep at least five hours a night.

Since the end of 2005, she had been thinking seriously of leaving school teaching as her primary profession. She weighed taking extended time off against pursuing a research position to which Angie had referred her. In early 2006 she applied to New York University.

E-mail from Alexander to Jhumki's parents, March 23, 2006

I dropped Jhumki off at her NYU interview location half an hour ago.

She's looking all professional in her new suit + shirt + pants (the purchase being a major accomplishment on its own merit!)

As always, everything was finished in the nick of time, but still Jhumki managed to get an unusual 5.5 hours of sleep last night!

Besides her brilliant self, she's bringing documentation the length of the Gulf War II attack plans :-)

Let's all send positive vibes in the direction of NYU's Steinhardt School. It's going to be a long day. After presentation and interviews, she's off for dinner. May not hear from her until 9 pm or later.

E-mail from Jhumki to her parents, the same day

Alexander copied, stapled, printed, organized, fed me, took out the trash, washed dishes, gave me his more professional-looking bag, downloaded my DVD, made back-ups, gave me an organized folder in which to put my stuff, did the visuals for my Powerpoint, gave me feedback about what to distribute during my talk. He got me flowers

*for when I got back and cleaned the apartment, all with
looming deadlines at his work. So, if I get the job, it's largely
thanks to Alexander.*

In late March Jhumki wrote to Angie that the NYU search
committee and department chair had recommended her
application to the dean for a position of assistant professor of
science education. Professor Calabrese Barton's reply was
uncharacteristic.

*YES!!! Jhumki, I am soooooooo proud of you!!!!!! That is
just awesome news—you made my day (whether you take
the NYU job or not!). I do hope you seriously consider it,
even with the concerns you've raised. You need to think
about what you would need for your "start up" package
(i.e., $ for equipment and so on), teaching reductions in
your first year, mentor, etc. Maybe Cath can share with you
what she had gotten in her start-up package.*
    Angie.

E-mail from Jhumki Basu to friends and family, May 1, 2006

*Just writing to tell you that I received the formal job
offer from NYU and am planning to sign and send it today.
Also, I formally gave my principal at my current school
notice last night. I am sad to leave SDL after three years of
the most challenging work I have done yet but also
extremely relieved to leave. It's been back- and spirit-
breaking, despite the immense progress I have seen in the
kids. I'm hoping that I've left the school in a more mature
place that will make the work less exhausting for new
teachers and administrators.*

*Thank you for all your support and advice; this is what
has made me take the risk of leaving my school to try
something new.*

✿

Mary Brabeck, Dean of NYU's Steinhardt School of Culture, Education, and Human Development, is a governor of the New York Academy of Sciences and recipient of numerous awards in education. She is one of the most convivial people Radha and I have met. In the desolate days immediately following the loss of our daughter, Mary and her husband, Michael, cared for us with great sensitivity. Today Mary is a mainstay of the Jhumki Basu Foundation.

"When I first met her in my office," said Mary, "Jhumki was a beautiful young woman, full of excitement and eagerness. She was very reflective and a bit wary of higher education. She was committed to working directly with kids and was concerned that if she came to the university, she would be pulled away from the world of urban youth. So she had all sorts of questions. She did the interview in what I came to understand was the typical Jhumki fashion. She was very thorough. She had done all her homework. She knew what her questions were. She knew what her concerns were. She knew what she wanted from the university."

Robert Cohen, chair of the Department of Teaching and Learning at Steinhardt, described Jhumki's waltz with NYU's selection committee.

"The amazing thing about Jhumki was this: People we hire want something. They want money. They want research start-up funds. They are looking for something for themselves. That is easy to deal with, because NYU has got funds. Jhumki was different. She *wanted* research start-up stuff and all that, but that wasn't the issue for her. The issue for her was about *conscience*. Could this job really be the platform to do important work that would have political meaning?"

Dr. Cohen, a slightly built, scholarly-looking history professor, spoke fast, absorbed in what he was saying. "She was doing meaningful work in the schools. She had *founded* a school.

She was very involved, passionately working with the students there. She was not sure whether being a university professor could really compare with that. NYU has a phrase, 'We are a private university in public.' Jhumki asked us, 'Do you *really* mean that?'"

After meeting Jhumki, Dr. Cohen decided they *had* to get her, but they would have to do something different. So he asked people not just from the Steinhardt School but also from other departments, people who were politically engaged, to let her know they were doing important work and to tell her that no one was isolated.

"I was making the argument," Dr. Cohen said, "that one can actually have more impact here than in a high school. That she had helped students in one school enormously well was great. But if she finds out that scholarship can change the way science is taught, and she publishes it in journals, it can affect the whole country—in fact, the whole world."

During the difficult process of deciding whether to join NYU, with long school days, advisory hours, late-evening classes at Baruch College for administrative credentials, Jhumki was also writing her doctoral dissertation. On the subway! It took an hour and a half by train in each direction from the Upper West Side to Crown Heights. Jhumki, hunkered over her laptop and oblivious to commuters, made the best use of every minute.

E-mail from Jhumki Basu to her parents, February 2, 2006

I slept a bit last night and had a really productive working morning—I feel like my second chapter is taking shape and I have a sense of where I am going. I also made a plan for research for the next several years, all the things I want to study and support. So that is cool. I think my research lens is Democratic Practice and Student Voice in Science Education. It made me realize how much I have benefited from Angie, but also how hard it was to think about these ideas at first (hence the challenges I faced teaching a program with her), food for thought for working with new teachers . . . the importance of small steps and goals each year.

Anyways, feeling excited and not exhausted, for a change!

Alexander, as always, is being a super-star support even though he has a big project due as well. Just his company is a good influence!

Jhumki accepted NYU's offer and became officially accredited as the second Professor Basu in our family after my father. During her first days she luxuriated in the presence of elevated minds and reduced pressure on her life.

From the journal of Jhumki Basu, Sep 2006

A new job!

Today I got food to eat for breakfast instead of buying a bagel that sits on my desk all day 'cause I'm too stressed to eat it. I made myself lunch, instead of relying on Alexander, and ate it at noon, not 4 pm or never.

Someone helped set up my office, moving things where I wanted them. Someone gave me office supplies. The administrative staff was friendly instead of yelling at me so I stop asking for anything. I got everything done on my "To Do" list. I don't have to get up at 4 am tomorrow to do all the work I won't do at work today.

I'm meeting a co-panning teacher at a coffee shop to help us plan. Later, she said, "Let's talk about this tomorrow again" (note: that's one topic of conversation discussed twice!) instead of "I don't have the time to talk about this right now" (note: and probably not ever).

There are people at work more experienced than I am who are willing to be mentors! I can go to yoga tonight and to dinner without thinking about how I really should be working. It's really nice to not be a teacher, for a change. I miss the kids, but I'll be seeing them on Thursday.

"Smart People"

We had a new faculty breakfast at Steinhardt. The school has the education department but also music, arts and public health. So they were all these smart people talking about piano recitals and electronic music analysis and breast cancer advocacy and teacher compensation economics research. Was fun. There are 26 new hires in the department, all reasonably young, though I'm definitely the kid! Was nice.

"Tenure?"

I've not been thinking much about my earlier concerns about taking this job: for what set of purposes am I doing this work? It makes me realize how being here is such a position of power to make change and how it can be confused with an opportunity to fulfill standards and live towards a future moment.

In some more concrete sense, it makes me feel that, while still at NYU, working at SDL this semester for four hours every Tuesday with science teachers and science students, is not only important because it informs and prepares my research, but because it is also my first commitment to making change in the world from the position of authority and freedom that I now have.

So, bottom line, I remember that if I work my hardest and do what I think is right and get tenure, great. If not, well, I've worked my hardest and done what I think is right.

After joining NYU, Jhumki put together her research platform at blinding speed. She defined her direction, applied for grants, outlined papers for publication, built relationships with other

214

NYU departments, set up links with under-resourced schools in the New York area, including SDL. Her application for a Spencer post-Doctoral fellowship is an example of her early academic work at NYU.

Exploring and Assessing Democratic Practice in Low-Income, Minority Science Classrooms

In this mixed-methodology study, I will investigate how democratic practice in science shapes student learning, within and beyond the context of science classrooms. I plan to explore the following questions:

1. *How do teachers understand and adapt literature-based definitions of democratic practice, assess the impact of democratic practice on students, and alter their ideas of democratic practice based on their experiences in the classroom?*

2. *How do youth experience teacher attempts at democratic practice, and how do these experiences influence student expertise, engagement and science identity?*

3. *How do identity, life history and cultural capital influence how teachers and youth experience and reflect on democratic practice?*

In assessing the impact of democratic practice in science education, I hope, through scholarship and community-empowering action research conducted with teachers and students, to positively influence the access, engagement and science identity of historically-disenfranchised youth.

28. BOLT FROM THE BLUE

The euphoria of that golden summer could not last.

Jhumki was spending the remnant of her holidays with us in California when Alexander called from New York. He had the most tragic news: his mother had died the previous night without any symptoms.

E-mail from Dipak Basu to friends and family, Aug 13, 2006

Jhomi and I left SFO for NYC on Saturday night after hearing the devastating news of Ilana's sudden death at their country home. J&A will leave Sunday evening for Greece. Radha is at home with Preetham and Vardhini. Alexander's sister Anna is with their father. Ariadne and her husband will arrive on Monday from Jerusalem.

This happened exactly a month after the happy events of July. What can one say?

Even in the short space of time we had known her, we had all grown to love Ilana. We loved her natural friendliness, her affectionate but firm handling of her mercurial husband, her wonderful cooking. The family lived and breathed around her. Without her they would be lost.

"She liked Jhumki very much," Alexander told Maithreyi. "She really got to appreciate her, enjoy her company. I was never afraid of my family not getting on with Jhumki. In general my family is quite accepting." He laughed as he added, "I am the least accepting in the family!" Sobering, he said, "Jhumki was there for me at the time, which was very important for me. The stability it gave me was very helpful."

History had repeated itself.

The new chapter of Jhumki's life with Alexander had begun with great happiness to be followed by great tragedy. If anything positive can be read into what happened, it is this: unlike the time of her aunt and uncle's murder, Jhumki and Alexander could stand shoulder-to-shoulder in the face of misfortune.

After burying his mother, a chastened Alexander brought his wife back to New York. They had little time to rebuild their lives. Akin to the time eight years ago when, free and footloose, blissfully unaware of the chasm yawning at her feet, Jhumki had strolled out onto San Francisco pier, the newlyweds, drawn close by one calamity, were hurtling toward another.

Anudip Foundation was expanding its work and needed our extended presence in India. With Jhumki settled in to her new job and a loving person to care for her, our American employment no longer a deterrent, Radha and I decided to spend four months in India through the winter.

On November 19, Jhumki's twenty-ninth birthday, we were in transit. From Brussels we wished her success in her new career and married life.

On the 21st, we were finishing a late breakfast with Viji in Chennai when my cell phone rang in the adjoining bedroom. I went to pick it up and found it was our daughter, calling from New York.

"Baba," there was no preamble, "is Mommy with you?"

My heart lurched.

When Jhumki began a phone conversation without a cheery "What's up?" or "Guess what?" something has upset her.

Radha came in, and I put the phone on speaker.

"Go ahead, Jhomi. Mommy's here."

"Listen. I had a routine blood test because my medical insurance is changing from New York schools to Alexander's company."

She stopped, and in the stillness I could feel my heart thumping.

"Okay," I said slowly, "and . . . ?"

"... and my blood markers are high, Baba."

There was another silence.

"Which markers, Jhomi?" Radha asked.

"CEA and CA 27.29."

Radha and I gasped and looked at each other in horror. She was referring to cancer markers in her blood that were regularly tested in checkups.

A full minute passed.

"Hello?" Jhumki said. "Listen. Alexander and I have done some research. They may be cancer markers, but everyone says they shouldn't be used by themselves for diagnosis."

When we still didn't say anything, she asked, "Baba, Mommy, you there?" to which there was a faint "Yes, Muppet" from Radha.

"Listen! Don't jump to any conclusions now. We've got to get scans and MRIs done. Then we'll see."

Radha was crying softly with her forehead on my shoulder.

"Look, Jhomi," I said, "let Mommy and me talk for a few minutes and we'll call you right back. Don't go anywhere. Are you at home? Is Alexander with you?"

"Yes, Baba."

"Jhomi, we understand the situation. Give us a few minutes."

"Okay, Baba," she said very quietly.

"Love you, sweetie. Bye."

I pushed the OFF button and sat back on the bed.

It *might* not be. It *could* not be. It *must* not be. It wasn't confirmed. There was hope. For five years, almost to the day, buoyed by uniformly negative results of biannual tests at Stanford Hospital, we had more or less ignored it. We had hoped against it, blanked our minds against it, shunned the unthinkable word, the root of nightmares.

Metastasis.

Synonymous to a word used by everyone every day: *spread.* Butter spreads. News spreads. Good cheer spreads. Cancer metastasizes. The sky falls.

Metastatic breast cancer is incurable. Statistics say that in eighty percent of cases, breast cancers do not metastasize. Viji's hadn't.

A pox on statistics!

What were the odds of a twenty-four-year-old contracting breast cancer in the first place? A fraction of a fraction of a fraction of a percent! Should Jhumki not now be offered a probabilistic reprieve?

Cancer markers in the blood are indicators of malignant cell activity. But, as Jhumki said, they are unreliable by themselves. A person with advanced cancer could have low marker levels and vice versa. But on that morning in Chennai, in my heart of hearts, I knew it was going to be bad. While I tried to keep a brave face, "the beginning of the end" was a phrase that kept sneaking to my mind.

I went to find my wife.

Radha was sitting in the other bedroom and staring at nothing. Her motherly big sister was holding her hand. We didn't have to tell Viji anything. She knew from our faces. She knew the implications. Usually voluble, Viji was quiet. When I came in, Radha broke down.

"What shall we do?" she cried as I held her close. "Oh, my God, what shall we do? She's our *baby*. What shall we *do*?"

There was nothing I could say to comfort her. Any reassurance would be an empty travesty. We could hope. We could fight. We *would* fight. We *had* fought. We would get Jhumki the best medical care. But I didn't need to tell her that. We didn't talk very much that day. Each knew exactly what the other was thinking. We called the kids back. Eight hours later we boarded a flight to San Francisco having spent three days of the four months we'd planned for India.

I have no recollection of the twenty-hour Chennaï/Narita/SFO flight, except trying to call Alexander from Tokyo and being furious that my cell phone did not work in Japan. We must have analyzed Jhumki's situation on the plane, talked, conceived scenarios, but I don't remember a thing.

We landed at SFO at noon on the same day we left Chennai and thanked the stars the time difference was in our favor. Jhumki and Alexander had already arrived from New York. We caught up with them on the second floor of the Cancer Center at Stanford. Alexander greeted us with a hug. We spotted our daughter sitting at a table in a corner and hammering away at her computer. She had not noticed us. I went and put my arms around her neck and kissed her head.

"Hi, Baba! What's up?" she said, turning around with a smile.

Then Mommy and Jhomi had a long embrace.

Jhumki sent an e-mail to friends and family a little later. No, it did not break news of the cancer recurrence. What it did was exemplify her matchless ability to rise above privations that demolish ordinary mortals, and look at good and happy things and so maintain her sanity.

> *I'm very happy [she wrote]*
> *Our wedding registry is up on the web*
> *Go to www.myregistry.com*
> *Login with mishti*
> *The password for guests is •••••*
> *I already put in for a National Geographic subscription.*
> *Now we can put in whatever we want*
> *Yippeee yaye yippee*
> *No napkin holders*
> *Jhumki*

The news of Jhumki's cancer metastasis spread (a hellish pun), and a tidal wave of concern and sympathy washed over us. Jhumki's team grew. "We are with you all the way," everyone said. "How can we help?"

At Stanford Hospital, Dr. Carlson affirmed what Jhumki had told us over the phone line to Chennai, that while the situation was worrisome, without the appropriate scans, no prognosis could be made. The results would be available the following Monday and we faced yet another weekend of waiting and worrying.

Tej and Jagjit Singh, dear family friends, had the four of us over for Thanksgiving dinner. Most people there knew Jhumki from when she was a child. We partook of good food, played board games, and caught up on news. There was no talk of cancer. During the weekend we planned the upcoming wedding. Jhumki worked on her Spencer Fellowship application, practiced yoga, and threw balls for Mishti to retrieve.

On Monday morning, we pulled into the parking structure of Stanford Hospital and after a relatively short wait, were led into an examination room. Dr. Carlson entered with a sheaf of papers. Jhumki's oncologist is a methodical man and knowledgeable physician who listens well and tells it like it is. Jhumki appreciated his attitude. After brief nods and shaky smiles, Dr. Carlson laid out his interpretation of the scan results.

Whole-body CT, PET, and bone scans all pointed to the same conclusion: lesions (abnormal tissue) had been detected in Jhumki's liver and hip. The lesions were small but they were distinctive. Other vital organs, including the brain, were clear.

We stared at Dr. Carlson while the deadly phrases reverberated around the small room. During the ensuing silence he looked at us in turn with concerned eyes.

"What is the significance of the size of the lesions?" asked Alexander.

"The largest liver lesion is 1.5 centimeters. We consider it small but significant. The others are micro-lesions, possibly cancerous, possibly not. The bone lesions are also small, but they are significant."

There was another silence. Radha's eyes were shut tightly.

"Can it be reversed?" I asked.

Radha's eyes flew open.

The room was designed for a patient and a doctor. Five made us a crowd. Dr. Carlson twirled meditatively on his revolving stool before he spoke.

"It can and it *will* be reversed," he said. "Therein lies our treatment plan."

At this marginally hopeful point we decided to adjourn and regroup in a half hour. Jhumki and Alexander went for a walk on the sunlit campus. Radha, brokenhearted, wept on my shoulder in the corridor.

"What shall we *do*?" she asked me again. "She's our little baby!"

I held her close and let her cry. I couldn't face the inevitability. I would die myself before facing a life without Jhumki. I knew her mother would too. The only thing I could tell her was that we could not give up. Jhumki was being a powerhouse, and we had to be strong for her. The cards she was being dealt were the toughest, least deserving, least reasonable, least plausible in the entire world. We had to fight back with her.

The kids came back, and we returned to the exam room. Jhumki looked serious and composed. She made us sit facing her. The doctor had not arrived.

"We've talked, Alexander and I," she told us gravely.

Just as she had done when the news of cancer first hit us in 2001, Jhumki had shaken despondency off and taken charge of the situation.

"It's rough," she said, "but we *won't* let it get us down.

Everything's changed, and nothing has changed. There's so much to do. We *will* have the wedding even if I have no hair. I *will* work. I *will* teach. I *will* write. I *will* run. I *will* travel. The first priority for my treatment, whatever they call it—aggressive, conservative, experimental—has to be based on this. And there's the question of New York versus California."

She looked at me.

"Will you help me with med bills and insurance and stuff?"

I nodded.

"Mommy, you have to help with doctors and treatment. You're good at that."

Mommy gave her brave girl a squeeze.

"Ranga can help with research. My friends can get access to cancer articles."

She turned to her husband. "Alexander will look after me." She took his hand. "We'll fight it, Alexander. We're gonna have a *good* wedding."

There was a silence and, as if on cue, a knock on the door. Jhumki gave Dr. Carlson more or less the same speech and waited while he cogitated. I wondered what his expectation had been. Outrage? Anger? Desolation? Tears? Fatalism? He had known Jhumki for five years. Had he expected anything less courageous?

"Give me your estimate, Bob," Jhumki said. "You know me well enough. Be frank."

After another pause, Dr. Carlson answered the question we all had at the forefront of our minds.

"It could be as short as six months, Jhumki. But I wouldn't be at all surprised if you came to see me this time next year. Two years is average. A small percentage live beyond ten."

"Thanks, Bob," replied Jhumki.

I don't know why.

The lesions found in Jhumki's liver and bone were renegade

breast-cancer cells that had escaped mastectomy and somehow survived chemotherapy and tamoxifen regimens. There still was a chance, though, they were not cancer cells. The biopsy would prove conclusive. We established that if the biopsy results were positive, Jhumki's options were threefold: hormone therapy, chemotherapy, or radiation therapy. Each treatment would focus on shrinking the tumors, ideally until they disappeared, and stayed that way for as long as possible—ideally forever—leading to full remission.

We read up about clinical trials and tried to find breakthroughs in cancer treatment. We found many brilliant options, but in mice, not in people. Lucky critters, those mice. Miracles happen every day for mice. For humans it takes years for a drug to be considered effective and safe. Mostly it never happens. There were no brilliant options for us. Everything boiled down to one thing: given all the "advances" in research and the clinical trials and the walkathons and the fund-raisers and the billions of dollars spent, metastatic breast cancer was— and is today—as incurable as it had always been. For a long time, the average survival rate has been two years.

Two years from when?

The literature is unclear. If it is two years from detection, wouldn't early or late detection affect the average survival time? Jhumki's runaway cells might have been in her liver before the cancer was first detected in 2001 and had survived chemo and tamoxifen since.

The following Monday, the biopsy report stared us in our faces and didn't require an oncologist to decipher. It confirmed that Jhumki had metastasis to the liver. Bone was another matter. Performing a biopsy of bone—inserting a needle and extracting tissue sample—is not only painful but dangerous, as it can cause fracturing. Jhumki had been complaining of bone pain for a while. Given the confirmation of cancer in the liver and the images of her bone, we accepted that she had bone mets too. Other common destinations of breast-cancer metastasis—contra-lateral breast, lungs, brain—were clear.

Did I invoke favorable probabilities and life's fairness for our valiant daughter? There were none available.

Oh, and by the way, it was December.

29. DISTANT THUNDER

No one was more aware of Jhumki's unflagging, almost inhuman focus on her goals in the face of obstacles than Peter Bing. Dr. Bing, an accomplished physician and philanthropist, first met Jhumki when she was looking for funding to travel to the Galápagos Islands as a Stanford sophomore in 1995. As they developed a profound friendship, the idealistic student and the elderly, but young-at-heart, chairman of Stanford's Board of Trustees, began referring to each other as co-conspirators.

"She really had an unconditional vision," said Peter in a phone interview with Maithreyi. "Jhumki saw the need, and she saw the solution. Unlike most of us, it is what she focused on. And of course that's what enormously successful people are able to do. They minimize the problems because, in point of fact, the problems *are* minimal relative to the enormity of the vision."

Thinking back today on Dr. Bing's words, I realize Jhumki saw her life's mission so clearly that she considered cancer—a thing that would devastate most of us—simply an obstacle and an irritant. And she treated it that way.

Peter felt that Jhumki went about her business with no interference from her ego. Most of us worry about a lot of things that involve ourselves: "How would I be perceived?" "Would this occupy too much of my time?" Jhumki believed that if something had merit, it was worth doing.

"Jhumki had something else which most of us don't have," said Peter, "an almost unlimited amount of energy, so that she could compress so much more in the same amount of time, so that all these things were doable, as it turned out. If it were for myself, I would have said, 'I will pick one thing.' She didn't have to do that. She was so incredibly productive.

"I was an enormous admirer of her abilities—mental,

emotional. I saw in her an embodiment of everything I would have wanted to be or would want to see in someone."

Maithreyi asked if news of Jhumki's cancer changed their relationship.

"I don't know that the relationship changed," Peter replied, "but my emotions changed. I am a physician by background and I did part of my training at Memorial Sloan-Kettering, and realized how desperate her situation would be. It wasn't something that we discussed. It made me profoundly sad of course, because I knew that there would be a premature ending to this remarkable life."

Dr. Bing spoke about their unique bond.

"I was not a mentor for her. That implies a major-minor relationship, the mentor being the major, passing on things to the minor, who learns at the foot of the master. That wasn't it at all. I was simply in awe of her and did whatever I could to be helpful. I wasn't a groupie exactly, but I simply wasn't her equal. I was certainly older, but I wasn't wiser. She was truly *sui generis* [unique], and never before and never since have I met anybody quite like her. It was like if a comet went by and you hung on a little bit for the ride."

Peter spoke about Jhumki the person.

"That same energy she brought to work seemed to power her sense of humor as well. I didn't know her when she was a young girl. Her sense of devilish humor, I am sure, led to lots of excitement for her parents."

Listening to the speakerphone conversation, I was reminded of the glowing MC at our thirtieth anniversary event.

"That unbridled energy of her work," Peter continued, "also came out in a sort of unbridled humor. It was wonderful to have that explosive happiness. She greeted each day—what's the right phrase?—as a glorious event! For most of us we get up and we drag around a little bit and try to get organized and get ourselves on the way. She just exploded into each day. For me it was such a burst of uplifting joy when she would explode into one of these humorous things she saw. And it was wonderful!"

The new year dawned.

Alexander and Jhumki flew back to New York. They had lives to live. They had to get away from the greyness called cancer. It was quite obvious that Jhumki's treatment would now have to take place in New York as a long-term—very long-term, we hoped—regimen.

Robert Carlson spoke to us about an intriguing specialist in New York, one of world's foremost cancer researchers.

"Some people find him difficult," Dr. Carlson told his patient. "But, Jhumki, I think with your personalities, you two will get along well."

We wondered what he meant and hastened to look up this strange-sounding specialist on the Internet. Here is what we found the website of Memorial Sloan-Kettering Cancer Center.

Clifford Hudis, M.D., is Chief of the Breast Cancer Medicine Service and attending physician at Memorial Sloan-Kettering Cancer Center in New York City, where he is also a professor of medicine at the Weill Medical College of Cornell University. He is co-leader of the Breast Disease Management Team at MSKCC, co-chair of the Breast Committee of the Cancer and Leukemia Group B, past chair of the Internet Services Committee and present chair of the Information Technology Committee of the American Society of Clinical Oncology ASCO. He is past president of the New York Metropolitan Breast Cancer Group and chair of the Scientific Advisory Board of the Breast Cancer Research Foundation.

A consultation with Dr. Hudis was scheduled for early

January. In inimitable style, Jhumki prepared a list of questions and e-mailed them to the doctor with a view to making the meeting more productive. To everyone's surprise, bang came a reply with "Yes," "No," "Don't know," or "Let's talk" marked beside each question. This highly unusual doctor/patient exchange became standard during Jhumki's later treatment.

On January 2, 2007, the four of us located Memorial Sloan-Kettering, the famous cancer institution, and nervously entered the outpatient area on 64th Street. Before long we were escorted to a standard-issue examination room and managed a few minutes of jittery conversation before the door opened and we were confronted by a young-looking, well-dressed man with a businesslike manner and honest eyes that surveyed us through glasses. As we talked it swiftly became apparent why Dr. Hudis was at the apex of his profession. It also became clear that when he had an opinion he did not hold it back. The exchanges between the celebrated oncologist and our daughter fell unconsciously into a rapid-fire patter of highly intelligent and professional people exploring complex issues.

From the notes of Dipak Basu at MSKCC, Jan 2, 2007

The Cancer:

Estrogen Receptor Positive—meaning the tumor grows through supply of estrogen hormones that are created by ovaries and, to a lesser extent, other tissues

Treatment Options:

1. *Stopping estrogen production—Pre-menopausal estrogen production is stopped either by elective ovary removal (oophorectomy) or by hormone suppression therapy*
2. *Chemotherapy—selectively kills cancer cells. There exist a vast variety of chemo drugs of different effectiveness, toxicity and side effects*
3. *Inhibition of new blood vessels—Use of an anti-*

angiogenic drug to inhibit blood vessels from carrying oxygen to cancer cells

4. *Bone strengthening—Reverse or combat bone weakening caused by spread of cancer cells to the bones through a bisphosphonate drug that blocks cells that cause re-absorption of bone*

Dr. Hudis prescribed a combination of the first and fourth options, and Jhumki's anti-estrogen therapy began at once. Two hormone-suppression drugs would cut off estrogen supply to the cancer cells and starve them. They would also place her in artificial menopause. A third drug would stabilize the bone. We hoped the grouping would halt and reverse progression of her cancer for a long time.

Children were what Jhumki lived for.

They were her passion, her life. In December 2006, after detection of metastasis, Jhumki realized that estrogen-inhibiting drugs could forever impair her ability to conceive her own children. Consequently, before cancer treatment began, she and Alexander decided to keep her maternal dream alive through the process of harvesting eggs at the risk of her cancer flaring. With the eggs they created several viable embryos, which were frozen and stored in a fertility clinic. In her first post to an online CarePage that she had started to provide updates on her health to her friends, Jhumki wrote:

> *We harvested embryos because I can't ovulate or carry a child, now that I've started the medication. We can get a gestational surrogate, but we haven't decided what our plan is with respect to having kids. I'll be on the medicine forever, unless something crazy happens in breast cancer medicine. The mortality prospects for women with metastatic breast cancer are pretty bad—you can find them*

on the Internet yourself. The doctors never cure metastatic disease, at best they manage it.

Jhumki's relationship with her doctor would be the bedrock of the rest of her life. Dr. Hudis' perspective on his unique patient and her yearning for children is best conveyed in his own words.

My introduction to Jhumki came by way of a very unusual e-mail. This e-mail described an unfortunate woman, newly diagnosed with metastatic breast cancer, but who was still considering or planning to move forward with the life plans of a young healthy woman, including starting a family. My initial reaction was skepticism and serious concern about her depth of understanding and comprehension regarding her diagnosis.

When I first met Jhumki in person, she described her plan, which involved getting treated for her newly diagnosed metastatic breast cancer but also bearing children or potentially starting a family through less conventional ways. This was a key focal point of our earliest discussions. In the very first few weeks of working together, I think she came as close as she could to firing me! I think the social worker at MSKCC talked her out of that, explaining that what she perceived as my harshness was actually something much deeper. I was providing an honest and scientifically based description of her reality. This was only meant to help her get to a place where she could do what was best for her.

In simple terms, she just did not like what I had to say.

Breast cancer is a disease that begins in the breast. It is a malignancy. The definition of that, from a practical point of view, is that the cells divide and grow in an unregulated fashion and in places where they don't belong.

The basic problem, not always understood, is that breast cancer spreads outside the breast to other parts of the body very early in its natural history. That means, to be cured of breast cancer at the outset requires two things. One is that you remove every bit of the visible tumor. The second is that you sterilize or eradicate the microscopic, undetected metastatic disease that is yet to be seen. This does not suggest that many people are not cured by surgery, but it emphasizes the point that many only appear to be cured, while harboring an undetectable burden of disease.

I describe all this because Jhumki's cancer went through these phases, years before she knew me. In a technical sense, unbeknownst to her or anyone else, she already had metastatic breast cancer before she met Dr. Carlson.

The clinical definition of metastatic breast cancer is a black-and-white thing—either you see it or you don't. When we detect it clinically we say the cancer "came back" and the patient now has metastatic breast cancer. But in truth that kind of artificial line is misleading. It seemed that when Jhumki met me, I was among the very first people to confront her with this reality.

How long did it take for her to accept it?

In retrospect, it doesn't seem like that long, but it felt very difficult at that time. This is not to suggest any character flaw, but this transition for her was among the harder ones I have had to navigate with her. Part of it was because she had such unbelievable energy and dreams and vision. The potential dashing of those dreams was something that she wouldn't allow to be true for a while.

Eventually, she came around and accepted these truths and very quickly became very realistic about the disease. As you would expect, once she really understood her situation, she managed it in a very rational way, making all the right choices along the way. But it was always a very hard thing for her youthful spirit. She was never bogged down by the workaday concerns of most young to middle-aged people. She was very youthful in her attitude. This is not to say that she was juvenile.

Instead, when she saw an issue, she analyzed it fully and then set about conquering it.

In terms of her treatment, Jhumki needed it to be evidence based. This meshes extremely well with the way I practice, which is why she had been counseled to give me another chance after we first met. The decisions we made were not really unique to her. In fact, virtually all of the decisions were the same ones that are made for any other person in a similar situation, and not just by me, but by most medical oncologists experienced in the treatment of breast cancer.

Once one accepts that metastatic breast cancer is not a curable disease—and that's a very big thing to accept—the focus of treatment becomes different.

Very reasonable questions that patients like her ask are, "Why should I get treated at all? If you are not going to cure me, then why do anything?"

The answers are in the middle ground where treatment done right can prolong survival—which is not the same as cure—and maintain and even improve their quality of life during the time that they do have.

In terms of the ever-present question of time, we are very careful not to be overly precise. These discussions are not melodramatic, as they are sometimes portrayed in the media. It's not like that in part because that ignores the unpredictability of individual cases.

In terms of specific treatments, this requires we balance the known toxicities against the potential benefits, so that our patients are able to make the most of the time they have left. In general this means that we pick the least toxic, the least noxious therapy that is defensible for the situation.

That is the paradigm that we followed for her, treatment after treatment.

Along the way, the measure of success, to be quite frank, is very modest. We ask, is the disease stable? Is it better? If instead it is worse, we change therapy, but otherwise we would continue what seems to be effective. The only other reason we change therapy in the middle of a regimen is when the treatment is unacceptably toxic for an individual patient.

The more unusual issue for Jhumki was her belief or hope at the beginning that the metastasis wouldn't stop her from doing other things like starting a family. I am not saying, "I told you so," but in a very predictable way the topic of pregnancy faded from the forefront as her disease inevitably progressed.

At the same time I have to mention the part I was very wrong about. When we first met, I noted that it took many years for her cancer to reappear clinically and that it first did so in bone. These are two factors that ring a bell in oncologists and suggest an indolent course and a tumor responsive to relatively nontoxic hormonal manipulations. Based on this I anticipated she would have a far better and longer course than the average patient.

She didn't.

30. HAPPY NEW YEAR

T he year 2007 had begun with a rush of activity. The excitement, while not overcoming the trauma of cancer, ameliorated some of Jhumki's pain. An e-mail from Jhumki to her friends, titled "Bike Girl," set the stage for the year.

Should I do the first one below or the second? They are both for women with metastatic cancer! I'm really interested in the 2nd ... J

AMAZON HEART THUNDER
United States, United Kingdom and Australia: In 2004 Amazon Heart launched its adventure programs with an inaugural motorcycle adventure, Changing Gears. In 2007 we'll offer Amazon Heart Thunder rides in the UK, US and Australia.

AMAZON HEART ODYSSEY
India, December 1–8, 2007: This December a daring group of breast cancer survivors will travel to Madurai in Tamil Nadu, South India, to spend one week building an orphanage for tsunami and AIDS orphans. Each member of our team will pay their own way to India, raise funds for the construction project and support local micro-finance programs for poor rural women and breast cancer projects. At the end of the adventure they will also meet with local breast cancer survivors to share their experiences.

She did not go on either of these trips, but they were examples of adventurous projects that she considered before taking on a big one, triathlon.

Loving the academic freedom of NYU, Jhumki threw herself back into professional life. She expanded her research programs to test innovative teaching models, while she enjoyed working compassionately and objectively with school kids. She now involved her family and friends in everything she did—especially fund-raising! Jhumki was a shameless fund-raiser, never hesitating to invoke the emotive aspect of her work to solicit money. One of our most satisfying contributions to her cause was sponsoring pizza and beer on Friday evenings for the beleaguered teachers at SDL.

From New York, Jhumki sent us highly irreverent snippets about bureaucracy, politics, friends and cousins, and their romantic entanglements, in a city that never stopped to amaze.

It was a red-letter day when she was allotted married faculty housing on NYU's campus in Lower Manhattan.

"Mommy, it's *palatial!*" she rhapsodized one morning, bright and early. Bleary-eyed, three time zones behind, we listened to her excitement on the phone call.

"It has *two* bedrooms! We can sleep in one and work in the other. Or you guys can stay in it when you visit. Or, wow, we can do both! I only have to walk across the street to my office. And we have it for a *song!*"

Nothing exemplified NYU's confidence in the prowess of its extraordinary faculty member and concern for her illness, than the allocation of so precious a resource, so close to her department. By severely cramped New York standards, Jhumki and Alexander's new apartment, a block from beautiful Washington Square Park, was spacious and sunny, if not actually palatial. The Steinhardt School was diagonally across from the apartment in one direction, and the physics department was diagonally across in the other. Thus, Jhumki's home epitomized one of her greatest triumphs: connecting the historically isolated science and education communities on campus.

৯

"There were no walls that she couldn't walk through!"

Dean Mary Brabeck was explaining this aspect of Jhumki's work.

"Sometimes the thickest wall of all was between the sciences and the science educators, and she just walked right through it and made friends. People straightaway grasped not only her passion to inform how to better teach science, but also her passion for understanding how students learned science. They saw the value in working with her in their own classrooms—that they could do a better job at teaching college-level science by listening to this very prescient and visionary educator."

Jhumki collaborated with Allen Mincer of NYU's physics department on two research projects. Out of the first project came a paper on what students remember about their teachers. This paper, which Dr. Mincer and Jhumki presented at a NARST conference, was titled "Situating the Preparation of Graduate Physics Teaching Assistants in Their Funds of Knowledge and Leveraging Their Potential as Agents of Critical Change."

The second project was on women and minorities in physics.

"It's clear that in physics there is a terrible problem of unrepresented groups," Allen told us. "There are very few women in physics. The first step is to recognize that there are things we can do to change this. Maybe many of those who fall by the wayside would have made excellent physicists, but in today's process we are weeding out particular ethnic or minority groups."

Jhumki changed the way Allen thought about teaching physics by inculcating her ideas of democratic pedagogy that drew on the students' funds of knowledge. "She set in motion many more things within the physics department," Dr. Mincer said. "Now I tell my students, 'You have sixteen years of biases about teaching. We will explore that.'"

The academic pace accelerated, and so did the recognitions. In February she received news that set her apart in her field of research:

> *Dear Dr. Basu:*
>
> *It is my pleasure as Chair of the Division K Awards Committee of the American Educational Research Association to inform you that your dissertation, How urban youth express critical agency in a 9th grade conceptual physics classroom, has been selected to receive AERA's 2007 Teaching and Teacher Education Outstanding Doctoral Dissertation Award.*
>
> *On behalf of the Awards Committee, I congratulate you on this stellar accomplishment. The award will be presented at the Division K Business Meeting and Reception on Wednesday, April 11th, 6:15pm–9:00pm in the Hyatt Regency Chicago, Grand Ballroom, Gold Level.*
>
> *I hope that you will be able to attend this event as I look forward to seeing you in Chicago and offering congratulations in person.*
>
> *Sincerely,*
> *Kim Fries, Ph.D.*

Jhumki showed her professional evaluation from NYU to her parents. It provided my first in-depth understanding of her accomplishments, and exposed me to the incredible amount of work she had taken upon herself.

Among her contributions during the year were an article on how students develop a sustained interest in science, and a book chapter on how students express agency in a physics classroom. Other articles were in the works.

With NYU colleague, Dr. Jason Blonstein, Jhumki received high marks for the first semester of NYU's Science Methods course, focusing on inquiry, reflective practice, formative and summative assessment. The course, which included a social-justice strand, became Jhumki's platform for publicizing her democratic teaching methods.

Another key contribution during that semester was a visionary plan for a cutting-edge lab for science teaching and research at NYU. Her ideas set in motion the establishment of a landmark Science, Technology, Engineering, Mathematics and Environment (STEME) institute with global impact. The center, close to where Jhumki lived in Greenwich Village, is nearing completion.

Planning for the future, Jhumki wrote in her evaluation that during the coming year she and Allen Mincer would conduct research on the development of graduate students' pedagogical tool kits. She would work with the computer science department at Columbia University to develop and evaluate engineering outreach programs for low-income, minority public school students. With Dr. Verneda Johnson, science head at Isaac Newton Middle School for Math and Science in Harlem, she would study experiences of NYU Science Methods students, as they synthesized ideas about standards-based science pedagogy and issues of social justice. She hoped to co-teach a doctoral course, contribute to NYU's doctoral committee by developing stronger program guidelines, recruit science-education candidates, and advise doctoral students.

With the ups came the downs.

"So they announced the internal research grants today," Jhumki wrote to us in April. "Four colleagues got awards. Two colleagues got two. I didn't get a single one. They awarded only one in the category in which I applied, to a senior faculty member. I guess I was the idiot who applied to the most competitive category. I also didn't get the Spencer Foundation award (for Fall). And I don't think I'll get the University Challenge Fund. And Knowles and Angelos grants are for the following year. So now I don't have funding for next year. When does a girl ever get a break?"

Also in April, Jhumki, while training for a triathlon—an event combining swimming, biking, and running—sent us this update:

> So, I had a good class today. I always forget that the week after cancer treatment does slow me down. I just get frustrated and discouraged 'cause I'm slower that week.
>
> Some small things are helping: the power bars and the oatmeal, and not working at SDL. Also, my swim technique is much better—I actually beat someone in class today. It's a miracle. I'm figuring out how to pace myself on the biking. And the best thing about triathlon is that the running is almost trivial—and even that, he's working on us taking weight off our hips and reducing impact—who would have known there was technique to running?
>
> I did 20 km on the bike, 2 km run and quite a lot of swim lengths and don't feel bad.
>
> I do have to get my act together a bit: get running shorts that work for biking, gels to eat on the way, and a wet suit and good bike.
>
> But even if I don't finish, I've gotten so much better.
>
> The person who started me on the class, interestingly, had leukemia when she was 8. We're very similar: she's a student of mine. Last time I saw her at the gym, she came to her competitive triathlon training even though she had bronchitis! She's by far my strongest, most hard-working student, totally organized and stressed by deviance from plan, turns in the highest quality work in class, teaches, runs triathlon nationally and manages an apartment building while dating someone seriously. We get along pretty well!

൭

On a flight from San Francisco to New York, Jhumki wrote a long letter to her husband who was in Greece. Alexander gave us a copy of the letter which revealed her thoughts on death and dying.

The take-off from San Francisco was spectacular. I saw the Golden Gate Bridge, Bay Bridge, downtown San Francisco and Oakland, the Bay and the Pacific Ocean. I could make out Presidio Hill Park and see to the Marin Headlands. And then the Sacramento Valley farmlands appeared and the Sierra Nevada, and then the dry lands of the west. Sometimes I'm so angry with my country and its leadership that I forget what is so beautiful about this land and space—I forget how different tribes roamed the plains with the bison migration, how jaguars once came all the way up to Arizona, and how settlers traveled with wagons through desert and swampland to settle the West. It's so easy to forget all this in the heart of a bustling city.

I think I want to come home. I want the sun to shine many days of the year, to see my friends at lunch and spend time with their children, to be outdoors, to be near my parents and Ranga. I've lived almost six years in New York, longer than I had ever imagined. If you think you can make friends, I would like to come back. If you think this is possible, I might start actively looking for jobs.

On the plane, I looked through all the photos on my computer. If I die, I want you to look through them with my family and choose some for my service. There are pictures of me with Ranga when I was little and with my dad and a goat and peacock wallpaper. I'm going to ask Preetham if he'll include in the Sangeet [musical event at their upcoming wedding] *some of these pictures of me with my grandparents and from when I lived in India. Maybe there are pictures of you when you were little and of*

Ilana and of your history that you want included too. Maybe Ari and Anna would talk about them?

I'm in a serious mood because I'm preparing for bad news from the scans. If things go well, there will be respite from this focus on preparing for dying. I felt so set in my mind last week and the week before that if I had to do chemotherapy again, I would refuse. But today, as I was between the gangway and the airplane door, I saw the blue California sky and felt the warm sun and thought about how we've had such little time together to share what is beautiful. And I felt sad about leaving you.

But I have to be honest, a part of me does feel selfish about dying (and dying quickly rather than in a drawn out way). I do feel relieved about certain things: not seeing my parents die, having our memories be of so much excitement together. I don't want to see the suburban malls take over parkland and the development in Costa Rica when we go back. I don't want to be around when elephants disappear from northern Africa. I suppose it's that other people's and other kinds of sadness seems too much to bear lately—I feel exhausted with my aunt and uncle and all the cancer and Ilana dying so soon after we got married. So being forced to die sooner would excuse me from all these challenges and from the decision about having children and exposing them to a tough childhood of illness. And, of course, I can't imagine living in a world where something bad happened to you.

Soon after writing this letter, Jhumki underwent a new set of CT and bone scans. In view of her improved physical condition, we expected a good outcome. We were wrong.

From CT/Bone Scan Report for Jhumki Basu, April 13, 2007

1. *New diseased lymph nodes*
2. *Nodules suspicious of metastasis in her lungs, an organ that had been clear before, and suspicion of lesion in the kidney*
3. *Increase in size and number of cancer cells in her liver*
4. *Increase in size, number, and spread of cancer to the bone*

We panicked.

Even Dr. Hudis was surprised that the scan results were so abysmal, because Jhumki had been feeling much better. It was clear, even to us, that hormone therapy had failed, her disease had advanced alarmingly, and that she had to switch to chemo.

Within chemotherapy there were several options. Dr. Hudis suggested Xeloda[15], an oral medicine that does not cause immune-suppression and hair loss. In conjunction with Xeloda, he recommended a controversial drug called Avastin that would cut off oxygen supply to cancer cells. Avastin held the possibility of dangerous side effects like high blood pressure and heart irregularity. To be treated with it, Jhumki would require regular EKGs and blood-pressure checks. For administration of the Xeloda/Avastin combination, Jhumki enlisted in a clinical trial in which her progress would be monitored carefully. Medical insurance did not cover Avastin's cost—a mind-bending ten thousand dollars per application—but Genentech, the drug's maker, picked up the tab since Jhumki was in the trial. It was

---

[15] I have generally used the brand names of the drugs that Jhumki used, rather than the more complex generic names. For example, Xeloda is a branded version of the drug capecitabine, that is brought to market by the Swiss pharmaceutical company, F. Hoffmann-La Roche.

end of April before we emerged from the medical quagmire. What would the future bring? Things looked pretty bad now. Would they get better? Would there be untenable side effects? Would Jhumki's professional life be affected? How would she look? A hundred what-ifs lay ahead. While we worried, Jhumki dusted herself off once more and regained her old resolve.

"Look, guys," she said to the three people who loved her the most. "The wedding's in two months. I've said I'll be there even if I have no hair. And guess what? We're going on that honeymoon come what may."

31. HEATHROW IN THE REDWOODS

The first message I received from Jhumki on the subject of her and Alexander's traditional wedding ceremony, dates back to August 2006.

I want all of you to know that the Ranchods [family friends] *informed me this evening at dinner that their son, Sanjay, had wanted an elephant for his wedding. He wanted to enter his wedding in an unusual way, on elephant back, and therefore, the desire for one. He called several zoos in the Raleigh-Durham area, but the only elephant available was too old. They offered him a camel, but he wasn't allowed to ride it. His wife felt that a horse might shy during the wedding procession. Remember Sandhya's wedding?*

Jhumki was referring to a cousin's marriage at our home, where I happened to unfurl an umbrella and make the groom's horse shy into a crowd of revelers. Luckily no one was hurt.

Jhumki's message set in motion the infamous "Horse vs. Elephant" theme for Alexander and Jhumki's nuptials, a topic of much friendly banter. Jhumki's good friend, Jenny Tran, made a wedding logo out of the rivalry, with a lotus ameliorating the combative animals.

Here is the story behind the graphic.

In the year 326 BCE, beside the River Beas in northern India, confronted by six thousand gaudily-decked and armored war elephants of the king of Magadh, Greek emperor Alexander the Great's all-conquering cavalry wilted and refused to fight. When this topic came up over dinner one day, our present-day Alexander staunchly maintained that the Greek army, after winning more than five million square kilometers, was tired and homesick.

This, I gingerly pointed out to Jhumki, was a recorded fact.

"Tell me another!" she snorted, losing all of a sudden her ability to be logical. And the horse-versus-elephant paradigm was born.

Two millennia after Alexander the Great died in Babylon, Greek and Israeli invitees to the forthcoming wedding wanted the event to be held in India. Indians, on the other hand, wanted to visit the Greek Isles and experience Jerusalem. Luckily, peace on Earth was restored when everyone agreed that Northern California in summer wasn't a bad deal after all.

Long before her illness, and before she met Alexander, Jhumki participated in this conversation:

> *Dipak: Jhomi, when are you going to get married?*
>
> *Jhumki: Oof, Baba! Who's gonna marry me?*
>
> *D: Why, lots of people will marry you. What about Tom and Dick and . . .*
>
> *J: Okay, okay! I get the point. Maybe one day I'll marry some sorry guy.*
>
> *Radha: Can we come?*
>
> *J: Where?*
>
> *R: To your wedding.*
>
> *J: Oh, there. Of course you can come, Mommy.*
>
> *[pause]*
>
> *J: We'll have a small wedding.*
>
> *R: How small?*
>
> *J: Oh, you know. I don't like to splurge on weddings 'n'*

stuff. Just a few people. You guys will have a quota.
  D: A what?
  J: You can invite five of your friends.
  [R and D gasp.]
  J: Okay, ten. That should fill a table.
  R: Ten friends?
  J: Okay, okay! Ten couples. Max.

In 2007, Jhumki was a different person. She wanted *everyone* at her wedding. Lots of family. Lots of friends. She wanted colleagues, mentors, teachers, doctors, kids. Lots of kids. Preparatory spreadsheets sprouted like flowers after a rain shower. There was a master wedding invitation list. A parents' (unfettered) invitation list. Alexander's invitation list. To-do spreadsheets cross-tabbed by priorities, responsibilities, and deadlines. Venue deliverables. Food deliverables. Costume deliverables. Transportation deliverables. Layout deliverables. Entertainment deliverables. Invitation deliverables. Lists of lists.

Petite and cheery, Jenny Tran, a New York graphic artist who was at Gavilan dorm at Stanford with Jhumki, volunteered to create the wedding invitation—quite unaware of what she was getting herself into. After weeks of wading through texts in five languages each with its own script, innumerable designs, outlandish fonts, many advisors, Jenny produced a masterpiece. The invitation was scripted in English, Bengali, Greek, Tamil, and Hebrew.

Very quickly our once-parsimonious daughter's guest list passed one hundred, then two hundred, and finally three hundred with enthusiastic support of quota-free parents. Every person who was invited had loved and cared for Jhumki at some time. Incredibly, close to a hundred percent of those invited came to the wedding. Of the 350 or so attendees, 75 were from abroad—India, Greece, Israel, England, Canada, Mexico. Later an especially witty guest remarked that diversity at the venue reminded him of Heathrow Airport.

Everyone who was invited knew Jhumki was fighting for her life. Everyone was aware she was doing so with absolute grace. There was no doubt in anyone's mind that her wedding had to be special.

Jhumki departed from the standard wedding template in other ways.

She wanted many students and teachers from New York to attend even though they could not afford to travel to California. To address this difficulty she cooked up a brilliant plan. On her wedding gift registry, together with *National Geographic* subscription, pillowcases, and spaghetti maker, Jhumki placed sixteen round-trip airfares. This category was the first to complete in her registry. Jhumki arranged housing for the group in a youth hostel at nearby Sanborn Park. For kids who had lived their entire lives on the concrete sidewalks of Brooklyn, staying in a cathedral forest of towering redwoods must have been a daunting and enriching experience.

Jhumki wanted kids of all ages to come to her wedding. If guests told her they would leave their little kids at home because they might "disturb" the proceedings, they got a glare and a growl—and brought their kids. The outdoor setting, with acres of sunlit grass for shouting and running and rolling, kept the children happy. She enlisted teachers to babysit tots at kid-size dinner tables and to help them with dinner.

The wedding was held on the grounds of a beautifully landscaped estate tucked away in the Santa Cruz Mountains. The flower-bedecked wedding platform had a backdrop of soaring redwoods. The soft serenity of nature in full glory welcomed the guests.

How can I describe our Jhomi on her wedding day? Gorgeous? Magical? Vibrant? Impish? Dazzling? Put all the words together, and you have an image.

No human being ever looked more stunning, more vivacious, more drenched with the joy of life, than she did on that July day. In meadows ringed by lofty trees, no girl ever danced more energetically or teased her beau more playfully. Yet few in the multitude knew that her neuropathy-affected hands, scratched and raw, and her feet, lacerated and bleeding in specially padded gold slippers, were breaking her parents' hearts even as they overflowed with love and pride.

On the night before the wedding, Radha and I were separately trying to write down what we would say at the reception. At 2 a.m., we both reached for the same thing. It was a nondescript, dark blue plastic dinner plate on which Jhumki had written a birthday poem for us in gold ink many years ago:

Hold Fast to Dreams
Years pass by,
And the leaves turn from green to gold;
Faces flash, and fade into hazy recollection.
Few remain in a chaotic life that never stops rotating;
Yet for me, there is forever a safe harbor.
'Cause when life is tangled and twisted in knots,
There is someone to share with, to cry with, to laugh with,
Memories of you, are what dreams are made of.
And in the end, though touching gold
Will leave me far away from home,
Through college and through life,
My heart remains wherever you wander,
And my dreams begin at your door.

Happy Birthday
September 17 and 18, 1992

"A History of Jhumki and Alexander's Wedding"
by Jhumki Basu

I got to California about 1.5 weeks before the wedding. We spent time with Jacquie, the tailor, right after I got there. Tej Aunty helped so much to design the dress for the Jewish ceremony and reception.

We served pizza at a homeless shelter. I remember the man there who once worked for De Beers, traveling all around Southern Africa.

On Wed, Thurs and Fri were the trips. On Wed everyone went to San Francisco. There were so many people there, I was a bit overwhelmed. But people were singing in Hindi, Hebrew and Greek. And it seemed like people had a truly enjoyable day at the Golden Gate Bridge, across Chinatown and at Ghirardelli Square. The next day, a small group went to Monterey: but none of the girls went because of the zoo.

The zoo! The zoo! The zoo!

We arrived in Oakland at 4:30 pm for the bachelorette night out. Ali and Joelle had food ready—hummus and vegetables and fruits. They were laid out on a picnic table with animal napkins and plates. There were 23 of us girls present.

Then we put up our tents on a field. It was lovely weather when we took an evening tour of the zoo. First the veldt—curious giraffes, peeping their heads over their enclosure to look at us, elands and various species of storks. Then the elephants: three females and a male kept separate, so he can be dominant and perhaps produce baby elephants. The elephants have "fingers" at the end of their trunks, to sort food and to scratch their eyes, which we saw! One elephant was chewing on an iron bar. They wear their molars down. One elephant throws things at evening visitors, so we had to stay far away. But I think we were quiet, so there was no trouble.

Then we went to the commissary where they have mealworms and crickets and blood popsicles and "enrichment" toys for the animals. We saw chimp night nests and squirrel monkey night enclosures and where baboons stay at night. You can't make a lot of noise or the chimps pound on the night enclosures.

We had a beautiful dinner—plants and yummy Thai food. I got the cutie pie elephant slippers then. Then we made enrichment for the fruit bats: long PVC pipes of flowers and fruit popsicles—nectar and fruit frozen in a little cup, which gets removed and hung from bat nets. We ate dessert and went to sleep in the cool outside air.

In the morning we woke up at 7 am and took a morning tour of the zoo. Howling ethereal gibbons, curious male and less outgoing female. We saw the chimps wake up and were warned that one spits. We saw one walking with a blanket, as if it were a skirt. We saw baboons and lemurs basking. They all interact—when the lemurs come out, the chimps get excited and excite the baboons and squirrel monkeys.

We saw the tiger enclosure with the heavy balls they roll around and Malayan and Island flying foxes lick up our enrichment. Then we packed, hugged and went home.

For the Sangeet event at my parents' home I wore Kalyani Paati's pink elephant sari with the chain of old rubies, made by Mommy. Preetham organized the whole event. I was so happy that Viji, who was ailing, got to sing to start everything off. There were so many people! I took a lot of pictures with the SDL crew. The kids looked great! Oh, they sang about me being a nerd.

Then the wedding day. Alexander set up the webcam for his grandmother in Greece—he stayed up late to get it right, *and it worked! Gia-gia saw the whole Indian ceremony. I had jewelry in my hair, Ilana's and Gia-gia's necklaces, and a diamond chain from Viji.*

The Hindu wedding started right away. There was the hand-painted platform on which four cousins carried me to the wedding, Alexander's family "arrived," Alexander was serenaded with Tamil songs. We exchanged flower garlands. After some Sanskrit hymns Anna and Ari tied my mangalsutra[16], then we took three rounds around the holy fire, then seven steps ending on a rock, and a final blessing.

Dressing for the Jewish ceremony was easy. We signed the ketubah[17] with the rabbi, with Jacky and Eitan as witnesses. There wasn't really a processional, but Alexander's family and our family came in together. The chuppah canopy was held up by men of his family, while others came to read and sing the seven blessings.

Rabbi Familan talked about unconditional love, the chuppah symbolizing a home made by people, not things, and being open so people could enter and leave with love. He also talked about peace in the world and bringing joy and support to people who have less access to this. He spoke in detail about our lives and in a lovely, personal way, about Ilana.

Bill Durham, my Stanford advisor, spoke at the reception on frigate birds, Paul Prokop on people from hard

---

[16] Thread of integrity—a sacred golden chain worn by Hindu married women, not only as a sign of their marital status, but also to ward off the evil eye and to protect their husbands from evil forces.

[17] A prenuptial agreement that is an integral part of a traditional Jewish marriage. It outlines the rights and responsibilities of the groom.

to get along countries, Kritika, Eitan, then Jacky, about driving Alexander home after he was born, Dimitris, his friend, about the journey of friendship. Then my parents and Vasilis spoke. My parents found a plate I wrote on a long time ago, and my mom cried a lot.

And then we thanked people and started dancing!!! I had lots of fun dancing. We cut the cake, which looked cute and scrumptious. And everyone liked it—there wasn't much leftover! Lots of people hung out dancing till 8 pm. I had lots and lots of fun dancing and I think Alexander did too. Then Alexander and I went to the Chaminade resort in Santa Cruz, drank champagne, ate dinner and slept, finally!

I felt sad Tuesday as we planted the tree at the wedding site 'cause everyone who came was gone. That day and week will never be repeated in the history of the universe. I wanted to plant something that will be left when I am gone. The tree overlooks where we got married and there will be a plaque remembering our wedding, as well as the approach trail in our name, and benches with Ilana's and Shanti's and SNA's names. Hopefully, the redwood tree we planted will live many years, maybe a thousand, and it will always look over that beautiful place where we got married on July 8, 2007. We are very lucky we had the money and so much help and love in planning our wedding. I think I've been thinking about it as an ending and feeling sad, probably complicated by having cancer. But I hope it's a beginning and we have a very long time of joy together. 'Cause I love Alexander, and our families have so much to share with each other. I could have never imagined a wedding or marriage like ours

32. OF HAPPINESS AND HORNBILLS

Dear Jhumki,

We have reached home after bidding you both goodbye at the airport and feel a deep sense of happiness and immense love. The wedding was magical and the two of you looked radiant and are truly the most beautiful and joyous twosome. May you always be as sunny and smiling and dance hand-in-hand while smelling the flowers. You know that we are forever beside you for all that life holds. Come back and see us soon!

Yours only,

Mommy.

ॐ

After the jubilation of the wedding, New York must have seemed a cold and hard place when Jhumki found herself back to mingling with gravely ill patients at MSKCC.

Since April she had been feeling generally better. Her blood markers were trending down. But nothing conclusively could prove progression or regression of the disease except scans that were scheduled three months apart. As her wedding had approached, Jhumki had decided to postpone scans to just before leaving for her honeymoon.

Her logic went something like this: "Hey, let's enjoy the nups to the fullest. Two weeks won't change anything anyway. If it's bad news, we'll be too immersed in our trip to worry. We'll deal with it when we come back. And if it's good news, those zebras and lions better watch out!"

Now, as the scans approached, I thought back to the disastrous results of April. What would the news be this time? Could Jhumki withstand another disappointment and pull herself back? Her blows had a history of appearing unfailingly after blissful occasions.

Then we received this e-mail:

I cried with happiness when we went to Sloan-Kettering and then we told Dr. Hudis that the anticipation of seeing him made me cry. Ha ha. And then Alexander had to say "We really like seeing you. It's just the hospital."

Galvanized, we opened the attachment to the e-mail. It was a long PDF report of her test results. We went straight to the summary . . . and rejoiced!

The cancer cells in Jhumki's liver had shrunk. Lymph nodes, while still prominent (indicating possible infection), were less pronounced. Cancer in the lungs was gone. The hip-bone condition had reversed. The news was good.

Correction: the news was *stupendous!*

Xeloda and Avastin were working.

With a big sigh of relief, Alexander adjusted gallantly to his wife's unorthodox concept of a honeymoon. Not Bali, not Barcelona, not Bora Bora. Their honeymoon began on the mean streets of Soweto in South Africa and went on to the wilds of Botswana.

Returning, after four years, to South Africa, a country she had loved, Jhumki guided Alexander around Johannesburg. About Nelson Mandela, she reminisced in her journal:

There's already a new airport terminal named after Tsambo, Mandela's mentor. Amazingly Madiba is 90 years old. Born at the time of WW1, great flu pandemic. His house was petrol-bombed. Two out of his three kids with Evelyn have died, and he divorced Winnie Mandela because of her politics. Now he is married to the first lady of Mozambique. I suppose he's a person among all the heroism. Perhaps he's lonely despite being asked to speak and be everywhere. When did he start to look old? Was Winnie resentful that

after waiting for so long and helping lead the ANC's
military wing that they no longer got along? When did he
start believing in non-violence? Was he tortured and
beaten? Why did they not kill him and killed Steve Biko?
Biko talked in such an engaging way. And his message of
Black Consciousness must have made the apartheid govt so
afraid, because it meant that each oppressed person started
to believe that he/she was powerful and skilled, when
oppressors want their subjects cowed, fearful and
deferential.

Flying to Botswana, she noted:

Plane to Maun—I am the only non-white person on the
flight. And there was only one black man on the Swissair
flight. Lawrence the driver said that there were lots of East
Asian tourists, but I see none, and it is clear that despite the
country being ten percent white, that these are the people in
the hotels, airplanes, business meetings, who hold all the
power and money. 33-years-old is the life expectancy in
Botswana. Does the HIV advocacy movement in the US feel
any affiliation with a true generation of bread-winners
dying here? If the epidemic does get put under control, still,
an entire generation will have to raise itself from childhood
on its own.

Jhumki's husband, attuned to sunny beaches of the Aegean,
told us later about the second night of his honeymoon. It *had* to
have been a coincidence, because even Jhumki couldn't have pre-
arranged what happened.

The newlyweds were settled for the night in a tent deep in
the bush of Botswana's Chobe National Park, when a pride of
lions killed a zebra a hundred meters away, and spent the night
crunching on its bones and body parts. Alexander stayed up
listening to *Panthera leo* dining, and unsuccessfully trying to

blank out the gory spectacle with images of sun-spangled Halkidiki beaches where Greek goddesses frolicked. *This is my honeymoon?* he wondered.

Jhumki slept on peacefully. She needed her rest. Later she recorded in her journal every animal, every bird, and every insect she encountered. The full list would be a zoology book, so here are only a few entries.

> *Red lechwe, white-fronted bee-eater, tsessebe, clawless cape otter, hammerkop, cape buffalo, slender mongoose, red-headed swallow, chacma baboon, glossy ibis, oxpecker, water monitor, roan antelope, kudu, bushbuck, hornbills. Lots of hornbills: Bradfield's, grey, ground, red-billed, crowned and yellow-billed hornbills.*

According to Alexander, Jhumki was at her best in Botswana. Here is what Jhumki had to say about him at the end of their trip.

> *Dear Alexander,*
>
> *This is my honeymoon journal. I am giving it to you so you have it to remember our honeymoon. This is my one and only favorite honeymoon, where we went to Bostwana to see the animals, Zimbabwe to see Victoria Falls, and South Africa to see my friends. I couldn't have envisioned a better honeymoon. And we even met some nice people— Dick, Stasia, Rob and Jouno and the many people at the lodges.*
>
> *I learned a lot, which makes it an even more special honeymoon.*
>
> *I love you very much and am happiest to be married to you. Everything you do makes me feel very lucky to be married to you.*
>
> *Love,*
> *Jhomi*

PART VI

SOARING WITH A
BROKEN WING

It is at the secondary level—in junior high, and more dramatically in high school, that the sense of human ruin on a vast scale becomes unmistakable.

Numbers cannot convey the mood of desolation that pervades some of the secondary schools; but certain statistics, even when you think you understand some of the problems of poor children in New York, jump off the page and strike you with astonishment.

From "Amazing Grace"
by Jonathan Kozol
Crown Publishers, New York, 1995
Reproduced with permission

33. A TIME NEVER BETTER

In November 19, 2007, Jhumki turned thirty.

How eventful were those three decades! How often had she turned a hopeless situation into one of meaning and purpose, creating new beginnings. For her birthday, her mother and I presented her with a plaque with an embossed poem by Tagore, a tribute to novelty and innovation. She hung it on her bedroom wall.

A Tribute to the New

Hail Nutan!
All things freshly born
When life's first happiness
Appears anon.

May thy beauty unfold,
May it melt the mist,
And shine radiant as the sun.

Sever the bonds of emptiness,
Liberate my spirit.
May victory of life ring out.
May it proclaim in Thee,
The eternal wonder of infinity.

The clarion sounds the dawn horizon.
In my soul
May eternal renewal herald
The day of my birth.

The closing months of 2007 were pivotal for Jhumki in many ways. Her career graph was rising logarithmically. She was working on research programs at SDL as well as at several schools in other New York boroughs. She was conceptualizing, developing, evaluating, and recording innovative science teaching methods that increased student engagement.

Her landmark paper, co-authored with Angela Calabrese Barton and two SDL students, Neil Clairmont and Donya Locke, titled "Developing a Framework for Critical Science Agency through Case Study in a Conceptual Physics Context," was accepted for publication in *Cultural Studies of Science Education (CSSE)*. In it she presents findings about developing the ability of high school students from low-income urban neighborhoods to think critically. She does this from an unexpectedly fresh perspective: that of the students themselves! Neil and Donya had participated with two others students in the earlier paper that Jhumki had presented in San Francisco in 2006. In the *CSSE* paper, the two teenagers reveal, through their experiences the importance of critical science agency in urban minority youth. Its results are based on a multiyear study of democratic teaching practice in high school science.

Three claims are presented:

1. *Critical science agency is intimately related to the leveraging and development of students' own identities*
2. *Critical science agency involves strategic development of teaching resources*
3. *Developing critical science agency is an iterative and generative process*

Another paper of Jhumki's, titled "Powerful Learners and Critical Agents: The Goals of Five Urban Caribbean Youth in a Conceptual Physics Classroom," was accepted by *Science Education* magazine. The abstract read:

> *Youth from low-income, minority backgrounds have often been marginalized from introductory courses, advanced study and careers in physics. Cultivating student*

agency may have the potential to improve access for diverse groups of learners. However, the implications of this lens for student learning have been minimally examined in the physics education literature.

In this ethnographic study situated in a ninth-grade conceptual physics classroom, I discuss students' critical goals—the intentions, motivations, and desires for change that youth hold. These critical goals were related to learning, voice, and participation in relationships and the world.

I also describe how student goals demonstrate the idea of "critical subject-matter agency" in physics: students positioning themselves as powerful learners envisioning subject knowledge as a tool for change in their own lives and world.

Jhumki sent us another bit of good professional news. "Looks like the Dean made my raise higher than what the department recommended," she wrote and added, "Congratulations to Alexander. He got the highest ranking at his work again this year!"

What a power couple!

It never ceased to amaze me the way Alexander was continually recognized for superlative professional performance and secured raises in a down economy, all the while lavishing care on our daughter while being dragged off to exotic places.

Then she wrote to me about her next "quarter birthday." This was a running tradition between us. Jhumki refused expensive gifts on her birthdays but agreed to "smaller" gifts at quarterly milestones, which we called her quarter birthdays. Everything she ever wanted on these occasions was to augment her teaching. On this occasion, the first item she requested in her e-mail was a NASA DVD containing a series of podcasts and guidebooks for secondary teachers. It was titled *Nanoscale*

Science: Activities for Grades 6–12.

The second was another DVD titled *Change and Motion: Calculus Made Clear*, by Michael Starbird of the Universities of Wisconsin and Texas. In the introduction, Professor Starbird quotes Bertrand Russell: "Mathematics, rightly viewed, possesses not only truth, but supreme beauty such as only the greatest art can show."

One of Jhumki's prized possessions was a "fun box" that she kept under her desk. It contained a longtime collection of personal writings from her students. Here are some pearls:

Contribution #1

> *You are beautiful*
> *You are a badass*
> *I want to be like you when I grow up*
> *Phenomenal Woman, that's you*
> *You have made a deep imprint on the world*

Contribution #2

> *Melanie asked her Granny how old she was. Granny replied she was so old she didn't remember any more. Said Melanie, "If you don't remember you must look in the back of your panties. Mine say five to six"*
>
> *A little boy was overheard praying: "Lord, if You can't make me a better boy, don't worry about it. I'm having a real good time like I am!"*
>
> *A little girl asked her mother, "Can I go outside and play with the boys?" Her mother replied, "No, you can't play with the boys, they're too rough." The little girl thought about it for a few moments and asked, "If I can find a smooth one, can I play with him?"*
>
> *Teacher: "What does the word 'benign' mean?" Student: "Benign is what you will be after you be eight"*
>
> *"Don't kid me, Mom, I know they're my feet"* - 3 year old

boy, when his mother told him his shoes were on the wrong feet

Contribution #3

> *random science fact #470: The fastest speed a falling raindrop can hit you is 18 mph.*

> *random science fact #3 trillion: A cockroach can live for nine days without its head.*

> *random science fact #2: The African Elephant gestates for 22 months (Yikes!)*

> *random science fact #99: There are 1600 calories in a pint of Hippopotamus milk*

> *random science fact #34,201: The silkworm moth has eleven brains*

After diagnosis of metastatic disease, Jhumki took on yet one more responsibility: cancer advocacy.

She became an active participant on the help line of Living Beyond Breast Cancer, an educational and support group that helps women affected by breast cancer to live as long as possible with the highest possible quality of life. Jhumki provided support for women who called in and required help in Russian, Hindi, Bengali, and Punjabi languages. Once while at Memorial Hospital, in the late stages of her illness, she took a help call and spoke bravely to the caller when she herself was close to dying.

E-mail from Matthew Zachary to Radha Basu, Dec 25, 2008

> *I am a survivor of pediatric brain cancer originally diagnosed in college, 13 years ago. In 2002, I quit my career to give back to other young adults with cancer and, in January of 2007, the 'I'm Too Young For This!' Cancer Foundation was born.*

> *Jhumki and I first connected in June 2007 when she applied to join our Young Adult Leadership Council, an all-*

volunteer brigade of young adult survivors looking for ways to give back to their peers and work towards improving both quality of life and survival rates. She was a brilliant, fervent advocate for us and significantly contributed to our efforts via various events in NYC including some grant writing strategy.

Sarah Beck is a professor of English education at NYU's Steinhardt School and chaired a staff committee, on which Jhumki served, for the training of doctoral students. Late in 2007 Sarah's sister was diagnosed with ovarian cancer. On the day of her sister's first surgery, Sarah had a class to teach, meetings to attend, and was distraught because she could not be with her sister. On her way to the first of these meetings she met Jhumki, who noticed that she looked upset and asked why. When Sarah told her, Jhumki urged her to put work aside immediately and be with her sister.

"I left the next day to go to Philadelphia," Sarah said. "From that point Jhumki frequently checked in with me to ask how my sister was doing and to encourage her to call with questions. She sent me links to resources for cancer patients and suggested questions we should ask the doctors. Any time I e-mailed her with a question or concern, she got right back to me with a detailed answer. Since neither I nor my sister has the kind of scientific background and medical knowledge Jhumki had, this was extremely helpful."

Sarah said she was in awe of how much effort Jhumki put into advocating for herself and other cancer patients, even as she kept up with her demanding work schedule, and managed the debilitating side effects of her treatment. Every time Jhumki saw Sarah, she would take the time to ask about her sister, listen intently, and offer advice—no matter how bad she was feeling.

34. HEARTBREAK

"It was the best of times, it was the worst of times..." So begins Charles Dickens's timeless classic, *A Tale of Two Cities*. Had he been Jhumki's biographer though, Mr. Dickens might have launched this book with a slightly modified opening:

"The best of times were the worst of times..."

Out of every cataclysm in her life Jhumki soared with a broken wing. Following every phase of untrammeled pleasure, she suffered a blinding debacle. As 2007 waned, Jhumki was forced to make an unexpected and agonizing choice.

E-mail from Jhumki Basu, Oct 17, 2007

Dear friends and family

So I've come to some realizations, perhaps because of the pressing need to make some decisions that have been hanging over my head for months, and the need to start moving forward instead of hoping for things that aren't going to happen.

Though we haven't flat out said it, I think Alexander and I are really not going to have kids, biological or adopted. I just don't think he can envision it working, and I don't think the sacrifices and challenges are worth it to him right now. The only reason, at heart, that I think he would have kids is to make me happy, and that's a bad reason—given the prospects of my being sick and dying in the next 2-3 years (yes! this is really likely), he'd be their primary care giver.

I also think some other things aren't going to happen.

I don't think we're ever going to get a dog or really even an aquarium. I think the responsibility of caring for living things, other than plants, is too much of a leap of faith for us because there is a good chance Alexander will be left caring for these things in addition to likely being our primary earner and the person on whom our health insurance depends. And what if they die? Given all the emphasis on dying, I don't think I could handle a zebra fish dying right now! I also don't think we are going to get a place outside the city or ever have a garden. There are questions like: How can we search for a place when I can't walk half the time? What happens when the plumbing breaks or the house floods, and simultaneously I can't walk and need medical attention?

All of this is hard on several fronts:

1. *I think I am the one who will have to say these things out loud because Alexander doesn't want to say them because he's afraid of hurting me. But it seems pretty clear that this is where we are heading by default, and the default process is very hard for me because I want some certainty, so I feel a need to say some of these things out loud.*

2. *However, such decisions mean admitting to give up on a lot of things that I care about a lot, and want in my life.*

3. *These realities mean embracing a decision-making process predicated on the belief that I will not be around long and will not be too healthy while I'm around. I think this belief is grounded in reality, but it's very hard for me to start living life with this philosophy. Of course, with regard to things that are about me, I don't have to embrace this philosophy; otherwise, I wouldn't know what I would get up and do every morning! So I'm going to still work on my book, train for triathlons, still apply to be an astronaut, still develop research projects, still support schools and kids and teachers. But around*

the joint decisions, I think we are choosing a "realistic" philosophy.

I've been very upset these past several days, in tears all the time, unusually distracted from work and unproductive. But perhaps this is just part of the process of facing reality rather than constantly fighting against it. I think it's going to take a while to get my mind around a new reality, and at least I know myself better than in times past, and know that I get solace from things like helping kids with college applications and helping teachers plan pyrotechnic demos that engage kids. But I think it's going to be a hard several weeks to months for me, and the process feels lonely and a bit private, because I just don't think Alexander is as deeply upset by these decisions and this mindset as I am. He's better at avoiding and getting on with what's normal, and frankly he can do all these things if I'm not around; he has time. And my parents are so upset by these same things that they don't provide much solace for me.

Just writing to all of you, so you know, because sometimes it's so hard to talk about all of this without just dissolving in a puddle of tears. I'm also writing because I value what you think and say more than the general world of acquaintances I have, so please feel free to write, but please feel no pressure!

So now I have to add that crafting this e-mail just made me say that we're not going to have kids, dog, house, to Alexander on the telephone. And he agreed about the kids and said we might consider dog and house, but I really, really don't think that when it comes down to it, it's going to happen. So that's the update.

I have talked to Paul Prokop about a few things:

1. *I've been feeling totally negative about myself and my life these past several days, wondering why I*

should get up in the morning and do anything 'cause I feel like I suck at everything and feel like a burden on other people and that if I died now versus in two years it wouldn't make a difference. We talked a lot about what are realistic goals and to believe that I can have a circle of influence but beyond that I can't single-handedly increase the number of urban students in scientist positions in just a year, for example. He also said that he does like talking to me and that other people care that I'm around. Which sounds stupid, but some of his concrete examples help. I feel really doubtful sometimes.

2. *We discussed that it might be helpful to me to make a concrete decision about kids sooner rather than later. He feels as if I'm putting the meaningfulness of my life on hold in anticipation of this decision. He said I'm going to have to see the world differently from two options:*

   a) kids—meaningful.

   b) no kids—not really meaningful, living the good life in New York to no purpose.

But that's exactly how I feel, and it's going to take a lot of work on my part to feel that my life is meaningful without the idea of a family. And given that time is short, it's better I start making that transition sooner rather than later, if I have to do it. Also, lots of other things are on hold: aquarium, garden, dog, house, really anything that isn't the status quo. But he said I also have to understand his perspective, where anything beyond what we have now doesn't feel like it has much value and is just more responsibility for him, especially if I'm not functioning at 100 percent. So we have to make some compromises about doing things I want to do that I might never get to do if I don't do them soon and having some stability and normalcy in our lives without huge additional stress.

We talked about what it means for me, in the short-run, to not have kids. I think I'm going to have to take some time off. I just can't make that decision and wake up the next day and write papers as if everything is normal and it's just a decision to check off a list. I think I might go to Seattle for a couple of weeks. Paul said we could talk about doing a little Japanese ceremony that people do when they have misfortunes or something that makes it feel as if it isn't a trivial decision. I went to their place for a few weeks when Shanti and SNA died, and I think I might do the same if we make this kid decision on the "not having kids" end. It's going to make me really upset, it already has, and I have to figure out whether my life can feel as meaningful or whether I just have to accept that it won't be. I also have to figure out what of all the many things I want to do, that I feel strongly about, and what I'm willing to put aside as impossible, given constraints of medical issues. I might work while I'm there, but I think I might ask for a "leave of absence" from meetings, etc. I think, in general, or maybe just tied to this kid decision, I need a bit of space to feel better about myself. I've been in tears every day since Sunday, and I'm finding it hard to be motivated or care.

Class went well last night, and that sort of thing helps. But I'm not doing too well overall emotionally, I think.

Love,

Jhumki.

When they had decided to freeze embryos a year earlier, Alexander and Jhumki were thinking that they would transform the embryos into a child (or children), if and when her health improved. Between July and October, Jhumki's scans and blood

271

test results became progressively better—in fact, significantly better than they had been before the embryos were frozen.

After their honeymoon, Jhumki wanted to move forward with having a child from the embryos through a surrogate mother. When Alexander said no, her world crashed. The shock at the possibility of never having children was immense. The anguish was searing as she wrote, and worse, she had to face the situation with hands tied behind her back. When Alexander chose not to move forward with the embryos, Jhumki had no other option to have a child, not even adoption. Her medical condition would eliminate their candidacy at an adoption agency.

On his part, Alexander was worried about the possibility of Jhumki's health deteriorating. He was disinclined to become a parent in case that happened. He was concerned about his ability to care for Jhumki while looking after a new baby. He also worried about the hereditary aspects of breast cancer, though Jhumki's genetic-transmission tests had been clearly negative.

Alexander is a logical person. He could address their lives and their situation analytically and scientifically on a long timeline. Jhumki, on the other hand, was driven by the unstoppable maternal force of a robust woman who was of childbearing age and desired children—an instinctive urge that defies logic. She was also driven by her ever-nearing horizon.

Friends in whom Jhumki confided told us that she became inconsolable when it was clear Alexander would not change his mind and her child would not be born. In the end she sent her friends and family the above e-mail and tried to accept and live with a situation she could not transform.

But, as she told her mother and me a few days before she died, she hoped that one day, even after she was gone, there would be a child.

35. THE TIGER HUNT

Alexander and Jhumki prepared to visit India over Christmas. They would see historic fortresses and palaces. With Ranga, Radha, and me, they would visit Corbett Park and try to spot tigers. There would be a reception in Kolkata. Radha and I, already arrived in India, were excited about introducing our son-in-law to people who had not made it to the wedding.

And then came worrisome news.

The trend in Jhumki's blood markers reversed direction. A new scan indicated that lesions in her liver had grown once again in number and size. Cancer was suspected in the lungs. Bone, though, was stable and unchanged.

Conclusion: after seven months, Xeloda/Avastin[18] had stopped working. The cancer had mutated, and it was time for a new regimen. But before that could happen, a three-week hiatus was required.

Bearing the bad news came a cheery voice.

"Three weeks, Baba!" Jhumki said over the phone line to India. "That's great. I don't have to worry on the trip."

I couldn't think of a single thing to say.

Jhumki and Alexander arrived in Delhi and stayed just six houses from the park in Saket where Shanti and SNA had lost their lives. Ranga was with them as they piled into the home of a close friend from our Delhi days, Jasjit Mangat, and his wife,

---

[18] On Nov 19, 2011, Jhumki's 34th birthday, the U.S. Food and Drug Administration revoked approval of Avastin for breast cancer treatment in view of its severe side effects. (Bloomberg Business Week, Nov 18, 2011)

Preet Dhillon. With them, Jhumki toured the monuments of the ancient city and slowly strolled past Shanti's apartment thinking of what might have been.

Then Radha and I arrived from Kolkata and the five of us drove the 150 miles to Corbett Park, one of a chain of Indian wildlife sanctuaries set up to protect the Bengal Tiger. At Jhumki's bidding we had booked the remotest accommodation possible, deep inside the jungle.

"What if you need medical help?" I had ventured to ask her then.

"I need medical help all the time, Baba. Let's go see a tiger, okay?"

Six hours after leaving Delhi, our vehicle followed a rough gravel path through dense deciduous forest until it disappeared into a wide, fast-flowing river with pebble-covered banks.

"Ramganga, sir," our driver declared, pointing at the river in case we had missed it.

Jhumki looked around and her eyes lit up like stars.

Coming ponderously along the riverside in our direction, with reeds protruding on either side of its trunk, was a big elephant. Behind it I saw a second pachyderm, knee-deep in shallow water, busy devouring vegetation.

Someone produced a ladder, we climbed aboard, and the two friendly animals ferried us across the river in golden evening sunlight. Sitting back-to-back on mattresses behind the *mahouts,* we swayed along on an overgrown track through dense forest. After an hour we arrived at the resort to find we had the entire place to ourselves. Other travelers might have thought it would be too cold and stayed away, but our tents had radiant heating and running hot water in attached baths. What luxury in comparison to our trekking trips! We relaxed on deck chairs, sipped gins and tonic, and munched on onion *pakoras*, while watching the sun go down in multi-hued flames. Dinner was excellent. Secure in the knowledge that the perimeter fence was electrified, we went to bed.

A distant commotion in the silence of the night woke me up. But as nothing noteworthy happened, I went back to sleep. Early the next morning a waiter knocked on our door with tea, biscuits, and the thrilling news that a tiger had killed a cow in the neighboring hamlet.

We assembled for breakfast and were animatedly discussing this development when the resident forest ranger arrived. The previous evening when he stopped by, I had told him about our Sundarbans tiger experiences, so he knew we were cat lovers.

"Well, Dipak-*ji?*" the ranger asked taking a noisy sip of tea. "When will you be seeing it?"

"Seeing what?"

"The cow, sir."

"The dead cow?"

"Yes, sir."

"I see."

A silence ensued while I rubbed my nose doubtfully.

"Where is this dead cow?" I asked after a bit.

"In the forest, sir." The ranger pointed vaguely at the trees around our resort fencing. "We can all go and see. Now itself, if sir wishes."

I thought carefully while Ranga and Jhumki watched me intently. They knew the score. They had read Jim Corbett's *Man-Eaters of Kumaon,* the definitive work on *Panthera tigris,* cover to cover. They knew how dangerous to human beings wild tigers can be. We were actually *in* the Kumaon, a Himalayan region made famous by Mr. Corbett. Alexander, not completely sure what was going on, looked at us quizzically. Radha dozed in the pleasant sunshine. A copy of *Man-Eaters of Kumaon* was open on her lap.

In the jungle-covered mangrove islands of the Sundarbans

where Anudip operates, one never steps off a boat to go into the forest—that is, if one wishes to return alive. Fishermen, honey gatherers, woodcutters, and poachers often do not return alive. Hungry tigers act blindingly fast when food is in the offing. 'Man=food' is the Sundarbans tigers' simple thought process.

And here was a guy, a forest ranger to boot, offering to take us to a tiger's kill as a sort of tourist attraction! Hadn't he read Corbett? Didn't he know tigers lie up close to defend their kills? Ridiculous! The man must be mad.

We went to see the kill—all of us except Alexander, who couldn't understand all the bother about a dead cow and preferred his afternoon siesta.

We traveled by elephant for a couple of miles into the jungle until we came to a steep hillside. Dismounting on a large and convenient rock, our ranger marched straight into the trees. The rest of us—Jhumki, Ranga, Radha, and I in that order—followed him in single file.

Dear reader, please be aware this is *not* recommended procedure in tiger country. Corbett says so. Sundarbans anecdotes affirm that the last person in single file is lunch. And I was it, that last person, heroically securing the rear, letting women and children go first. Even though it was quite cold in the shadow of trees, we became warm after twenty minutes of uphill walking. Suddenly, with a shock, I realized, in the protective manner of Sundarbans woodcutters with their axes, I was carrying my rolled-up jacket against my jugular vein—the point where tigers sink their fangs.

I know. I know. My thoughts were gruesome. I couldn't understand how Radha and the kids could blithely follow the confounded ranger deeper and deeper into the jungle. No trails, no tracks, no cell phone signal, just up hill and around trees and rocks, any of which could be a perfect site for an ambush.

And then, without warning, we were upon the cow. It was a

young, black animal, quite dead, lying on its side with its eyes open, fang marks you know where. No part of it was eaten. I looked around furtively. Any one of the surrounding clumps of undergrowth could conceal the brute. Unobtrusively, I bunched us up closer.

If you are expecting a climactic end to this story, you will be disappointed. The drama was all in my mind. I took a picture of the unfortunate cow and urged everyone to beat a retreat. I am pleased to report we made it back to our elephants safely, and twenty minutes later we were back at the resort.

"That was cool, Baba!" Jhumki pronounced, and went to wake her husband.

We had tea. Later we rode the elephants through the jungle and along riverbanks. We saw deer and monkeys of several varieties but no cats, striped or spotted. The next day, at the outset of the drive back, at Dhikala village which borders the park, we found everyone agog with excitement. A bus had hit and killed a tiger in the night!

Oh, dear, I thought, another precious feline down the slippery slope to extinction. Was the casualty the very same tiger that had killed "our" cow? And was it why things had been quiet when we visited its kill? I will never know.

Much later, while reliving our tramp through the forest to the tiger's prey, it struck me that it was Jhumki who had led the way lockstep with the ranger. Upon dismounting from her elephant and before I could caution her, she was into the trees. The rest of us had followed. She knew there was real danger. Was her intrepidity natural? Did the proximity of death no longer cause fear? Did the image of a snarling tiger fade before the visage of cancer?

I will never know.

ഇ

Radha and I returned to Kolkata. Ranga went back to the U.S. Jhumki and Alexander flew to Udaipur, a city of spectacular palaces and lakes. Alas, there they both came down with a nasty stomach virus. Jhumki recovered enough to see some sights on their last day, but Alexander barely made it to the airport for the flight out.

When in Kolkata, Radha and I usually stay at the historic Tollygunge Club and enjoy its many amenities. But Jhumki wasn't falling for the fancy club stuff. Her favorite aunt, my father's sister, Jhumki's Pia Didu, and her husband, Choto Dadu (little grandpa), who officiated as master of ceremonies at her wedding, have a house in Kolkata's Salt Lake locality. Jhumki was determined that she and Alexander would stay with them. Her decision no doubt was influenced by the prowess of Shefali, Pia's diminutive cook. Many a recipe has Jhumki extracted from Shefali's mind-library by patiently having her qualify "fry nicely" and "add a *good* bit" and "when it looks *just* done." While at Salt Lake, Jhumki liked to go shopping at the neighborhood bazar with old Jagadish, Pia's housekeeper for over forty years.

Jhumki and Alexander's reception was held at the Saturday Club in central Kolkata on a lovely, sunny afternoon. Friends and relatives, young and old, came to check out the much-vaunted Greek entrant to the Basu family. Jhumki had several cousins in the city. Three of them had traveled all the way to California for the wedding. For the youngsters it was a historic reunion filled with jollity. My Aunts Biva and Shobhana, aged ninety-two and eighty-six respectively, who had seen a lot of Jhumki when she was child in the eighties, were overjoyed when she spent quality time with them and explained her work. Later they shed tears with Radha. Why couldn't they, living well past their allotted lifetimes, exchange destinies with one so young, so cherished, so full of the promise of life?

And then the roller coaster of fate began its journey down.

Radha's big sister Viji had been integral to our every happy occasion. She was a survivor. She had fought off breast cancer, diabetes, and heart disease, enduring crisis after crisis to keep going. At the time of Jhumki's wedding we noticed that Viji was getting uncharacteristically irritated and ascribed it to stress. Afterward, at the homes of her sons—Preetham in California and Nandu in England—she suffered fainting spells and memory lapses. An MRI in Bristol revealed a large brain tumor, and the subsequent biopsy indicated glioblastoma, its most malignant form.

Viji never recovered from that biopsy. She became increasingly confused and slipped into a coma. Nandu and a physician from Apollo Hospitals in India transported her from Bristol to Chennai. During the next four months Radha and I visited her at Apollo, as did her sons and daughters-in-law. Vardhini was with her when Viji passed away.

It was December 29th.

Alexander was to fly the next day to Greece and we encouraged Jhumki to leave the depressing environment and go with him. But Jhumki was firm. She *would* be there for her mother at Viji Aunty's funeral in Chennai.

36. BEING NOTICED

In January 8, 2008, Radha sent this e-mail to friends and family:

We are back from India but not home yet. Yesterday was a difficult day at MSKCC. Jhomi is stoic but knows that the next treatment may limit her lifestyle. We are terribly worried BUT determined to fight every step and keep at it as long as there are options. One thing that Dr. Hudis said that was mildly positive is that she looks and appears clinically better than 12 months ago when he first saw her.

After I wrote the above, we have decided on Gemzar as the chemo agent and Jhumki started treatment last night. It was a painful infusion and she became distraught and jittery, perhaps due to Decadron, the steroid administered against infection. She slept ok but we will watch her today, she might have a fever.

Poor baby, she wants to live her life amidst all the rigors and side effects and the uncertainty of treatment. She still plans to go to Seattle to visit the Prokops on Friday, then to San Diego on Monday for a NARST conference where she is presenting, and then come home for a week. She is really looking forward to seeing all of you before starting the semester.

Dipak and I are living our lives around her needs. She wants to come home once a month, and go down to see Ranga in Southern California or up to Seattle more often.

Love you all a lot. Your love and support makes us strong to keep fighting.

During one of her treatment days at MSKCC, Jhumki met a young chemo suite nurse named Morgan, who could find a vein in her wrist right away without poking around and hurting her unnecessarily. Morgan had the great quality to look her distressed patients in the eye when she spoke and feel their suffering as they anguished through chemo. She loved her job and was extremely good at it. Morgan and Jhumki became friends, and Jhumki always asked her to perform intravenous infusions on her.

Our daughter spent many hours in the waiting area at MSKCC when she could have gotten work done over the Internet. Appalled by the sight of seriously sick patients thumbing listlessly through old magazines and making one another even more depressed, she wrote to management and demanded that they install free Wi-Fi for patients' use. MSKCC agreed to her request and everyone became a bit happier.

How she got through the activities of that spring semester— teaching two courses at NYU, conducting research at far-flung boroughs, taking long subway rides in icy weather, applying for grants, publishing papers, keeping up with friends, working cancer hotlines for other sufferers—I will never comprehend. Was she racing away from shadows that were coming closer? Did the finality of being unable to have children drive her to drown herself mercilessly in work? Was she able to tolerate the physical suffering of cancer because the emotional pain went deeper still? Was she able to devote herself relentlessly to serving others, despite the fact that every fiber cried out to stop and rest, because resting would mean reflection on loss?

In March she was hospitalized with pain and high fever, symptoms that are always worrisome during chemo. She developed a blood clot in her arm, and her white blood cell count dropped. Pale and weak in a hospital bed, Jhumki raged about how cancer treatment was wreaking havoc on her work schedule. The current regimen was abandoned and Taxol, a venerable but toxic cancer drug, became her primary therapy. Scans in June showed that her lungs were clear, the liver lesions were reduced or gone, the bone was unchanged, and her blood markers were down.

Jhumki had a reprieve, but at a cost. Her hair was gone, as were her eyebrows. When she went out she wore one of her fashionable hats or classy bandanas. In the evenings her head ached and needed rubbing as she lay, spent, on the living-room sofa. Her legs and feet ached from neuropathic pain. She applied palliative cream to the soles of her feet and wore crocs.

And then, Jhumki's oscillating destiny went straight from nadir to zenith and pulled her out of misery.

> *Good Morning Radha,*
>
> *I am delighted to tell you that Jhumki has been selected as the Castilleja Distinguished Alumnae Award recipient for her outstanding and innovative contributions to education. I understand that she is planning to attend the Centennial Symposium on Saturday, May 3rd in Palo Alto and we were hoping to present the award at lunch. Head of School, Joan Lonergan suggested that you would know how best to contact her to give her this special news. We would love to have you present too.*
>
> *Many thanks,*
>
> *Maggie Ely Pringle '71*
>
> *Alumnae Director*

This news broke amid a flurry of activity. There were just ten days to go before the Castilleja award ceremony, and Jhumki didn't even know about it. Radha was in India on a work trip when Maggie's e-mail arrived. I happened to be in New York and the sunshine came back to her tired face when I told Jhumki.

"But, *omigosh,* Baba! I've got so much going on . . ."

As she said that, I could see from her expression how proud she felt. I knew wild horses would not keep her away from beloved Casti. She moved staff meetings, doctors' appointments, lesson planning, triathlon practice, and heaven knows what else, to make it to California for the weekend.

Mommy, desolate in Kolkata, would miss the award.

Jhumki's flight arrived at SFO after midnight and I met her at arrivals. From a distance she gave me a brave and weary wave. I took her backpack, gave her a hug, and managed to get her into the car before she fell asleep.

The following morning the April sun shone brightly on Castilleja Green, around which Jhumki had spent six rich years. Spring flowers smiled from the periphery. She wore a sleeveless dress with pink and red floral patterns, matching belt and hat. I took her picture in the thriving garden she had started as a science teacher nine years earlier, and which is now formally dedicated to her memory.

Centenary celebrations were underway in the main auditorium when we arrived. Condi Rice had sent a video message from Washington. Mark Hurd, CEO of Hewlett Packard, was speaking. At the entrance we met Doris Mourad, and the two science teachers caught up on news. Then we sat down and listened to the speeches. It was hot inside and Jhumki took off her hat.

At noon we walked over to the well-remembered school cafeteria for the award luncheon. Joan Lonergan, the school principal, was there with Doris and several members of Castilleja Alumnae Association. Anjelika Deogirikar, association president, read the commemoration and presented Jhumki with the memento. I was taking pictures when I realized Jhumki wasn't wearing her hat. I was about to remind her, but something made me stop.

Jhumki did wear a hat after that memorable day—but only if she needed to keep out the cold.

In early 2008 Jhumki applied for a research fellowship from the Knowles Science Teaching Foundation.

KSTF's programs support outstanding early-career scholars who conduct research to gain insight into the complexities and challenges of preparing and supporting high school science and mathematics teachers. The executive director of KSTF, Angelo Collins, is a forceful and deceptively motherly-looking lady. She had much to say about the process of Jhumki's selection for the coveted fellowship in competition with a "goodly" number of others.

"Jhumki's submission was one of four that were ranked as fundable that year," Angelo told Maithreyi during her interview. "After determining this, I spoke with her several times because her task was to summarize her entire research project in one page for our Board of Trustees. These people are not educators, not teachers, not scientists, but financial and businesspeople. She sent me the first draft and I told her it was absolutely beautiful, but my Board will read the first sentence and say, 'What does she mean by democratic pedagogy? This woman doesn't know what she's talking about because she's using all this jargon, and it's not going to work.'

"In one of our conversations Jhumki said, 'I've finally got it!'

"She was going to write it for a grandmother or an aunt, I think. And once she got that idea, the one-pager came out just perfect. Thereafter, the Board had quite a serious debate about the final two proposals. Both were concerned with helping underprivileged children by providing them with really strong teachers. It was the quality of Jhumki's one-page presentation and the clarity of her writing style that persuaded the Board this was the proposal it would fund."

Here is the one-pager:

How New Science Teachers Interpret and Enact Democratic Science Pedagogy

Implications for Teacher Induction, Development and Retention and Student Learning

Student empowerment in science depends on teacher empowerment. Retaining qualified science teachers is of major concern in America's urban public schools if we are to address the grave challenges that urban, minority students face in gaining access to STEM disciplines and science education. However, limited research exists on factors supporting the induction, development and retention of science teachers in early stages of their careers.

In this study, I introduce the idea of democratic science pedagogy as a teaching philosophy and practice designed to address issues faced by students historically disenfranchised from a high-quality science education and, in turn, important for developing and retaining teachers. The study is innovative in that it will explore how urban science teachers theorize and practice democratic science pedagogy, how their experiences connect with professional development and satisfaction, and how their practices influence student learning and engagement in science.

The body of the KSTF proposal contains Jhumki's vision of empowering science teachers to engage *all* underserved youth in science through democratic pedagogy. It is written in no-nonsense style and with full academic rigor. Angela Calabrese Barton acted as a referee in support of Jhumki's application. Her letter to KSTF read:

Dr. Basu holds the stance, and I believe rightly so, that many youth from low-income, urban backgrounds have an interest in and a desire to succeed in science, but that teachers struggle with the strategies and tools they might deploy in support of real student learning. Her study should offer teachers and curriculum developers with new insights into how one might better reach a population of students so often left on the margins of science education.

Dr. Basu is one of the most driven and rigorous young scholars I know. Dr. Basu is an experienced teacher, and draws extensively upon this personal practical knowledge side by side with the literature as she seeks to understand youth learning in school contexts. Indeed, I believe that Jhumki has a remarkable future ahead of her in academia. She is just the kind of person that Knowles Foundation would be pleased to have as a Young Scholar.

After Jhumki received the KSTF award, she spoke with Angelo about the budget for the fellowship. Only at this point did Angelo learn about the cancer.

"She wanted to know if her illness was going to change anything," Angelo recalled. "I told her no. We were interested in the quality of her work and how it fit with our mission. So there was no problem at all.

"You will smile," Angelo continued, "when I tell you what I told Jhumki. 'You have written into this two-year grant, five years of work. You cannot possibly do everything.' She was going to do some survey work. She was going to trial the surveys and design teaching modules. She was going to publish them. She was going to author a book. I told her, 'Jhumki, in two years as a junior professor, you cannot possibly do it all.'"

The astonishing thing is that Jhumki did it all.

In eight months.

E-mail from Jhumki Basu to her parents, July 11, 2008

So I wanted to tell you that things are sort of good at work, despite all the stupid cancer stuff:

- *3 grants supporting 3 doctoral students*
- *7 papers published, 4 are independent research, 2 reviews, 2 in the pipeline for this summer*
- *got good course evaluations for the semester, despite hospitalization, etc.*
- *got a perfect 5 score from the undergrads I teach*
- *things are good at SDL with respect to research, and I'm starting at another school close to our house*
- *thinking about the book prospectus and laying foundations for it with the article writing and the new doc students*

Good, right?

Good? It was the understatement of the millennium. These were fantastic achievements.

As the year progressed, five of Jhumki's academic submissions were published:

1. Basu, S.J. (2008). Powerful learners and critical agents: The goals of five urban Caribbean youth in a conceptual physics classroom. *Science Education, 92(2), 252–277.*

2. Basu, S.J. (2008). How students design and enact physics lessons: Five immigrant Caribbean youth and the cultivation of student voice. *Journal of Research in Science Teaching, 45(8).*

3. Basu, S.J. (2008). Empowering communities of research and practice by conducting research for change and including participant voice in reflection on research. *Cultural Studies of Science Education.*

With her colleagues at Steinhardt:

4. Milne, C., Kirch, S., Basu, S.J., Leou, M. and Fraser-Abder, P. (2008). Understanding conceptual change: Connecting and questioning. *Cultural Studies of Science*

Education. (online publication Feb 2008).

With Neil and Donya, her students at SDL, and Angie:

5. Basu, S.J., Calabrese Barton, A., Locke, D. and Clairmont, N. Developing a framework for critical physics agency through case study. *Cultural Studies of Science Education.* (online publication June 2008).

In 2008, in addition to KSTF, Jhumki received two grants, the Rudin and Petri Fellowships. She decided to utilize all the money to fund four NYU doctoral students under her guidance. One of the four, Frank Signorello, worked at the New York Hall of Science, where he set up experiments for droves of visiting school kids.

"Jhumki was very open to everything I threw at her vis-à-vis ideas about the way that I teach," said Frank. "She espoused many of those methods: ideas of reform-minded pedagogy, democratic ideals, giving students voice, giving them choice in what they learn and how they learn. They come to the Hall of Science for free. We don't tell them what to do. They can play. It's guided play. They can take a workshop."

Jhumki was receptive to Frank's ideas. She suggested that her doctoral students incorporate methods that were used in Frank's informal techniques into a formal classroom environment.

"The one thing I really enjoyed as I was working with Jhumki," Frank added, "was she wanted us to be equals. But I would look to her for experience. I was always very in awe of all the experience she had at a very young age because I was older than her!"

৵

The world was paying attention to Jhumki's crusade. Through academic neglect, territorial politics, and parental apathy, kids in urban American schools were increasingly being left behind.

Neil Clairmont (above)

Donya Locke graduates
from Lehman College (R)

In the Sundarbans with Radha

Clifford Hudis   Susan and George Remsberg

With Alexander (above)

Wedding pictures (below and right)

Castilleja Distinguished Alumni Award

Mary Brabeck and John Sexton
at NYU Reception

Keynote Address at School for
Democracy and Leadership

Maithreyi Nandakumar Interviewing SDL Teachers

Alexander, Rob, Radha, Vardhini, Preetham, Jhumki, Ranga and Dipak
at Point St. Catherine, Gabon

Jane Goodall (center) with Sci-Ed Fellows and staff of Jhumki Basu Foundation at Sci-Ed Innovators Symposium & Expo February 11, 2011

Parents, schools, school boards, and governments were discouraging science either overtly or implicitly. Most science teachers in under-resourced New York schools were untrained in science. Young science teachers with dynamic ideas were the first to be laid off because of state budget crunches. America was losing the scientific innovations that had made it great. Students from affluent families—those able to afford private education—and foreign students were filling the demand for scientists in corporations and universities while inner-city youth languished in an unending cycle of poverty.

A dying educator was saying:

> *Rise up, America!*
>
> *The flower of your youth is fading. See your lost children. They are your future. Love them. Respect them. They have the solution. They are the solution. Here is the way.*
>
> *Give them a good education. Give them all a good education. Bring out their best. It is their birthright.*
>
> *They are my legacy.*

37. A VARIABLE SUMMER

Good morning, Mommy!" came a cheerful voice on a transcontinental call.

"Jhomi, why are you so happy?" Mommy asked suspiciously.

"Oh, nothing. I'm just happy. Maybe because I'm with Alexander."

But Mommy would not be sold the Brooklyn Bridge.

"You *didn't!*" she said with growing incredulity. *"Did* you?"

No reply.

"You ran it?"

"Ran what, Mommy?"

Jhumki's voice was ever so innocent.

"You ran the triathlon!"

It turned out our daughter was calling with her neuropathic feet still in the shallow waters of a cold upstate New York lake, where swimming, the third and last part of the Pawling Triathlon, had just completed. The other parts of the race, running and cycling, had finished earlier. Jhumki was overjoyed because, even in her debilitated state, she had actually completed the event. Earlier, Radha had forbidden her to participate on account of her health. Quite naturally, Jhumki completed the event and *then* called to tell her about it.

Our daughter restricted complaints about her illness to their adverse impact on her work. On just a few occasions did she break down and lament, and that only with a few people—her mother, Alexander, or friends like Paul, Kritika, James, and Jeremy Just once in a while did the suppressed frustration, misery, and hopelessness burst forth in a childish cry for justice—as in this message to Alexander.

Stressaroonie.

I am the biggest loser in the whole world.

I am a big loser.

Why can't everything be like it was when we first met?

And how come everyone is having a family?

What about us? I'm only meant for dying?

Why is our life so screwed up?

I don't want to have cancer anymore.

I want it to stop being like this.

Why can't they fix it? And why is my life a big torture?

Why couldn't the hormone therapy work, and then I could live a long time and have a normal life and have a family with you?

Why isn't anything working?

Why am I so cursed? It's not fair. I love you and want to be with you and I can't be 'cause of this shitty situation. And it just doesn't stop.

What can I do to make things better?

Why can't we have a nice family like Celeste?

Are you angry at me?

Are you disappointed?

You married me when I was pretty and going to do all these things with you. And now I'm not.

I want to get better.

Why is this happening? I'm only 30 years old. Nobody in my family got this.

Everybody thinks I'm a loser and good for nothing anymore.

Are you mad at me?

Am I doing my job badly?

Is it going to be scary to get sick and die?

Is it going to happen soon?

What's going to make me less afraid?

When we got married in Greece, I never thought this was going to happen. Not even once. I had such a small lump, and the doctors never said anything about metastatic cancer and how yucky it was. What if it's in my stomach in these scans? Then am I going to die of starvation?

You're worried?

Do you think it's going to get better, and our lives are going to be normal again, and it's just a bad period? And in twenty years, we'll look back on it and have grown from it? And we'll have kids and a family?

I wish they'd find a cure for my kind of cancer, not just Herceptin and hormone therapy, but for me too. Why are they so dumb? They get so much money, and there's no cure and no new drugs and nothing.

I'm only 30.

I'm little.

Through the early part of summer 2008, while Taxol held the killer at bay, Radha and I suffered no illusion that it would last for long. Inside our daughter, cancer cells and chemo antibodies were in tumultuous battle. She was now on her third regimen. The drugs were working for lesser durations, a clear and expected warning sign. Long-term toxicity of chemotherapy was beginning to cirrhose the liver. The literature says that after the third treatment regimen, things don't usually go well. Soon it would be two years from the diagnosis of metastasis, the average survival period. When I thought of this, my heart beat madly. A few times Radha broke down and wept uncontrollably.

"Why *her*?" she would ask. "She's never done anything but good for others. It's a curse on the family."

Then the two of us would regroup and steel ourselves and close our minds to a life without Jhumki. That actually wasn't hard to do. It really was impossible to think of life, of a world, from which Jhumki was absent. A blank white wall would show in my mind's eye when my thoughts went there.

Once, after Jhumki had spent a weekend at home while I was traveling, Radha sent me this e-mail:

> *Kissed her au revoir. She said that the weekend was really nice. How to share with you the emotions of the last three days? The joy and awe of the special child that we have created and the choking sorrow that this unique, unmatched, vivacious, independent, unwavering, silly, tough, childish, brilliant, nimble, determined, hard-working, tender, loving, full-of-life, young angel could be lost to us and to the world. I would give everything dear and my own life to make her better. I do not know if my tears are for the joy of having her or the thought of losing her. She is truly a blessing. Just wanted this weekend to keep on and never end.*

๛

Jhumki and Alexander decided to distance themselves from New York for a while and spend the summer of 2008 in the San Francisco Bay Area.

During the subsequent days, while Alexander worked from a rented Palo Alto apartment, Jhumki spent most of the day at home with us, ensconced in her usual spot at the kitchen counter, where she had once grumbled through grading Casti papers. She watched her mother cook her favorite dishes as she typed up the latest research paper. At ground level Mishti pulled on her pajama legs for a ball to be thrown. Often Jhumki went out with the dog accompanying her and performed yoga exercises in the open air. Now and then she took a break to read Pushkin or Maya Angelou. At other times we would find her stretched out on a sofa with Mishti curled up on the floor below her, both sound asleep.

That summer, when Jhumki and Alexander were away in

different places, Mishti sent Jhumki an e-mail message. In our ultimate geeky family, even the pooch has an e-mail account.

> *Dear Jhumki,*
>
> *I miss you. I hate my food. I looked in your room and under the bed and pulled the covers off but you were not there.*
>
> *I got so mad at your parents for sending you away that I threw up on the stairs while people were around.*
>
> *There! You better come back now.*
>
> *Love,*
>
> *Mishti*

Mishti had copied Alexander on her doggy-blues message, and *boing!* came the reply.

> *Dear Jhumki,*
>
> *I miss you too. I hate my empty apartment. I looked in our room and under the bed and since you were not there, I decided not to make it.*
>
> *I got so mad at my work for keeping me from Chicago that I caused my program to run in loops.*
>
> *There! You better come back now.*
>
> *Dear Mishti,*
>
> *I hear your pain, woof, woof.*
>
> *Alexander*

38. A STELLAR DAY
IN BROOKLYN

How was Jhumki able to work so hard in the face of cancer? Nancy Gannon, Jhumki's principal at SDL, believed it was because Jhumki made her insane work ethic something matter-of-fact, something one just did.

"Her energy was only one part of it," Nancy said. "Jhumki had this humility that was really remarkable—her authenticity in the way she lived her life. She never sounded a false note. She wouldn't make a remark that later she couldn't stand by. It's really hard to live one's life like that."

On May 24, on a lovely spring day in Brooklyn, when the first batch of students graduated from SDL, Radha and I understood why Jhumki drove herself so hard.

We arrived at the school in Crown Heights as special invitees and were welcomed warmly. We looked around with pride as the auditorium filled with red-robed, mortar-boarded kids. Many came over to say hello and to give us a hug.

"Where's Ms. Jhumki?" they asked.

It was getting late. Where *was* Ms. Jhumki?

The auditorium was full when someone tapped on my shoulder, and there she stood, looking perfectly lovely. On her slight, straight-backed frame she wore a lacy white blouse, a flowery blue-and-white skirt, and white Crocs. Glasses gave her a nice schoolmarmish demeanor that was belied by a smile that wouldn't stop as she chatted and surveyed the festive hall.

The bedlam quieted, and Jhumki went onstage with the other guests, including Nancy Gannon, who was expecting her first child any day. Alexander took up a strategic position with his high-power camera.

The program featured the Honorable Darlene Mealy, council member of the City of Brooklyn, as keynote speaker. In no-nonsense language, Ms. Mealy spoke directly to the graduating class. She detailed how far they had come from the mean streets and declared how proud they should be of their accomplishments.

Yes!

SDL graduates had every reason in the world to be proud. Their achievements were simply phenomenal. Compared to their community's demographics, they were off the charts. The high school completion rate in the Crown Heights area of Brooklyn is 30%. The kids who attended ninth grade at SDL when it started were from the Crown Heights community. The class of 2008 had all but one student graduating, thus hitting a 95% high school completion rate.

Jhumki was an important factor in their success, but as Nancy has rightly pointed out, she did not do it alone. She was part of a team of teachers—young, smart, dedicated to their students, infused with a passion to try new teaching methods and new ways around the horrendous obstacles Crown Heights kids faced in just getting through the day. Reinforcing Nancy's view of teamwork, graduation levels at SDL have stayed in the nineties in the years after Jhumki left, a testament to the school's lasting commitment to new ways of teaching.

The students applauded Councilor Mealey for her advice, but it was abundantly clear whom they were waiting for. When Jhumki got to her feet, the audience went up in cheers. There were claps, whistles, and roars. She stepped to the podium and held both arms above her head. The megawatt grin connected to her groupies. The cheering intensified and subsided as Jhumki began to speak.

Good afternoon!

What an honor it is to speak to you today! Of all the things I have done in my life, the most rewarding is to look out at all of you and know that you have completed the many steps required of you to graduate.

While I am, of course, proud of you at this one moment, I am even more proud of and do remember the work you have completed to make it TO this moment: you have read and written, solved equations, risen to the challenge of a science fair over and over again, used art to speak for social justice, tackled a Change Project every year, tutored, interned, studied, and defended yourselves during Portfolio. Many of you have overcome many challenges in your personal lives to make it to today.

Earlier today, I asked some of you about concrete things you have achieved of which you are most proud. I want to tell you some of the things that you told me.

These are just a small sample of the many, many things you have achieved since you attended the School for Democracy and Leadership. I want each of you, in this moment, right now, to think of something you have accomplished of which you are proud and which has taken hard work. Pause. Picture this accomplishment in your mind.

When you face challenges in college or in your life, I want you to draw on this memory you have just chosen. It can be easy to feel defeated, as if you cannot do what people expect of you, easy to feel alone or unsupported, as if the challenges are large, and you are small.

But remember, in drawing on this memory, that you have a track record of achievement, evidence from your past that you can and will achieve. Remind yourself of your accomplishments regularly and know that you have developed the skills to face the challenges that life will bring.

I also want to tell you about some of the things you have done that have made me most happy to work with you.

One of my favorite memories is of when my tenth-grade advisory organized a talent show and raised enough money to take the whole group ice-skating, to play laser tag and enjoy Indian food. Do you remember? You came to my apartment and spent the day with me—I had such a feeling of solidarity with you and such a feeling that you could accomplish what you set your mind to—the talent show took organizing and public speaking, money management and creativity—and then you put the earnings to good use in ways that built your own community.

I have been especially proud of you at the yearly science fair, where you have defended your ideas to real scientists, laid out smelly experiments, and shown that you are explorers and scientists.

But I have particularly enjoyed working with you in one-on-one moments. Do you remember when you got stuck building a parallel circuit in my physics class and needed help or had trouble graphing an inequality so you came to my office? Some of you have come to NYU to visit me and apply for scholarships. Some of you have worked with me to teach your science class. And we've talked about colleges, Regents Exams, making up history essays, and sorting through disputes with friends and with teachers. It is in these small conversations with you that I have most appreciated you and learned the most about who you are— the great unique potential and strengths that each of you holds.

When I graduated from high school, Condoleezza Rice, the current secretary of state, spoke at my graduation. She is the first black woman to hold that office. She comes from a racially segregated community in the South and used her education to make herself one of the most powerful, accomplished women in the world. I want to end by telling you the three things she told me because they have served me well over the past fifteen years.

1. *The first advice that Condi Rice gave at my high school graduation was "Honor where you come from." As you know, my family is from India. My grandfather was the first open-heart surgeon in India, and I come from a family that believes in service. My parents were immigrants, like many of yours, and they built a life by drawing on their education. Where do you come from? Who has shaped you? What are the values of your families or your mentors? Take just a moment right now and think of these. Pause. Remember these as you move forward—to honor where you come from and to think back on the people who have supported you in getting to this point.*

2. *The second piece of advice that Condi Rice gave me is to "Find your passion." My passion has been working with you, being in this school, teaching science, because I believe that the best way to make decisions in the world is to look at data and evidence. When I have been tired or frustrated or disappointed, knowing that I have been doing the thing about which I am most passionate, has allowed me to keep working hard and achieve my goals. So you should make sure to find your passion, to seek classes and jobs and lives about which you are passionate, even if it takes you time to find these. You will do your best work in your life around what you are most passionate.*

3. *Finally, Condi Rice told me that whenever I failed, I should "Get up and try again." You already know how*

to do this, how to reapply for a scholarship when you have been denied, how to try for a higher score on a Regents Exam, how to come to school when you've had a tough morning at home or on the walk to school. It's something I've had to tell myself a great deal lately, while I've been treated for cancer. No matter how hard every day might be, I can start each new day by trying again, by aiming for the best in myself, by reaching for all that is possible.

The people in your life will continue to support you and believe in you. We will be around when you need a small conversation or a little help. But you are also at that important place where you are more independent than ever before and can shape the world in which you live. Congratulations on this important day when you should be most proud. But also remember that there is plenty left to achieve.

I think I speak for your teachers and families and mentors when I say that we expect the world of you in the years ahead. We expect you to be scholars, thoughtful parents, responsible partners, good friends to each other, and accomplished scientists, business owners, web designers, activists, and poets. We expect this because we are so proud of you and know how much you can accomplish. We expect you to find your passions and aim for success even when the road is difficult. We do expect you to be a source of positive change in the world.

Thank you for the honor of speaking to you on this special day, and congratulations again with the greatest admiration and love!

39. OF TEACHING AND TEACHERS

On a hot afternoon in July 2009, a little more than a year after she delivered her keynote address there, Maithreyi Nandakumar and I took the long subway ride to the School for Democracy and Leadership to talk to a group of teachers who had worked closely with Jhumki.

The resulting wide-ranging conversation was a no-holds-barred deep dive into the real work that goes on in tough schools in tough neighborhoods with tough kids from tough family situations. Like nothing else it opened up my mind to the significance of Jhumki's work, the crying need for it, and the esteem with which her colleagues held her as a friend and leader.

※

Maithreyi: *Will you please introduce yourselves?*

Maggie Schwirk: *I am currently a biology teacher, still at SDL. Jhumki was my mentor for three years.*

Emma Heeschen: *I was an English teacher the second year the school opened. Jhumki was my assistant principal and my mentor and one of the few people that I could turn to here in the first couple of years. Now I am the assistant principal at SDL.*

Max von Euw: *I am the eleventh-grade chemistry teacher. Jhumki was basically my savior that first year.*

Kelly Houston: *I am the twelfth-grade science teacher and also head of the science department. I knew Jhumki as my mentor for the last three years of my teaching here.*

Joanna Yip: *I taught at SDL during the first two years of its existence. Jhumki and I were on the original planning team with Nancy Gannon to write the grant to start SDL. I taught ninth-grade English, and Jhumki was our team leader the first year.*

Maithreyi: *What are your memories of meeting her for the first time?*

Max: *A genius—like, that was definitely without saying. The amount of good ideas and information that came out of her head was phenomenal. She had ten projects for me the first time I met her. Yeah, definitely, the science department as a whole agreed that she could come up with good projects like nobody's business.*

I was teaching living environment, which wasn't my forte, and starting with genetics. I was struggling because while I knew the information, it didn't mean I knew how to teach it. I went over to Jhumki's office, and we started to connect the idea to our students that genetics is not only a code but we are actually made of this stuff ourselves. Jhumki came up with this idea of drawing a picture, about going from a little DNA strand, attaching a human to it, and having a magnification of a skin cell just to connect the ideas.

She started explaining this idea, and she took a look at my face, and I was like, "How am I supposed to do this?" Then she helped me create a worksheet with tangible steps.

Maggie: *My first memory of Jhumki was when I came to interview at SDL and she was doing fifty million things. I remember sitting with her. It was her office plus advisory room. The first thing I remember was just how all the kids were flooding to the room and they all loved her, they adored her. I remember thinking, like,* Wow, if I can be a teacher like that, that the kids come to, ask questions, just go to for any info, or any troubles they have.

Emma: *In her office on my interview day, she was doing a million things. But she didn't look like she was doing a million things because she made everybody feel like they had her undivided attention. She was giving some kid a yogurt from the fridge and helping some other kid with an application and answering a question from a third kid and meeting me for the first time. It felt like we all had her undivided attention, and she was never frenzied.*

Kelly: *I remember Jhumki with this air of calmness. She always helped me to see the end goal. I would get caught up in the day-to-day stuff with kids and their behavioral problems, and Jhumki would always revert to the same question: What do you want your students to get out of your classroom? What do you want them to get out of your teaching? This would always put things in perspective. I would have a million questions about how to put this project together, and I have an idea for an experiment but I am not really sure how it's going to work out. She would always be able to figure it out. Not do the work for me but guide me to where I needed to go.*

Maggie: *She knew how to solve every discipline issue. She would say, "For this student you just have to call their home, and for that student you should let them do an errand for you once or twice a week, and then they will be on perfect behavior."*

Emma: *Jhumki knew each kid as an individual, which is the same way she relates to us as adults. She had these relationships with so many of us, and it was true for every single classroom engagement. She knew how to make the most difficult concepts fun and interesting for the kids and connected to their lives. She was always doing experiments and blowing things up. The kids wanted to go to her class. They wanted it to be orderly enough so that they could do these fun and engaging things she had set up for them.*

Kelly: *In regard to discipline, nobody really hears you when you are yelling. People yell because they feel like they are not being heard. And that almost never works for students. We all have had that moment when we want to just scream, just be heard, especially when a class of, like, twenty kids are talking over you. Jhumki never resorted to that tactic. She always knew the best route was to go through the relationship and seek out whatever a student needed to be, and she had the time to do that. Jhumki seemed to understand the path to connect with everybody she met, which is quite extraordinary.*

Maithreyi: *What strikes me is this needs so much effort in getting to know every student. Is that sustainable? Is that possible on a daily basis for you who are working here still?*

Maggie: *I guess it's possible. It's difficult because you need to give up a lot of what is your own time. You need to do that in order to call every parent before the school year begins and keep in contact with every parent throughout the year. I don't think I have done as good a job as Jhumki in developing relationships with students and parents. But it's one thing out of a million that you're like, "Oh, I am going to do better at that!"*

Maithreyi: *There is a lot more freedom for the kids at SDL. They get power to choose and have a say. Does that work all the time?*

Joanna: *Democratic pedagogy was something we struggled with a lot. We started the school with broad ideals of creating a democratic space for students, particularly for students who often don't have any voice in their communities. We were hoping that this would be that place for them. There were lots of ways in which that happened. We had a youth court. A pretty strong advisory system. Students had lots of extracurricular activities where they could choose ways they could get involved in the community. We had an activism club that did a two-year research project about the campaign for fiscal equity. But there were also moments of deep struggle, as democracy can often seem a very alien concept for underprivileged students. It is hard for them to understand their role in it. It was a big learning curve for all of us, teachers and students.*

Kelly: *One of the biggest struggles we had in terms of making democratic teaching work on the ground is the difference between democracy for an eleven-year-old and democracy for an eighteen-year-old. We struggled at first with our middle school students about how to balance the need to have a voice for kids who are just trying to find their voice in a variety of ways. They may not know what that means to them yet. It has definitely been an ongoing struggle and one that I think Jhumki just understood.*

Maggie: *I am thinking back to when Jhumki was doing her research at NYU and she used to come in and meet with us. We would come up with specific tasks for our class surrounding democracy. I had never thought about some of those things. Through the discussions with her I was reminded that we have choice in democracy in our classrooms and we still don't even know it! We don't necessarily think of representing a lot of the things we do that way, but we are doing it that way anyway. The reason social-science teachers are doing it is because of her influence.*

Maithreyi: *I would like to understand some of the serious day-to-day difficulties Jhumki faced.*

Joanna: *One day Jhumki didn't show up for work and she called and told us she couldn't get off her back. She wasn't able to move; she was lying on the floor, and she couldn't get up. So we told her, "Okay, you just rest." The next day we told her, "Just stay home until you get better," but she called me later that afternoon saying, "Joanna, is there any way you can come pick me up to go to work tomorrow?" I said, "Are you serious?" She is like, "Yeah, I need to be at SDL." So I went to pick her up, and she was able to walk very slowly. She came anyway, and that's just one of many instances.*

Emma: *I was in awe of Jhumki. I remember one day when she was writing her dissertation, and she was teaching here, and she was being the assistant principal, and she had just got married, and was living in the Upper West Side. Though she was living an hour and a half away, she was here by seven o'clock every morning, and was one of the last people to leave the doors. I remember when, about to step in the elevator with her, I asked, "How do you do it? Why are you not exhausted? You commute for three hours a day!" She looked to me and said, "Well, I get to work on my dissertation. I never have time to work on it except when I am on the train." That was her answer. That was her three-hour commute.*

Kelly: *Once Jhumki and I were trying to coordinate a time to meet, and she finally said, "Well, do you mind coming to my chemotherapy treatment on Friday night? We can plan there." So I showed up in Manhattan with my books. Alexander had brought her some kind of a disco ball to hang up on her IV stand to make it a little more festive. It was Friday night in New York, and here she was in her late twenties having chemo. She sat there, got hooked up . . . it was a little painful for her, and she had to have a cold compress on her arm. But we sat there and we planned for the entire hour. It was the most productive session. She definitely had a way to make you feel comfortable. She could read somebody when they wanted to ask a question but didn't know if it was okay to ask. She was open about where she was in her cancer and how she was feeling both mentally and physically. I was amazed because planning curriculum would be the last thing I would do if I was having chemotherapy treatment. She was a trooper.*

Joanna: *Jhumki and I were the only two teachers who lived in Manhattan. So almost every day we took the train back into the city together, and that was our debriefing session. I think her struggles aren't different from struggles any of us have as teachers. It's the way that she dealt with it after that's different. Students may have yelled at her in physics because she set*

306

really very high standards and students that weren't used to having to reach a higher bar. She dealt with it by talking to other teachers, by talking to her family and Alexander. I don't think she went through it unfazed. She always felt whatever struggles we were having as a school or in her relationships with her students; there was always a solution.

Kelly: *Jhumki helped me see the bigger picture and the end goal. It was the same in dealing with a student because it's very easy to tune that student out and say there is nothing that can be done. Lost cause. But Jhumki took the harder route. She always believed there was a solution. It might be difficult to get to, but it could be done. I always keep that in mind when I teach. No student is ever lost. One should never give up on a student.*

Emma: *It was hard as time passed and she started getting more visibly sick or more tired. I never expected Jhumki not to have any energy, because she had always had the most. And then I went to dinner with her and she talked about how she had come to the really hard decision and realization that she wasn't going to have children. That was one of the first things that she had let go of. She was starting to think she might not live. For the first time I was thinking about it too.*

40. OF DADS AND SILVERBACKS

Good morning, Cliff!"

"Hi, Jhumki. How's it going?"

"Oh, you know, the usual stuff. Nothing I can complain about that I haven't already."

There was a silence while Jhumki studied a framed Monet print on the wall of the exam room, then her doctor.

"Okay, Jhumki, what's up? I'm listening."

"Oh, nothing. Just that my dad wants to go to Gabon."

"Your dad wants to go do what?"

"Gabon."

"What's a gabon?"

"It's a country in West Africa. They speak French there."

"Ah, at least I've learned something new today. And you are telling me this because?"

"Oh, he wants to see lowland gorillas. My dad does."

This exchange was gleefully recounted by our daughter and more sedately by Dr. Hudis.

"Jhumki, can I check you out? How's the nausea?"

Dr. Hudis knew full well there was more to come, but he refused to give Jhumki the satisfaction of asking her. In the end it was his patient who caved in the mind game.

"It's my dad's sixtieth birthday," she said, hopping onto the leather-upholstered table.

"Really? And he wants to go to Gabon for his sixtieth to see gorillas?"

"Uh-huh." Jhumki offered the dutiful daughter look. "I have to go too, don't you think? I mean, it's his sixtieth 'n' all."

Our Jhumki had another side. This was a side distinct from her passionate, untiring drive to help America's poor teenagers.

It was a side that treasured pure enjoyment of God's creatures, especially primates, in their untrammeled homeland. *Gorillas in the Mist,* the story of Dian Fossey's life, was her favorite film. Jane Goodall was her lifetime hero.

Even with her devious approach Dr. Hudis would not have allowed Jhumki to go completely off the map. For example, we could not go to Rwanda because viewing gorillas there requires much walking, and Jhumki's feet were in pain from neuropathy. She convinced her doctor that lowland gorillas in Gabon, unlike their mountain cousins in Rwanda, required little exertion.

In actuality things never happen as planned. Deep in the trackless Mikongo rain forest of Gabon, the guide leading Jhumki and Alexander's group managed to lose his way and our daughter ended up walking seven kilometers with broken nails and bleeding feet. A furious Alexander had muttered bloody murder in the direction of the guide, who, luckily for him, did not know Greek, Hebrew, or English. Thankfully, after bathing her feet in warm water and drinking a glass of wine, Jhumki was none the worse.

But before the trip to Gabon, there were several important activities. Alexander went to Greece to see his family and Jhumki came to California to stay with her parents. We had now begun a routine whereby Jhumki was never alone. She may have balked about invasion of her privacy, and we tried hard not to invade, but being under no illusion of the stage she was in her illness, she did not rebel.

Camaraderie of the chemo suite was a unique Jhumki thing. She liked a "quiet" person to accompany her to the clinic, where she got a lot of work done on her laptop. If she had to "entertain" the person accompanying her—for example, a goodhearted relative from out of town—that was a bummer. A comment like "Jhumki, you poor thing!" or "Don't you worry; everything's going to be all right" was grounds for immediate dismissal as chemo escort.

On July 22, 2008, Jhumki flew from San Francisco to the annual KSTF summer workshop in Philadelphia. NYU had arranged a low-cost flight for her with a connection in Atlanta. Radha, anticipating everything that could go wrong for a fragile girl traveling alone, booked her on a direct flight, just in case. As it turned out, tornadoes hit the Southeast and the connecting flight was canceled. Thanks to her mother's foresight, Jhumki, with aching legs and hands, flew direct to a room at the Renaissance Hotel in Philadelphia where the conference was to be held.

"I would never have survived hassling with the airline and getting an overnight place in Atlanta," she called to tell her mother. "Thank you, Mommy, for getting me to Philly."

Jhumki got down to work at the three-day summer conference. There were three hundred science teachers, mostly fellows. A very few attendees, like Jhumki, were research scholars with multi-year funding.

"After all those phone conversations, the very first time I met her was at that 2008 workshop," Angelo Collins recalled. "You read about people who are ill, who do not let their illness conquer them. She was thin. She had lost her hair. But she participated in every session. She conducted a workshop for our teachers on democratic pedagogy, and on how to use their environment for science teaching without the need for fancy equipment. 'Just use what's around you to do that,' she told them."

For the workshop Jhumki defined her vision of democratic science pedagogy and listed several reasons for the desperate need for new science-teaching strategies in America:

- *Low-income, minority students face significant challenges in gaining access to and succeeding in science classrooms and careers*

- *Minority students are vastly under-represented in the number of degrees awarded in the physical sciences, computer science and engineering*
- *Urban teachers, particularly new ones, face constant challenges and frequently change schools and leave the teaching profession entirely*

In Jhumki's presentations, there was a preponderance of video, an integral aspect of her work. At NYU she had procured several camcorders and meticulously recorded her research data, or had her doctoral students record every teaching method that came out of their research. The team spent hours cataloging and archiving their findings.

On the third morning of the conference I landed in Newark and drove to Manhattan to collect suitcases from Jhumki's apartment. Then I drove to the Renaissance and found the KSTF session rooms. The doors to one room were open and I saw Jhumki busily going from table to table and talking to people. Wearing the same outfit and glasses as she had worn on SDL graduation day, she looked slim, elegant, and professional.

She caught sight of me and her face lit up. Several fellows turned and looked in my direction curiously and I felt extremely proud. She gave me a thumbs-up and a nod indicating that she wouldn't be long. At 4:30 p.m., out she came bouncing on her crocs.

"Let's go, Baba. I can't wait!"

I could sense her excitement. She was avidly looking forward to the trip. We drove the short distance to Philly airport, returned the car, checked in, went through security, and settled into the transatlantic flight. True to form, Jhumki fell asleep with her head on my shoulder as soon as the plane took off. I tucked a blanket around her, leaned her seat back, and fervently hoped the holiday would be everything she wanted. I wished it would never end. Gabon was her dream trip. She knew in her heart that it would be the last big one with the people she loved.

The plan was for everyone to meet up in Paris on July 26 to catch the Air France flight to Libreville on the next day. Alexander would come from Greece. Radha had already left for Europe on a business trip and would be waiting for us. Ranga had been urgently required for a scientific meeting in, yes, Paris! Preetham and Vardhini had gone early for a French vacation.

Jhumki and I found Mommy at a Roissy hotel near Charles de Gaulle Airport. Preetham and Vardhini were staying in the city center. Ranga hadn't surfaced. Jhumki, tired after the trip, went to sleep in our bed. Alexander arrived in the afternoon, collected his wife, and went with her to see the sights. Everyone finally got together for a raclette and crepes dinner in Montparnasse.

The next morning we survived a bomb scare.

As we were checking in at CDG, a large number of gendarmerie suddenly appeared and our departure terminal was evacuated of thousands of travelers. Very soon the only thing visible in the gaping hall was a single small suitcase on the ground. Crowded together in the entryway, we watched cops wave their hands and shout at one another. Suddenly, a shrill police whistle blew a long blast. At once there was a loud bang, and the suitcase exploded into bits. No one told us whether the bomb inside the suitcase blew up, or if the suitcase was detonated in a controlled explosion.

The whole thing had taken two hours. Would we miss our flight?

As it turned out everyone made it aboard.

At Libreville baggage claim, Jhumki jammed her feet against something hard and unyielding and broke a toenail. Alexander, ever vigilant against infection, became very concerned about the bleeding. He called New York and tried to get through to Dr. Hudis, but managed only to reach an oncology fellow. It was probably the strangest call the man would receive in his medical career.

"Who is this?" the fellow asked.

"I am calling for Dr. Jhumki Basu," replied Alexander.

"Okay, but why can't the doctor call me himself?"

"*She's* an educator. I'm her husband. She is Dr. Hudis's patient."

"I see. OK, what seems to be the problem?"

"She's broken a toenail. It's bleeding."

"I am so sorry to hear that. Can you bring her in right away?"

"No, we can't. We are in Libreville."

"Upstate, right? Well, she *should* come in right away for a blood test, you know."

"No, it's in Gabon. We're in Africa. French West Africa. Listen, we're on vacation. What can I do to help her?"

At that point the fellow gave up conjuring scenarios and concentrated on the medical problem. He advised Alexander not to remove the nail. He told her to wash the wound with clean water, put an antiseptic cream, and bind it. We did not record the fellow's name to thank him for his sound advice. Jhumki followed his recommendations and there were no complications.

Our guide, Robert Barber, met us at Libreville's airport. Rob had led Jhumki and Alexander's honeymoon safari in Botswana, and the three had become very good friends. This time, Rob organized our Gabon trip from a thousand miles away in Maun. We all liked the big bwana-type man who, while quite young, had an I-can-fix-anything attitude. He treated Radha and me like parents, and would not let us carry a thing. After a few protests I relaxed into the elder statesman role. Jhumki was very comfortable in Rob's company, for which I was grateful. By evening she was keeling over with laughter at the Sofitel bar. The quality of humor, fueled by the potent combination of the boys, Rob, Ranga, Alexander, Preetham, gin and tonic, went predictably and quickly down the toilet. Jhumki egged them on. Vardhini laughed at their jokes.

Radha and I watched them. Then we looked at each other and sighed. Let her be happy, were our unspoken words. Let her be pain-free and enjoy her cherished holiday.

The following morning, at Libreville's domestic terminal, we were waiting to board a small plane to the Mikongo rain forest, when an airport worker approached our group and wanted to know who Monsieur Basu was.

"Oui," I said, and put up my hand in case he thought my language skills were poor. The worker took me to the check-in counter, where our bags were still stacked. I turned to look back at our group as I left the waiting area. They seemed worried.

"Est-ce le vôtre, monsieur?" Is it yours, sir?

The worker was pointing to a duffel bag with my name tag on it. Before I could answer, I heard it: a whirring from inside the bag. I looked for a moment at the bag and then looked around. Several big men in uniform were staring at me somberly. The police whistle at Charles de Gaulle airport sounded in my ears. But I didn't panic. I fished around inside the bag, found the offending device, and held it up for all to see.

It was my battery-powered toothbrush, vibrating vigorously.

"Qu'est-ce que c'est?" asked one of the men, backing away.

"Toothbrush!" I replied, and, as I had no clue about its French equivalent, mimicked brushing for good measure.

There was a moment's silence while everyone stared at the toothbrush, then at me, and burst into laughter. I joined them, thankful that Gabonese police did not blow up bags first and ask questions later. I returned to the family fold and an almost tearful welcome. Everyone was sure I was even then being driven away to a Libreville dungeon. They laughed when I described my little adventure.

"Baba, don't you know you always have to take the batteries out of . . ."

I grinned at her.

"Oof, you're hopeless."

Three memories illuminate my remembrances from that thrilling trip.

First, there was Evengue Island. We got to Evengue by boat along the narrow Mpivi River, with its reed-encased banks overhung by willows resplendent with iridescent kingfishers. On the most overhung parts we were beset by—*Dr. Hudis, please skip!*—tsetse flies. They were small, brown, unremarkable insects with the fearsome reputation. Rob had advised everyone to wear beige clothing, because tsetses avoid that color, with long sleeves and long pants. It worked, and none of us contracted sleeping sickness. And, Jhumki opined, Ranga had the disease anyway.

The entirety of Evengue Island is a gorilla sanctuary supported by a Dutch nonprofit, Apenheul whose friendly scientists, Nick and Boanna, took us to visit their resident family of eight gorillas. Among them was a monster twenty-eight-year-old silverback named Mabeki. When Mabeki came out of the trees in a fenced enclosure all of us sank to the ground, cast our eyes down, and made sure our teeth didn't show. The huge ape looked from left to right and back again and moved around slowly and regally. Then he went berserk and galloped up and down the periphery of the enclosure in a strange, crab-like manner, simultaneously beating his chest with a frighteningly loud sound. Boanna, a naturalist of Jhumki's age, told us he was demonstrating alpha behavior.

Later in the hotel bar, Nick listened attentively while Jhumki described her interest and experiences with primates and the great significance of the visit for her.

The next day Radha and I went by boat to see the local attractions—translucent green cathedrals of giant bamboo groves, and a rusted, all-metal church brought piece by piece from France and re-assembled. Jhumki had some mysterious project going on with the scientists, and the boys didn't want to stray from the beer. When we returned Jhumki was waiting for us at the dock. From a distance we could tell she was very excited. We came closer and she bounced up and down while we tied up.

"Guess what, Mommy?! Guess what, Baba?!" she gushed, hauling us out of the boat. "Guess what happened to me?!"

"You haf won ze Lotto Gabonaise, *oui* Mam'selle Jhomi?" I said.

"*No,* Baba!" She bounced higher. "Guess *what?*"

"You swallowed a sunset?"

"No. No. Better than *that!*"

She finally settled down enough to tell us everything. Nick had taken her—the first-ever tourist to be accorded the opportunity—to visit Evengue's resettled orphaned gorillas, whose parents had been killed by poachers for bush meat. The baby gorillas had been brought to Evengue, habituated, and released back into the forest on the island.

Once in the forest, Jhumki and the others donned masks and overalls to avoid infecting the apes, walked a mile to a glade, and sat down on a log. After a while several gorillas appeared from the surrounding jungle. Initially they were hesitant with the unfamiliar person in blue. Then one of them became friendly— overly friendly—and tried to pick Jhumki's camera out of her pocket.

Jhumki spent more than an hour with the gorillas. Her happiness was so boundless that we didn't know what to do. She had wanted to be close to wild gorillas all her life and it had happened. If there is a primate paradise, she had just been there.

Evengue is a wonderfully relaxing place. Cool breezes play through the open windows of its guest cottages. The tree-lined river ripples in the distance. Late in the afternoon of Jhumki's gorilla encounter, I filmed our idyllic surroundings. I forgot about the clip in the difficult times that followed. More than a year later I played the video back and realized with a shock that there was a voice singing in the background. It was Jhumki, rendering her favorite Beatles song from the next tent, her melodic voice floating on the tropical breeze, softly singing the lyrics of *Hey Jude*.

My second memory is from Loango, where the whale watching is superb. In fact, it is primate-famous Gabon's best-kept secret. We were in a high-speed, low-noise rubber raft fifteen kilometers out on the Atlantic when, all around us and frighteningly close, humpback whales began to leap out of the water like gargantuan fish in a lake. Male humpbacks shot out of the water without notice, launching their full sixty feet into the air, and fell back with tremendous splashes. This mating ritual was a fearsome sight. Once, two whales, one on either side of our little raft, rose gracefully into the air and fell away in a crashing welter of foam that violently rocked us. Strange, I mused as the boat settled. If the target of this colossal tomfoolery is below the surface, how can she see their antics?

On our second day at Loango, whales notwithstanding, Jhumki decided to skip the rocking in the open ocean that brought on nausea. Instead, she wanted to spend an afternoon fishing on a quiet river. I stayed back with her while everyone else went to watch more humpbacks. On the fishing boat with us were a nice guide and a young newlywed couple. The boat was well stocked with rods, bait, lures, hooks, and beer. We chugged along while the guide fixed shiny lures, threaded little fish onto hooks, and showed us how to cast. He told us to watch a cloud of diving terns and to make our cast so that the hook dropped among them.

I thought of asking whether we were catching terns or fish, but felt the this humor would be out of place. Jhumki and I studied the agile seabirds, and had an ornithological discussion about whether there were any arctic terns that annually migrate twenty thousand miles from Pole to Pole and back. To Jhumki's joy, the guide said there *were* arctics in the lot.

The husband of the newlywed couple was a master fisherman. While his wife tired of the technicalities and fell asleep, he arched his pole perfectly and landed the hook exactly in the middle of the terns. He hauled in the line. Nothing. He did it again. Nothing. He changed lures, rods, bait, and kept at it. Nothing. I was impressed by his patience and skill.

Meanwhile, Jhumki sat on a barrel and fished.

She made a cast. One cast. The boat moved, and the lure moved through the water.

"Try again, miss?" the guide asked.

"No, I'm cool," Jhumki replied. "Thanks."

An hour passed. The guide took us to several locations. Jhumki made a second cast and sat on her barrel. Our friend, the fisherman, had made maybe a hundred casts with no success.

"Baba, come here! I may have something."

I quickly went over and grabbed the rod just as it dipped and was about to be snatched out of her neuropathic hands. The line ran madly. The guide and the newlywed clustered around us. Everyone showered advice.

"Pull!"

"Reel her in!"

"Let him run!"

After ten minutes of this, Jhumki's catch was landed, a fifteen-pound red snapper. She was proud as punch.

It was getting late when we chugged back to the Loango pier. The others had not returned. We docked, and Jhumki did her bouncing act while she waited impatiently for Alexander.

"Where is he? Where is he?"

The returning whale watchers, drenched by another glorious marine mammal display, were showered with Jhumki's excitement. Everyone admired the catch. That night, the non-vegetarians in our party feasted on her bounty, accompanied by good Pinot Grigio. And another unforgettable day in French West Africa came to a close.

My third memory is crushing.

We spent the last day and night of our trip at Point St. Catherine, a small island with wide beaches, coconut palms, and our tiny rustic camp. We spent most of the day lying on deck chairs, trying hard to push back the looming reality of life. The evening was billed as Baba's birthday and our farewell dinner.

The dining room of the resort was rather nice considering the remoteness. After we assembled for dinner I thanked my travel companions for their kindness. We went around the table, and each of us spoke about our most enjoyable moment. I tried to be creative, but it was nothing like the inspired poetry I had generated on my fiftieth with the kids in the Rockies, just before our Everest trip a very long decade ago. With my rambling, I didn't convince even myself that the trip was memorable, let alone others.

Then it was Jhumki's turn. She began to say something, stopped, and stared at me with enormous eyes. I went quickly around the table and hugged her close. She didn't cry, but others did. Then she shook herself, returned my hug, and called out, "Okay, guys, bring it on!"

And then, at the remotest place imaginable, there appeared just for me a perfectly baked cake, with not candles but sparklers firing! I was completely overcome.

"Blow 'em out! Blow 'em out!" chanted Jhumki from across the table.

Yeah, right. *You* try blowing out sparklers.

The pyrotechnics wound down.

I made a wish.

It didn't come true.

PART VII

STARBURST

"The truest, most fulfilling form of happiness can be found in serving other people, and working outside of one's self-interest."

Sreyashi Jhumki Basu

41. GOING DOWN

"**S**he thought," Radha said, laughing, "I could do *anything!*"

We were reminiscing about the time when Jhumki wanted to keep the trip to Gabon a surprise for me as long as possible.

"What about immunizations?" her mother had asked her. "Baba has to get his shots, you know."

"Oh, you can do it, Mommy," Jhumki replied, unperturbed.

She really did believe that she could distract me enough, or that I would be so sound asleep, that when her mother jabbed me with a yellow-fever shot, I wouldn't feel a thing!

"She truly took us for granted," Radha said with a bittersweet sigh. "In a very good sense. But she took us for granted. She knew we were always there, and so she could go far and be adventurous. She might say, 'I do fun things with Baba,' but she always depended on Mommy to get things done."

During the teenage years of rebellion, Jhumki used to think we were very corporate, very strait-laced parents, and rightly so. At the same time it is interesting that when she went to Russia, when we supported her in Russia, when she had problems after Shanti's death, and even when she most fervently fought with us, Jhumki never for one minute believed that her parents would not support her. It became an intrinsic part of her personality.

"Hold fast to your dreams," she had written on the dinner plate for our birthdays in 1992. Young as she was then, she felt that no matter where she was, whatever she did, we would be there for her. It made her a freer spirit. We were her safety net. Because of us she could fly free.

"Alive and real! Flying free!" her mother summed it up. "That was Jhumki to me."

Jhumki was unwell upon our return from Gabon.

The journey back to Paris, compressed into a single day, was epic. We went from Point St. Catherine to Loango by boat, Loango to Omboue in a Land Rover, Omboue to Port Gentil in a small plane, Port Gentil to Libreville in a bigger plane, and Libreville to Paris in an even bigger plane.

In Paris, Jhumki looked grey and felt tired and queasy. She slept in our hotel for the afternoon. Later she went with Alexander on a *bateau* ride on the Seine, and the two had dinner out. Our routes diverged on the morrow. Jhumki and Alexander went to New York, Preetham and Vardhini to San Francisco, Ranga to Los Angeles, and Radha and I to India.

Breaching humpbacks, tsetse flies, berserk gorillas, fireworks on cakes, faded to a land far away and a time long ago.

On August 12, Jhumki sent this message to her fellow travelers:

> *Scans are back. Lungs are still clear but liver mets have grown in number and size. Not surprising, given that liver function tests are up and blood markers as well. Bone mets are stable.*
>
> *I also clarified to Cliff that, lest he has forgotten, I do have a life. I recommended what Ranga suggested, that they start paying me for my time spent at the clinic.*

The news was bad once again. Taxol, the great workhorse of breast cancer, had stopped working. To mark the event Jhumki, in inimitable style, held a classroom discussion on evolution versus creation. An ardent disciple of Charles Darwin, she pointed out to her students that *she* was the clearest example of Darwinian theory.

"Look at me!" she said with vehemence. "These stupid cancer cells in me aren't that stupid. They mutate—they *evolve!*—they change every three months to survive chemo attacks. If that isn't pure Darwin, I don't know what is."

Taxol treatment was discontinued in favor of yet another intravenous chemo drug. If not transfused properly, this drug, Navelbine, caused tissue damage around the vein. Low blood counts, as well as other depressing things, were side effects of the drug. More than ever, Jhumki depended on nurse Morgan to do her job well.

In spite of her failing health, Jhumki's keyboard clattered away. She submitted two book chapters that were accepted for publication. And, in keeping with her uncanny way of making light of the toughest situations, on the day of her decision to use Navelbine, Jhumki "scientified" Elizabeth Barret Browning in a message to her friends:

XLIII. "How do I love liquid nitrogen? Let me count the ways..."
Jhumki Basu (1977–)

> *How do I love liquid nitrogen? Let me count the ways.*
> *I love LN2 to the depth and breadth and height*
> *The vapor can reach, when feeling out of sight*
> *For the ends of Coldness and filling empty Space.*
> *I love thee to the level of everyday's*
> *Most quiet need, by roses shattered by candle-light.*
> *I love thee freely, as bubble wrap strives for Right;*
> *I love thee purely, as air in balloons changes phase.*
> *I love thee with a passion put to use*
> *In my experiments, and with my childhood's faith.*
> *I love thee with a love I seemed to lose*
> *With my lost LN2 access code,*
> *Soap, hot water, explosion—I choose,*
> *I shall but love thee better after the* kaboom.

℘

Rani Elwy, Jhumki's cousin, lives a few miles outside Boston. Eight years older than Jhumki, Rani holds a PhD in health psychology from Kings College London and is a professor at the Boston University School of Public Health. Her oldest child, Lucy, is a bright and curious teenager in whom Rani sees much of Jhumki. She has two other children, Benjamin and Charlotte. Jhumki and Rani had a long-standing friendship that they conducted mostly over e-mail.

"Ben's coming into my life changed my relationship with Jhumki," Rani told Maithreyi at her interview.

Ben is an extremely intelligent and artistic child. Sadly, he has a rare and painful neuromuscular disorder which makes it difficult for him to walk.

"His surgical treatment brought us cousins closer," Rani said. "Very few people can understand what Ben is going through. Jhumki took the time to stop and think about us and follow Ben on his CarePage. During the last six months of Jhumki's life, we really bonded."

When Ben first required hip surgery, no one knew the prognosis, so it was a huge leap of faith when Rani and her husband, Shirin, agreed he go through with an operation called femoral osteotomy. They did the first surgery, and Ben was okay after a longish period of rehab. In August 2008 they did a second surgery following which he was in immense pain.

"And I became the mother from hell," Rani remembered tearfully. "I had said in the CarePage that Shirin was getting mad at me because I was getting mad at everyone all the time. I just thought no one was listening. I said, 'You've got to get him out of ICU. Got to get him to orthopedic ward. Got to take him off meds right now. It's not helping him.' My nice methods did not work, and I lost it."

Jhumki had just come back from Gabon. She read in Rani's most recent post that Ben was being given so much pain medication that he was hallucinating. Lying in intensive care, he had said, "We are so far in outer space that we won't get back in time."

"My son never says this!" said a distraught Rani.

It was at this point she received this message from Jhumki.

> *Hi superstar mom,*
>
> *Been out of town for two weeks. I was reading your recent post and wanted to write a bit.*
>
> *I don't have much that is wise to say, but I feel this is what I do all the time in the hospital with the nurses and technicians and sometimes the doctors. I feel bad being so angry and combative, but I also think there is often something de-humanizing about being in the hospital. One can be in so much pain and need, and one is treated in some systematic way. I am also angry a lot at the world—in my case, anxious and defensive about how people see my lack of hair, quick to be hurt and easily offended. I think my mom has some similar and some different feelings. And negotiating differences of opinions with one's spouse under pressure is yet another challenge to responding to chronic disease.*
>
> *Always thinking of you and sending much love, Jhumki.*

Rani loved and was comforted by this message.

"She would have been such a great mom and would have had the luckiest child ever," she said in tribute to her cousin.

Immediately after returning from Gabon, Jhumki developed a fever. Five days later it became so high that Alexander took her into urgent care. The application of Navelbine wasn't going well. In addition to pain, nausea, and exhaustion, insomnia was affecting Jhumki's alertness, and depleting her energy reserves. Through Alexander's electronic updates to India, Radha and I felt her distress, and once again we cut short our trip and flew back to the U.S.

When we arrived in New York, we were horrified by the change in our daughter in the two weeks since we were in Gabon. Exhaustion was clear in each dragging step; pain was evident in dark rings around her sunken eyes. She had no desire to eat and was wracked by nausea. Jhumki was very ill.

We moved in with our friends, the Kumars, who wrapped us in love in their home, just as they had done in the dark Delhi days when Shanti and SNA died.

August flowed into September, and Jhumki's condition worsened. She was now on ancillary drugs to treat side effects of cancer medicines. These drugs had their own side effects, and so on down the line. A complex spreadsheet was required to administer Jhumki's medicines per multiple doctors' orders. In addition, she was exhibiting signs of extreme anxiety. We, her caregivers, were at our wits' end.

In early September, Dr. Hudis said, "Stop!"

He refocused treatment toward managing the pain and stabilizing her condition. He ordered a pain patch called fentanyl, which became a talisman on her arm. Navelbine was discontinued. In spite of all this, Jhumki kept going downhill. A blood test showed she was severely anemic.

Wanting to work, unable to work, hugely depressed, wildly excited, railing about bureaucracy, raving about wanting to help her students, e-mailing when her fingers weren't numb, Jhumki was going through a spectrum of extreme emotions. On September 7th she was admitted to Memorial Hospital in a highly anemic state and underwent a blood transfusion. It had an immediate effect. Her anxiety subsided, and her strength came back. Two days later she went to see Dr. Hudis.

The previous time she had seen him, Jhumki had been in dire straits. Chemo had been stopped and home care ordered, an acknowledgment of the terminal stage of a disease. On this occasion the four of us were present in the exam room when Dr. Hudis pushed open the door and entered.

"Hi, Jhumki. Mornin' folks."

"Cliff, how are you?"

"I'm fine, Jhumki. *You* look much better."

"Yes, Cliff. I am now going to sing you a song."

Dr. Hudis was becoming adept at keeping his face straight against Jhumki's impulsive nature. I could imagine him thinking, *now what?* While we watched, Jhumki fired up her iPhone and pressed a button. Tinny ukulele music accompanied the voice of a male singer, and Jhumki sang along with him:

> *I am a vampire*[19]
> *I am a vampire*
> *I am a vampire*
> *I have lost my fangs.*
> *So I'm sad and I feel lonely*
> *So I cry and I'm very angry*
> *And I hate some garlic*
> *So I'm no more sad and*
> *Ache yeah yeah.*
> *I am a vampire and I am*
> *Looking in the city*
> *Pretty girls don't look at me*
> *Don't look at me*
> *Cause I don't have my fangs*
> *But I have lost my fangs.*

[19] From "Vampire," lyrics by Leo Bear Creek. Reproduced with permission.

Jhumki stopped the music.

Dr. Hudis stared at Jhumki while she looked back at him with a little smile playing at the corners of her mouth. A full minute passed.

"Okay, Jhumki, you win. What was that about?"

Jhumki explained that she felt weird about having someone else's blood inside her. Like a lost vampire. Cliff got it.

Dr. Hudis was encouraged by Jhumki's improvement.

"You're teaching too?"

"Yes, Cliff. I taught two classes last week. *And* I've been directing my doctoral fellows."

He couldn't believe it, but he swung into action. Hospice stopped. Jhumki came back under his care.

The sinusoidal nature of Jhumki's life once again kicked in at this point. In the midst of all her suffering, something wonderful took place.

Her third-year review, a mandatory event for all NYU tenure-track positions, was approaching. For the review she had to submit a detailed self-evaluation, but she was in no position to do so.

"I'll help you, Jhomi," Radha said when the subject came up, and Jhumki had gone into a black depression.

"Yeah, right!" she said angrily. "You *can't* do it, Mommy! How can you when even *I* can't do it? Do you know how much work it is? Do you know how much stuff's gotta be extracted? Gotta be coordinated, catalogued, documented?"

"No, I don't," Radha told her. "But I can help with the boring things—the sorting, the copying, the filing."

For three weeks, mother and daughter slogged between bouts of illness. They concentrated on creating and collating the review material. The finished product would have made any academic highflier proud.

On September 14, Radha and Jhumki marched into the office of NYU's director of faculty affairs and deposited a small plastic filing cabinet with a carrying handle. Inside was her third-year self-evaluation, catalogued and filed. A duplicate of everything, including the cabinet, graced her living room.

The cover letter was compelling. In it were two paragraphs that would receive widespread attention and be quoted often in the context of social justice in education:

> *Central to my work is the belief that a diversity of youth should gain expertise in scientific knowledge and learn to think logically, investigate original questions and innovate in ways that fulfill needs in their lives, community and world.*
>
> *In my research I am most interested in investigating ways in which young people from low-income minority backgrounds who are deeply under-represented in science, can gain access to quality education in this field.*

Jhumki wrote about expanding her work with Allen Mincer to include study of under-represented communities in the natural sciences. She talked about a new program she had been pursuing since her Renaissance Charter School days of 2003: linking school kids with university professors to develop interest in different aspects of science. Through the years she had obtained college internships for many inner-city students and had proven the model. She wanted to scale it up.

"We hope to first run this program with the collaboration of NYU and Polytechnic scientists in the summer of 2009," she wrote, "and begin research-based evaluation of the impact of this program on teacher practices and student learning in science."

It was still summer 2008. Jhumki was planning for the summer of 2009!

Her cover letter concluded: "I look forward to spending the

fall of 2008 developing a book prospectus on democratic science pedagogy."

Jhumki was planning to write a textbook.

It was mind-boggling.

42. THE IMPORTANCE OF BEING JHUMKI

In mid-September, amid the wreckage of Hurricane Ike, Jhumki made a difficult trip to Houston for a second opinion on her treatment at the MD Anderson Cancer Center. It did not go well, and she received a pessimistic prognosis from the specialist she visited. The flight back to New York was hard, and we were too depressed to remember that it was September 17th, Radha's birthday. Weak and totally worn out, Jhumki went to sleep after she got home.

And then, wonder of wonders, early the next morning, she sprang a huge surprise.

"Happy birthday, Baba!" she sang out cheerfully, pushing open the door of our room as Radha and I, still in bed, sat up in astonishment. Our birthdays are a day apart. Jhumki got into bed with us, and I reached over and pressed her hand. She chattered brightly about old memories, Delhi driver Jaipal, the dog Tiffany, Shanti, our conquest of the Rockies, Gabon.

We had with us a Jhumki that was totally different from the Jhumki of the last few weeks.

She went on to talk about summer camp at Castilleja when, while lying in bed and moving her body to the rhythm, she began to sing camp songs. One song followed another until she came to a favorite about the three little elves of the famous Kellogg's cereal box. She sang it with obvious enjoyment, as she remembered the doting little girls of Discover.

> Snap: "Snap, what a happy sound/Snap is the happiest sound I found/ You may clap, rap, tap, slap, but Snap makes the world go round/ Snap, crackle, pop—Rice Krispies!"
>
> Crackle: "I say it's Crackle, the crispy sound/You gotta

have Crackle or the clock's not wound/Geese cackle, feathers tickle, belts buckle, beets pickle, but Crackle makes the world go round/Snap, crackle, pop—Rice Krispies!"

Pop: "I insist that Pop's the sound/The best is missed unless Pop's around/You can't stop hoppin' when the cereal's poppin'/Pop makes the world go round/Snap, crackle, pop—Rice Krispies!"

She kept going, while, mesmerized, we listened.

After some time she got to Bollywood, and I was amazed at how many Hindi songs she knew. As with "Snap Crackle Pop," there was one clear favorite. She got out of bed, turned her laptop on, and sang along:

All the hot girls put your hands up and say,
"Om shanti om!"
All the cool boys come on make some noise and say,
"Om shanti om!"[20]

After a few more songs, she became tired and the fragile look came back.

"Go to sleep," I told her gently. "You've made this the best day of my life."

"Thanks, Baba." She gave Mommy and me a kiss and went back to Alexander.

More than a year ago, Jhumki had written:

If I'm dying and if I'm in New York, I want my friends to come visit me and then I want to move back to California for the last couple of months.

I'm scared to move if I'm sick, 'cause I don't want to

[20] From the 2007 Bollywood movie, *Om Shanti Om.*

334

move away from Dr. Hudis—he and I have as clear an understanding as I think we can about my values around living, dying and medical treatment. But maybe I can trust Dr. Carlson if I come back to California. Dr. Carlson already knows that I will come back to him, and he'll coordinate with Dr. Hudis. Before I leave New York, I want us to have a pot luck party, where everyone comes.

As Jhumki's cancer became worse and it became apparent that she needed a break from teaching, we invoked this desire of hers and began to talk to her about moving back to California.

On Sept 9th, Jhumki applied for and received a leave of absence from NYU. She took this step with great reluctance, and only after she came to terms with the fact that she was unable to concentrate enough to prepare for class, and didn't have the strength to teach for two and a half hours at a stretch. Her co-instructors, Drs. Verneda Johnson and Susan Kirch, agreed to take over her two fall classes.

From a CarePage posting by Alexander, Sep 21, 2008

Dear Friends,

We would like to organize a small going away/packing party on Saturday, September 27th. It would be an open house between 11am and 4pm at our apartment. We will have food but if you want to bring potluck and/or drinks that would be great. Please let me know that you have received this because I may not have the current addresses for everyone. Feel free to bring your partners and kids.

We plan to leave for California on October 5th. Jhumki is unlikely to be able to see many people one-on-one before that time, so we ask that you join us next Saturday.

The die was cast.

Jhumki had acknowledged that (1) the disease was overwhelming her physical and mental strength, (2) care and comfort would be superior in her parents' home, and (3) she was leaving New York for good.

Or so we thought.

Events were to prove her wrong on all three counts.

On the day of the open house at her apartment, I was dispatched to Bagels on the Square to collect supplies of New York's best, and instructed not to forget ample cream cheese.

Alexander got the knives out. Cucumbers, tomatoes, and feta were sliced efficiently and regrouped in olive oil and lemon juice. Radha made *idlis* out of rice flour and embedded them with nuts and herbs. Guests brought fruit, salads, appetizers, cakes, and chocolates, and soon every inch of Jhumki and Alexander's dining-room table was covered. More food waited on the kitchen counters.

Jhumki stayed in bed for most of the day. When guests arrived in the evening, she appeared, sat with them for a while, and then went back to her bedroom to rest. Later, Teachers College buddy Edna Tan helped her to eat, while Jhumki, with pinched face and circles around her eyes, sat surrounded by the people who loved her: friends from New York, Stanford, Castilleja; colleagues and students from SDL, NYU, Columbia; Angela Calabrese Barton from Michigan; Madhu Anand from San Francisco. Jeremy Dodd sat down at the piano and a Beatles medley rang out in chorus. After a bit Jhumki got up, walked slowly to the piano, and sat beside Jeremy. She began to sing along with the people who meant more to her than life, people whose smiles and tears flowed unashamedly that evening as they watched her sing.

More guests kept coming, and no one wanted to leave, even when Jhumki announced she was going to lie down and hugged everyone good-bye. People stayed on, chatting in low tones, not wanting to lose her aura.

༝

Jhumki had reached a stage when one of her caregivers or a trusted friend would accompany her wherever she went.

Two days after the open house, at Jhumki's request, I walked her to NYU's Pless Hall. After the elevator doors opened on the fourth floor, she disappeared into a conference room and shut the door. I settled into a comfortable chair. While I waited, several other people came up the elevator, and went into the same room, and shut the door behind them. Time passed. People kept going in and out of the room. Someone left hurriedly and came back with a pitcher of water. That worried me. After an hour, the door opened wide and I saw Jhumki emerge, breeze out with a big smile, and, before I could get to her, disappear down the stairs.

Oh, my God, I thought, she'll fall down the steps and Alexander will kill me. I rushed out and saw her, a flight below me.

"Jhomi! *Wait!*"

She stopped and looked up. In the overhead light I saw her face shining.

"Jhumki!" I admonished as I caught up with her. "Don't you know you are never to . . ."

"*Baba!* I forgot *all* about you! Guess what happened?"

"If anything happened, Alexander would have . . ."

"Baba, *listen!* I was videotaped!"

And just like that, Jhumki had pulled off another coup. Worn out, sick, weak, unable to focus, about to retire, Jhumki had just been filmed presenting a cogent discourse titled, *How Can Science Educators Engage Minority Youth?*

It is a bravura performance.

The video, which is proudly displayed on NYU's website as tribute to its brilliant and courageous faculty member, shows Jhumki, fragile, wearing her "good" white blouse, and a dusting of returning hair, sunken cheeks and rings around her eyes. The speech is faultless, delivered with the confidence of a consummate visionary declaring her life's mission with sincerity and truth.

Transcript of NYU recording of Professor Sreyashi Jhumki Basu, Oct 2, 2008, reproduced with permission

There is a body of knowledge of science to be taught. And generally the way we teach science is, there is a textbook and we say, "Let's go through textbook page 1, 2, 3, 4, 5, 6, 7— finish!"

Maybe you cut out a couple of the few interesting chapters on electromagnetism—students are too dumb for that anyway!—and after we do that, we say, "Content for that semester done."

I think it's also important to insert into those courses the idea that students are familiar with materials and maybe even experiences related to funds of knowledge related to their backgrounds and beliefs and experiences that are either materials that are connected with science, or beliefs in materials connected with actually doing science. There is also science that relates to things that kids are familiar with.

And then the second point is that science doesn't always have to be—in fact, science is not perpetual accumulation of informational knowledge. If we didn't ask questions in science and attempt to solve them, we would never move forward in science.

It's just that often the questions are so technical in the fields that students work, that they don't have the specialization to pursue those questions. But I think students can still get hints of those questions in all sorts of different ways. They can work in the lab of someone senior and develop questions. If it's a teacher who does that, then they can go back to their students and do a quarter on what that material was, bring in the scientist, do an overview of that topic, and spend a chunk of time setting up the foundation to explain how that was a question, and that it wasn't just a mental exercise, or a memorizing tool.

So you know, a lot about where we lose kids—we lose them, frankly, in history as well—it's a belief that "Oh! Okay, I just have to memorize the book, and then I get the passing grade." But it's not actually interesting. If I had a question, I would not look up a science book. If I had a question, I would look up the Internet! So there is this idea of process, that there is an interesting way of answering a question, there is a set of methods, there is an interesting process. It has been relied upon in diverse forms for thousands of years. To not know that means you are missing out on something really important. You are missing out on inquiry as a mode of thinking.

And I think we lose so many black, Hispanic, and female scientists every year, and other students, students from low-income families, students who don't get an adequate science background, students with various disabilities whose needs aren't met. I feel we really miss out on those students in particular, in part maybe because they are not willing to jump the step every time they are told to do so. They want something more than that. And those are the students whom we want. We want those students who say, "I don't want it just the regular way, I want it to be meaningful to me, and I want it to make sense to me."

Now that's a generalization. I can't say that every kid in the world is going to be interested in science, but I hope that every kid is in some level is interested in science, if not for their entire lives, then for some moment, something really sticks out to them.

43. DEAR PROFESSOR

"Guys, no adria today!"

The day following her video recording, after being rehydrated at MSKCC, Jhumki made this sudden announcement. Morgan, poised to insert an I-V needle filled with adriamycin, paused. All of us looked at Jhumki in surprise. She smiled and her wan face transformed, the old mischief glimmering in her sunken eyes.

"I can't be beat on this weekend, you know!" she said.

We laughed as we realized what she meant.

E-mail from Dipak Basu to friends and family, Oct 4, 2008
Re: Jhumki and Madonna

She was incredibly beautiful and strong. I refer to both the ladies in the subject line.

To begin the day Paul's arrival in New York put a smile on Jhumki's face. Then Vasilis arrived and his gruff jokes made us feel better.

Then Jhomi got dressed in a smart blue skirt, white coat and silver slippers, and appeared from her room to a speechless audience. She looked tall, slim, enchanting, angelic. To see her so poised, wanting to look good for Alexander with the last of her strength, made us cry. Vasilis, Anna, Priyanka and Paul applauded and gave her a sendoff to the Madonna concert.

The four of us drove to Rutherford, NJ. Thanks to Radha's pre-work over the phone, we received VIP treatment from the IZOD Center. The head of security himself came to get us. He swapped J&A's tickets, gave Radha and me comps and took us to a private box!

The sights, the sounds, the power and spectacle of Madonna's music were awesome. J&A have looked forward to it for months. We doubted if Jhomi would be well enough to go, if she would be able to stay more than a half hour. Jhomi stayed the full show and danced in the box with her husband. She was wiped out at the end but ever so happy.

On the drive back to Manhattan, I thought Jhumki was napping in the backseat, when a voice spoke above the radio.

"Mommy," it said. "Do you think I'll be able to vote?"

Unsure how to answer, we were quiet.

Two days later, Jhumki's world changed completely.

Dr. Perry Halkitis of NYU Steinhardt, who arranged the celebratory event as a complete surprise at short notice, contacted Alexander just before the weekend. To keep it secret, Jhumki was not shown the official invitation. She was simply told there was to be a special farewell party and she should dress appropriately.

Perhaps she had a premonition. Perhaps she thought it might be her last NYU group function. Whatever the reason, she dressed for the occasion in a formal black suit, white blouse, and good shoes. It was the same outfit that Alexander had bought for her NYU job interview. Mommy convinced her to add a touch of makeup, something she never did. She walked to Pless Hall holding Alexander's hand. Vasilis, Anna, Radha, Paul Prokop, and I fell in behind them. Jhumki's eyes widened when we got close to Pless Hall, and she saw her dearest friends from Casti school days, Eric Beerbohm, Kritika, and James, waiting.

"Oh, hell, this must be big!" she said. "Baba, what's happening?"

More friends, Jeremy and Libby Garland, joined us as we entered the building together and crammed into the elevator. On the fourth floor Jhumki exited to applause. The large common room (where had I waited while she was being videotaped) was now filled with her colleagues and students. Everyone hugged her. Then Jhumki noticed the provost and did a double take. But before she could say anything, the elevators doors opened with a loud clack and everyone looked around.

It was himself! John Sexton, president of NYU.

People who could find seats sat down. Others stood bunched together. Dean Mary Brabeck, whose brainchild the event was, introduced Jhumki and her family. I noticed Jhumki's smile had become rigid. She was overwhelmed.

The provost announced her promotion to Associate Professor, something extremely rare for an academic of two years, then the Goddard Faculty Fellowship Award, and then her tenure!

Everyone gasped.

There were loud cheers.

President Sexton rose to his feet and the august member of New York society walked over to where Jhumki was sitting stupefied, and went down on his knees before her.

He spoke, but not to Jhumki, but to Alexander.

"I liked and respected you before we met," Dr. Sexton told him. "Thank you for giving us Jhumki. And for encouraging her genius."

The president got back on his feet and gave a stirring speech that was laced with humor. Jhumki hid her face in her jacket in embarrassment.

Then a student from Jhumki's Teaching Methods class unrolled a multicolored poster and presented it to her.

Dear Jhumki,

If one day we become great teachers, it will be because we followed your lead. You have modeled excellence, resiliency and compassion to us all. We will always remember you.

NYU Methods Students.

Dean Mary Brabeck spoke next and was followed by Jhumki's colleague and friend, Fabienne Doucet. Tongue-in-

342

cheek, Fabienne told everyone what the Steinhardt faculty really thought of Dr. Basu.

Jhumki's Third Year Review Celebration
Congratulations from the Faculty

On behalf of the faculty members of the department of Teaching and Learning, I wish to present our heartiest congratulations to our beloved colleague, Dr. Jhumki Basu.

Jhumki, you are nothing short of extraordinary, and your impressive work ethic and dedication make you more than deserving of this recognition and celebration.

For those present who have not had the privilege of getting to know Jhumki as I have, I wanted to share what I believe to be the top ten reasons Jhumki is such an incredible success.

10. She refuses to behave. We've all heard the saying, "well-behaved women seldom make history." Well, Jhumki embodies this to the utmost, abiding by her convictions even if they are unpopular. She's not afraid to write scholarly work with high school students, she speaks her mind in meetings, and she always forces us to reconsider why we do things the way we do.

9. She has no patience for committees where no work gets done. She comes to meetings, laptop in hand, starts typing feverishly, and by the end is prepared to disseminate a "to do" list. She also does not shy away from hard work herself and typically takes on more than her fair share.

8. She can find a relationship to science no matter the topic of conversation. Whether it's mixing drinks, planning a wedding, or walking through the park, you can be sure that you will learn something scientific along the way.

7. She isn't afraid to get close to teenagers and let them know she believes in them, in their dreams, in their promise.

She lets them into her life and effortlessly weaves mentoring and friendship in a way that I find admirable.

6. She also talks to three-year-olds like they're real people. Since I have one of these specimens in my own home, I can tell you that they are an amazing source of wisdom. Jhumki recognizes this, taps into it, and runs new research ideas by them!

5. She works hard and plays hard. She cherishes good times spent with good friends, and this gives her energy to tackle tough projects.

4. She isn't afraid to ask for help. Jhumki has taught me the beauty of delegating, and I have learned to appreciate collaboration in a new way thanks to seeing the way she works.

3. She really means it when she asks how you're doing. Jhumki knows that you can't get very far in life if you don't know how to treat people well, so she always has a warm smile and a kind word to offer.

2. Further advancing the cause of "science in the everyday," Jhumki is, I'm pretty sure, the originator of the Ecological-Adventure-Vacation. She would rather swing from trees in the Amazon or go spelunking in Transylvania than sit on a beach reading a book. And the number one reason Jhumki is such a success:

1. She writes thank you notes on paper made from elephant poop, again seamlessly weaving science into every aspect of her life. Now that's what I call dedication!

So Jhumki, thank you for inspiring us all to excellence and to embracing life full-tilt. In gratitude, I want to present you with a small gift from us, your colleagues. The wise King Solomon once said, "a happy heart is good medicine." Your happy heart has been good medicine for us all. The contents of this box are intended to return the favor.

Finally it was Jhumki's turn to speak. She stood up hesitantly and faced the crowd. Stunned and shaky, she fumbled and dropped the microphone. Alexander came to the rescue and held it for her.

"I don't have experience in this," Jhumki said, and looked at her mother. Turning to the audience she added, "I don't know what to say." Then she remembered something and pulled out a piece of paper from her jacket pocket and read from it.

"Thank you for gathering with me on such short notice. I don't feel particularly meriting of any kind of honor of this kind. The achievements are entirely due to the ecosystem of staff and students with whom I have been privileged to collaborate. I feel like my work is just beginning. I'm also sad and a bit taken aback at having to take a leave of absence at this moment, when things seem to be fitting together. I hope to work as best I can from California at the high level of quality appropriate for this university. Thank you to everyone who organized this, particularly Perry Halkitis. I hope you enjoy yourselves.

She sat down and Mary gave her a long letter. It informed her that she was being promoted to associate professor and included her achievements, pages of them.

The meeting broke up for a wine-and-cheese reception.

Jhumki was leaving for California in two days. Nobody knew when or whether she would return. Everyone tried to keep emotion out of their voices as they said congratulations and bid her adieu. They were all adults and understood her precarious situation. No one told her, "Have a good time."

Crimson-and-gold in the fall sunset, Washington Square Park was gleaming when the Basu entourage emerged from Pless Hall and walked the short distance to Jhumki's apartment. She held on tightly to her mother's arm and did not say anything, but implicit in her action was gratitude for the tenure review dossier that she and Radha had delivered two weeks ago. I was walking a few paces behind them when Radha suddenly stopped and hugged her daughter emotionally. She later told me what had made her do this.

"Mommy," Jhumki had said in wonder, "my work really means something, doesn't it?"

This realization was to have momentous impact in a very short time.

44. AWAY OUT WEST

The apartment was full of boxes on October 7 when Radha, Jhumki, and I left Vasilis and Alexander to pack and drove to MSKCC. On the way we stopped at a flower shop. At the clinic Jhumki presented bouquets to Dr. Hudis's nurse, Maureen; Iris, our helpful appointment scheduler; and Morgan. They were really touched. No patient in their memory had given flowers to cancer-care staff. Jhumki saved the biggest bouquet for Cliff. Did his professional ice crack just a bit on that day?

We returned to the apartment.

Jhumki's estate attorney, Carolyn Glynn, came over—at least one New York lawyer does house calls. She was armed with documents and a witness to execute Jhumki's last will and testament.

After Ms. Glynn left, Alison Rosen arrived. Dr. Rosen is a counselor who had worked with Jhumki from the time she'd come to MSKCC. The two retired to the study to talk in private.

Ruth Oratz came next—at least one New York oncologist does house calls—to offer Jhumki encouraging advice. Dr. Oratz is a remarkable cancer specialist who developed a close bond with Jhumki. She works mostly with young breast-cancer victims, a small and special needs subset. She has a personal, feminine, reinforcing approach and tries to help her patients maintain an acceptable quality of life for as long as possible. Jhumki would visit Dr. Oratz periodically to discuss how her primary care was going. She always felt better when she returned from the visit.

"Some people live seventy, eighty, ninety years," Dr. Oratz said later, "and never have in life what Jhumki had in those last few years. Spectacular, but that's because of who she was. She brought out the best in everyone, everyone who came in her circle. You felt like you were in this circle of light. She radiated a kind of peacefulness. There was never anger. She never was bitter. She never complained about why did this happen to me.

"She wanted to feel well. When she felt the treatment was too harsh, she thought, 'No, this doesn't make sense, and it is interfering with my ability to do the things I love to do. I am willing to have treatment, but only if it is going to enhance my quality of life and afford me more time and more energy and more ability to do the things that I want to do in ways that would be creative and productive.' That was the only time she would be upset or angry or annoyed, but she never had a feeling of being victimized. That's very unusual."

By the time Dr. Oratz left, Jhumki was spent.

Paul fed her dinner, and she lay down with her mother sitting by her bedside. Alexander, Vasilis, and I finished packing the cartons in time for FedEx to pick up.

After that there wasn't much left to do.

Early the next morning, as our limo pulled away from the curb, I looked back at the apartment building longingly. We were leaving behind a city of happiness and sorrow. Would it be for good?

Later, much later, after she had been to hell and back, Jhumki told us she had no recollection of going to California.

There were five of us going west: Jhumki, Alexander, Vasilis, Radha, and I. Alexander's sister Anna would have liked to come, but someone had to hold down the fort in New York. I toyed with the idea of chartering a jet to reduce the stress on Jhumki, but the economics didn't work. So we flew United.

The morning after we arrived home, Jhumki felt better and went on a two-mile walk between Radha and me, along roads she knew from her school days. She pointed out the direction in which Tiffany had once run away for a week. Later a home-care doctor and nurse came to examine her. The next day she went to

Stanford, saw Dr. Carlson, and had adriamycin administered. She went to see Preetham and Vardhini's new house and commented that her apartment would comfortably fit in their kitchen.

And then she began an alarming decline.

She asked us to cancel her weekend open house and refused to meet even dear Casti friends like Joelle, Kritika, Sehba and Celeste. Her anxiety was uncontrollable. She could not sit or lie still; instead, she wandered around the house with someone always hurrying beside her to make sure she didn't fall. Nothing, not even Mishti, interested her.

On October 14, in the small Stanford examination room where metastasis had been confirmed, Dr. Carlson took Jhumki's hand, gently guided her to a chair, and sat on a low stool facing her. Alexander, Radha, and I stayed quietly in the background.

"Jhumki," Dr. Carlson told her, "I'm listening. Tell me your objectives. What would you like to do?"

I truly consider what happened next to be a pivotal miscommunication.

Dr. Carlson had looked after Jhumki for seven years and was a trusted care giver. He wanted to know Jhumki's expectations about her treatment regimen. Jhumki, on the other hand, thought he was asking about her career plans. Guilelessly, she told her doctor about learnings from the fall semester, her temporary leave of absence from teaching at NYU, exciting ideas for her Teaching Methods class in the new year, continuing work with SDL kids, writing papers and a book, a Greek trip over Christmas.

Dr. Carlson listened attentively and waited for her to finish. Then he opened a folder and checked the test results from the previous week. Closing it, he looked her in the eyes, as always, and began to speak.

He told her she was very ill. He told her that things were not looking good. He told her some of her plans were over-ambitious. He told her he did not believe continuing adriamycin was beneficial.

There was silence that went on for an eternity. I seethed, waiting for Jhumki's face to crumple. It didn't.

"Thank you, Bob," she said in a small but steady voice.

"Do you have any questions?"

"No, Bob."

Dr. Carlson left the room. It was the last time we saw him.

We sat there shell-shocked for some more time. Then Jhumki shook herself and got to her feet. The dark rings around her eyes were very pronounced.

"Well, that's that. Let's get out of here and go to Cafe Borrone."

It was a beautiful day in Silicon Valley. At Jhumki's favorite coffee shop in Menlo Park, we ordered sandwiches and coffee. It was just past noon, and the place was packed. We found a table in an outdoor enclosure and crammed in among hi-tech professionals chatting animatedly about products and venture capital and business plans on their lunch breaks. When we had settled in with our orders, Jhumki quietly and clearly made an announcement.

"Look. I am going back to New York."

Aghast, we stared at her.

"When?" I asked.

"Now, Baba. Tomorrow."

Shock, consternation, and attempts to dissuade her could not shake Jhumki. The decision had taken hold of her anxiety- and trauma-shrouded mind, and it drove all subsequent thoughts, words, and actions. She viewed us as forcing her to remain in California, imprisoning her. She *was* going back to New York.

"Take me back, Alexander. *Please.*"

Weeks later I recognized that under the frenzied external agitation, a razor-sharp intellect was beating panic-stricken wings against the golden cage of California.

The award ceremony at NYU had stunned her. Its reinforcing impact had been enormous on her flagging self-belief. It had opened boulevards of possibility for her life's mission. Professors had toasted her. Doctoral students had been abandoned. She had been put to pasture in an uncaring land. The California sun shone on a dreary desert land of infirmity, where Professor Basu would shrivel until snuffed out.

Dr. Carlson's pronouncement, made in completely good faith, propelled Jhumki to desperate, headlong flight.

I would not wish her harrowing return journey to New York on my worst enemy. Frightened, drugged, agitated, restless, speechless, uncoordinated, Jhumki experienced the ultimate plane ride from hell.

Even in the state she was in, Jhumki knew—though we didn't—that she was turning her life around. Nothing was certain except she had a few days, a few weeks, perhaps a month, maybe a little more, before the end. There was so much left to do. She wanted to run and do it all at once.

From the interview of Ted Diament

I picked them up at Kennedy Airport, and she really seemed to me to be quite the worst I had ever seen her. On the way back Alexander was driving and Jhumki was in the front seat. I was in the backseat. I think Jhumki was disoriented, and she wanted us to stop the car. I was a bit concerned that she might die in our car! That's how bad it looked to me. I don't think I have ever been with a person in that state. Alexander, I thought, was very strong. We did stop the car to get her oriented. That happened twice. She was very agitated, reaching for the door of the car.

E-mail from Dipak Basu to friends and family, Oct 18, 2008

Jhomi was very agitated the early part of the night after the return to New York, intensely-tired and over-medicated. Around midnight she started to relax and sleep for two hours at a time, eating and drinking in between. In the morning she told us she was happy to be home and endlessly walked around the apartment supported by Alexander or me, coming to a stop every time in front of the plastic box with a copy of her tenure dossier.

Her favorite pictures and decorations are back in place and the house looks inviting. She listened to usual morning sounds outside her window—garbage truck backing up, street cleaning vehicle going by, NYU security staff loudly changing shift, sirens on Broadway—and was happy.

The next day, however, Jhumki's anxiety returned in full force.

Her hospice physician, Dr. Bakalchuk, was out of town and told us of dire outcomes over the phone, while a stand-in physician dubbed Jhumki's situation "terminal anxiety" and that she had a short time left.

"Days. Perhaps hours," said the physician.

The next day her friends, Eric, Kritika, James, and several others, came to see her. Jhumki refused even to let them into the apartment. She was short with us and used dreadful words she had never used before.

On Sunday evening, at the recommendation of the hospice doctor, a strong dose of phenobarbital, a drug used to control epilepsy, was administered. Jhumki sank into a deep slumber. Hospice arranged for a night nurse to take up station outside her open bedroom door, and the four of us—Jhumki, Alexander, Radha and I—slept through our first full night in a long time.

On Monday morning Jhumki would not wake up. We shook her. At last she arose to have some soup and medicines, and then fell asleep again. It was not looking good.

And then, while Kritika sat with her in the darkened bedroom, Alexander took Radha and me outside, and handed us a five-page document. It had been written by our daughter sixteen months ago.

I looked at the title.

It read "Planning for an End."

45. PLANNING FOR AN END

*A*lexander, Mommy and Baba,

This document is proof-read by Paul Pawel Jerzy Prokop.

I'm writing this today because Paula, the woman who gave me the idea of the CarePage is in the hospital, very sick because of side effects of chemotherapy. Ironically, her cancer is in remission. But she's on an IV and they don't know why her hands and feet are swelling and more gory details I don't need to include. Though people keep telling me that I don't need to worry about dying, reading about real people with metastatic cancer makes me realize that side effects from chemotherapy can quickly turn into serious illness. I've done a lot of work preparing for a time before and after I die, and I don't want this to disappear because something unexpected happens. I've put this in Paul's safe-keeping because I don't think it's necessary to give it to you yet.

I would like how I die to not have an entirely tragic feeling, and thinking of Carey, I would like how I die to be a reflection of how I live. It's a good way to be remembered; I know that from experiencing Carey's service. I'm going to make this a checklist so it's easy for you to follow instructions. :)

I don't want to be put on life support at all. It's just not worth it to me after struggling through so much medical care. I have done my struggling and waiting. I do not want to do more.

Oregon is the only state in the nation in which a terminally ill patient with six months or less to live can legally ask a doctor to prescribe a lethal amount of medication. Please keep this in mind. I do not want to be alive if I cannot be active, think, work and enjoy life in ways I did before.

Ted Diament helped me fill out my healthcare proxy and other information. Paul and Alexander should have a copy.

If my organs can be donated, please do so. But I might not qualify because I have cancer.

On my computer are my logins in the file called "Important Hospital Stuff." Ask Alexander for them. It will help to update people through my CarePage. Also, you can use my cell phone or the "Master Wedding Spreadsheet" for calling people and getting their addresses to mail some of the things I have listed below.

If I'm dying, I want photos from everywhere printed for the room I am in, from places I have been and places I want to go: Africa (Gabon), Argentina (tango pictures), Alaska, India, and growing up, the Kenya and Japan trips, the hotel Furama in Hong Kong.

If I'm dying in NY, I want to go to lots of Angel Corrella performances at American Ballet Theater and Baryshnikov performances with Hell's Kitchen Dance.

I want to go to Half Moon Bay one last time, walk up Sanborn Park, to San Francisco at Ghirardelli, camping somewhere with all of us. I want Ranga to come. And I want to spend every day with Alexander.

Maybe we can have a bed in the living room so I can see the view every morning, and then a place in the kitchen, so I can be with everyone when they visit. I want Preetham to hear my whole list of food and make a menu every day.

If I'm dying and have time, I want the service I've described below to happen once while I'm alive minus all the sad things, so I can experience the music, food and people. Then you can do it again after I die. That way I get to enjoy it too. We can make an e-vite together. I want it to have the Caravan song as an mp3. I want my book out and things that I like, maybe the album from NY that I've hopefully made and other things we choose together.

Maybe we can put up a map of the world and put up

pictures each day of a different place I've visited. We're not going to make it too cheesy, okay?

Mommy, you and I should sit with our jewelry and decide who it's for. I know during the wedding, you liked finding notes from people long gone; we should do the same for others.

Please consider doing something nice for my doctors. I don't know what they would want or would consider meaningful.

I don't want the "thing" after I die to be called a funeral. A "service" sounds less grim. Also, I want to be cremated. An open pyre like in India would be preferable to a crematorium, but my idiot country might not allow this.

Here are poems I want read at my service; they are some of my favorites. Maybe ask Kritika and Carolyn and James to read them—you can find them in the Norton Anthology *and* Handbook of Heartbreak—*these are in the white bookshelf in the entry of our apartment bottom-most left shelf.*

- *Gwendolyn Brooks:* I Hold my Honey
- *Shakespeare:* This time of year though mayest in me behold
- *John Donne* Valediction Forbidding Morning: *This is to be read for Alexander. Ask Cissy Lewis to read it, she first introduced me to it*
- *Some poems marked in* Handbook of Heartbreak—*James can read these and then keep the book. He gave the book to me a long time ago and will find the marked pages.*
- I carry you with me always because I carry you in my heart *(to borrow a line from e.e. cummings).*
- *Something from Billy Collins that Libby reads.*
- *I have something for Kritika to read.*

I would like Preetham to sing Ragupathi Raghava, *Ama to sing* Sitting here wanting memories *and Kamron/Chisara/Ama to sing* Sail to the Lord, *though I'm not religious. They can sing this stuff to me in the hospital. We should attribute service ideas to Carey Davis.*

I want to make a program explaining my choices.

We can send an e-vite for the dying pre-party with that Caravan *song as invite.*

James made movies of messages I have to people I care about. Please ask him to send these to people, and maybe play them at the service, if you think it's appropriate.

There are lots of lots of photos around: Baba, can you make an album for Alexander and for yourselves, so you can have something cheerful to look at instead of feeling sad all the time? Jenny can lay it out if you give her the pictures. There is a whole set of pictures on my "Personal Folder" under "Family and Friends." You can use those too.

At my service I want Australian Shiraz and Gewürztraminer to be served. It can be the kangaroo labeled Shiraz. I want there to be yummy food cooked by Preetham, Baba and Mommy. You can get help from Neela Aunty.

I don't want a Hindu religious service, just something fun and light, where people can meet and catch-up and have fun. Maybe it shouldn't be at home. Maybe Sanborn or somewhere beautiful and outdoors.

There's a yoga CD that Melissa used to play that I really liked. It has a male singer's voice. Perhaps ask her for her music. Also, the music can be from the list I sent JJ, the DJ for our wedding—what I like, such as Indigo Girls and Annie Lennox and Ella Fitzgerald and Paul Simon.

You can put out some print-outs from my CarePage because I don't think it all has to be flowers and joy. There were things that were hard, and I want people to know. There are other things to put out: Costa Rica pictures and my howler monkey video and the South Africa video (all in the top drawer to the left of my desk).

Joelle can sing some of Carey's songs with Katie Isenberg.

Ama can sing When I Die Tomorrow *or* I Am Sitting Here Wanting Memories—*these are from Talisman.*

Ranga, maybe you can talk a little about growing up together in Saket, tell some funny stories.

I've sorted letters to people and want you to give them back to them, so they don't gather dust forever. Libby will tell you what to do.

What will you do with all my stuff? Try to donate clothes without being too sentimental, and donate books to libraries or well-organized schools. Don't be too sad about donating things: think about the people who will actually use my yoga mats, instead of them languishing in a closet. Maybe donate all my books at home to the library.

Please give my research materials and books to Angie or let her decide what to do with them. You can give her all my research tapes, in case she wants to organize them, and she can finish my book. I've spoken with her about it already.

If I pass away, I'd like all my office books to go to Angelo Collins at the Knowles Foundation. They have a science and math education library and work with 300 teachers and will pay for shipping.

Did you like the list? Is it in good Jhumki style? I guess there's too much for one service, but that's how it always was when I taught—too much to do and say in too little time.

Love you, try not to be too sad. Death is part of life, and I've lived more in my 30 odd years than many do in a lifetime, partially due to a life of privilege, particularly in my education, partially because of how you (Baba—adventure and curiosity, Mommy—determination, hard work and savvy-ness) taught me to live in the world. And in the time since I was diagnosed with metastatic cancer, I've learned something about what I really enjoy and care about in the world, in contrast with what I think I "should" be doing with my time. An important lesson.

Recently, everything good in my life has been in light of being with Alexander, especially what has brought me comfort, joy and a lot of silly-ness—how lucky I am to have met someone completely unique in the world.

Love,

Jhomi.

46. WHAT HAPPENED IN THE NIGHT

At two o'clock that afternoon, Jhumki awoke suddenly and sat up straight in bed. Radha, dozing in a chair by her side, hurriedly got to her feet. A little earlier we had been trying to decide whether she should go to the emergency room, or be watched closely as the hospice doctors were suggesting.

Radha put the alternatives to her daughter.

"Mommy, take me to emergency. *Now!*"

Jhumki said this with complete authority and with no ambiguity whatsoever.

One complains in New York when an emergency vehicle goes by every fifteen minutes with its siren screaming. After that day I shall never complain again.

In response to our 911 call, two paramedics in big boots and yellow jackets came to Jhumki's bedroom with a gurney. They gave us a choice: they could take her to the closest hospital, or to a hospital of our choice, provided it took less than twelve minutes to get there. We selected Memorial Hospital, and the ambulance, with siren shrieking, made the trip from Greenwich Village to the Upper East Side in eleven minutes flat—an impossibility in my reckoning.

Jhumki was awake when the paramedics came.

"Hi!" she addressed them. "I am Dr. Basu."

"Hello, doctor," said one paramedic, getting things ready to transport her. "What's your specialty?"

"I am Associate Professor of Science Education at New York University."

"No kidding. Science Education, huh?" mused the young

Filipino, wheeling her along the hallway to the elevator. "I gotta tell you this, doctor, I didn't much like science in school."

"Really?" Jhumki asked. "Why?"

"Oh, it was kinda tough. Teacher wasn't interesting. You know, the usual stuff."

Jhumki tried to sit up but failed since she was strapped to the gurney.

"Listen, science can be fun. It's *good* for you."

"Yeah?"

"Yeah."

As she was being inserted through the back entrance of the ambulance, Jhumki said to me, "Can you give him my contact info?" and to the paramedic, "Let's talk later, okay?"

He looked at her strangely as she lay back and dozed off.

Even though she was under private hospice care, MSKCC had kept open the option of Jhumki being taken to Memorial Hospital in a crisis. At the emergency room, Jhumki was fortunate to come under the care of a wonderful physician, who assessed the situation and took rapid action.

E-mail from Dipak Basu to friends and family, Oct 20, 2008

> *The conclusion today by Dr. Shanu Modi is that Jhumki was highly over-medicated. She has ordered intensive intravenous re-hydration and the meds will take another day to fully drain away. Jhumki's color is better after hydration and she is sleeping, relieved of anxiety. When awake she completely follows all conversation around her. Hudis will come over tomorrow.*

Jhumki was now battling for her life.

October 21 began with little change in her condition. Slurring, irritation, anxiety, drowsiness, panic, debility, all piled up on her.

It was a very rough day emotionally. Dr. Hudis came could not do much as Jhumki was completely distraught. She sobbed uncontrollably several times while telling her mother, "I don't want to die. I am 30. It's so unfair," and cried herself to sleep.

"There is nothing more heartbreaking for a mother," Radha wrote to her friends. "It is unbearable to watch her sorrow and pain. The attending doctor would not administer heavy medication and the anguish was not easily controlled. I wish and pray desperately for her last days to be peaceful and calm. Is even that mercy not possible?"

On the evening of October 21 there was no change in her condition. Jhumki was comatose, close to death. As night deepened we asked Alexander to go home and get some sleep. After he left, Radha went to nap on a sofa in the waiting lounge a few doors away. A nurse came by now and then to check Jhumki's vital signs. The hospital was silent, somnolent in the eerie glow of minimalist halogen lighting.

Around 2 a.m. I was sitting beside Jhumki's bed when she stirred and tried to get up. Hastily I got on my feet to clear away the various tubes and lines around her.

"Baba, I gotta go."

"Wait a sec, Jhomi. I'll get Mommy. She's just around the corner."

"Baba, I gotta *go!*"

Wheeling the I-V stand along, I helped her to the bathroom. She went okay, came back, and sat on the bed. I was wrapping a cotton blanket around her when Radha walked in, looking worried. She must have known telepathically that something was going on.

"Hi, how's everything?" she asked. "Why's she sitting up?"

"Oh, she had to . . ." I began and was interrupted when from somewhere came a throaty, humor-filled, long-forgotten voice.

"Maw-mi, you wanna know somethin' funny?"

362

We stepped back in shock and stared in the dim light at the hospital-gown-clad skeleton with enormous eyes that was our darling child.

"Y'know, Mommy? I hadda go, and Baba wanted to find *you!*"

She said it like it was the biggest joke in the world. About to protest, I stopped, and the two of us hugged her spontaneously. She lay back, sighed, and went back to sleep. I held my wife while she cried "can-it-be?" tears.

On that day I understood the phrase "a heart bursting with happiness." It was a miraculous, miraculous day, every minute of it, as we watched a new Jhumki emerge, little by little, a beautiful butterfly emanating from a cocoon of anguish.

By 5 a.m. she was wide awake and ravenously hungry. I was dispatched to find the breakfast menu. She wanted every item on it, but there was a problem. Patients couldn't order before 7 a.m. This upset her.

"Don't patients need to eat?" she grumbled, settling for crackers Mommy managed to scavenge from a break room. Then we went for a walk. She was adept with the hospital's wheeled walker. I trotted alongside her, pushing the I-V stand. We did several turns of the hospital corridor until she suddenly noticed the wall clock said seven.

"Gotta order. Gotta order. Let's go, Baba."

We found a phone, and Jhumki called in cornflakes, croissant, cranberry muffin, scrambled eggs, french toast. Then she was told it would take forty-five minutes for the food to arrive.

"I mean, Baba, croissants? Cornflakes? Forty-five minutes?! Will they go to the market to buy them or what?"

A nice nurse came by, studied Jhumki, and suggested she visit the art room.

"Let's go, Baba!"

Radha was sound asleep in a chair in the hospital room. We took the elevator down two floors, through a set of glass doors, and into a large carpeted area with several partitioned sections. Jhumki walked across to a piano and stared at it for a while. I stood by her and watched quietly. She reached down and pressed a key. *Plink!* it went. She sat down and pressed another key. *Plonk!* Then she pressed three keys together with fingers of one hand, turned it over, and looked at it in wonder, then at the other. Her hands were not rigid and claw-like anymore! She got up and stared at me for a bit as though seeing me for the first time. I wished I knew her thoughts, but didn't want to break into the metamorphosis taking place in front of my eyes.

The pinched face and constant frown, constants ever since Gabon, were gone. A new softness permeated her gauntness.

We walked slowly to a table with plastic baskets of crafts. An attendant in a blue coat came over and laid out some kits for her. Jhumki sat and selected an earthenware plate and little multicolored ceramic tiles—stars, crescents, leaves, snowflakes. She glued them one by one carefully onto the plate. While it dried, she found a clear plastic parrot and a chubby dinosaur and painted them in yellow, pink, and green watercolors. Her hand was steady. Not one splotch.

I felt a presence and turned. It was Dr. Rosen, Jhumki's counselor.

"Baba, can I spend a few minutes with Alison?"

"Careful!" I was about to tell her—she was going unusually fast with the walker—but stopped myself in time.

Radha and I were in the hospital room when Dr. Rosen brought back Jhumki and left. Her breakfast had arrived on a big tray laden with several covered dishes. She lifted a lid in anticipation and her face clouded. It was some kind of mush. She lifted another lid. More mush. And so it went on. Croissants, muffins, scrambled eggs, toast, pureed to perfection, reduced to pulp. After she lifted the fifth lid, I knew she was going to cry.

"Steady, Jhomi," I said. "Stay right there. I'll be back in a moment."

I dashed to the elevator and down to Starbucks on the busy main floor of the hospital; bought two of their fattest croissants, a big blueberry muffin, and a café latte; and dashed back. I have never watched a child—sorry, a professor—eat with such gusto.

In the middle of breakfast, Dr. Shanu Modi walked in with a following of junior doctors and residents.

"How are you, Jhumki?" asked Dr. Modi. "You *do* look better."

She sat down beside Jhumki and measured her pulse while we recounted the night's happenings. The young doctors, all men, stood in a tight bunch facing us.

"I do feel better, Dr. Modi," Jhumki said. "And do I have a treat for you."

She lifted the lid off a container on the tray, and then another, while naming their contents. From there on it was vintage Jhumki.

She lectured the massed doctors and residents roundly on the ills of pulverized muffins, the inhumanity of croissant pâté, and the inadvisability of doctors asking patients to eat food they wouldn't themselves touch. The young professionals stared at her pop-eyed while Dr. Modi, Radha, and I fought hard to not laugh.

The siren was not screaming this time.

Alexander and I sat in the back of the ambulance taking Jhumki home from the hospital. We had been driving along First Avenue for a few minutes when she turned to us from her gurney with her eyes wide.

"How did I get to the hospital?" she wanted to know.

"In an ambulance like this, Jhomi," Alexander told her.

"Really? I don't remember it at all. Who decided about the ambulance?"

"*You* did! Remember? You woke up and said, 'Take me to ER right now.'"

She stared at us in disbelief.

"I did? Was I very sick?"

"Yes, Jhomi." I reached out and squeezed her shoulder. "We thought we'd lost you."

She was silent for several Manhattan blocks.

"Have people been asking about me?"

"I have a long list of phone calls, and your inbox is full," Alexander said. "Many of your friends were at home when the ambulance came to take you."

"They *were*?"

"Yes. Kritika and Ted and Eric . . ."

"Kritika was there?"

"She was. But you weren't well enough to talk to her."

We were stuck in traffic. No siren, remember?

"Baba, can I use your phone?"

I handed it across, and she called a number.

"Hello, who's this?" I was near Jhumki and could hear Kritika answer, probably from Harvard. My phone number would have been unfamiliar on her display.

"Hi, this is Jhumki!"

There was an astonished silence and then a *"Jhooooomki!!!"*

"Yeah, it's me." Jhumki grinned on the gurney. "You know, just checking on how your dissertation's going an' all!"

She was back in her groove or, as Chris Emdin would say, her zone!

The previous ambulance trip had taken eleven minutes. This one could happily have lasted eleven hours. She had talked to Kritika, Ted, Paul, and Eric before we reached her apartment, and was itching to get off the gurney by the time she was wheeled inside. A beaming Vasilis and a brand-new walker welcomed her home. The apartment was spotless. Everything that had gone to make her a final home in California was back in New York and in its former place. Anna, Alexander, and Vasilis had worked themselves to the bone to make the apartment ready for her second return from the dead. Jhumki rolled off the gurney and went to each room with her walker. She checked out everything as though looking to rent the place. She studied an oxygen cylinder in a closet, handicapped railings on the bathroom wall, a plastic stool under the shower, an I-V stand in a corner, food in the fridge, newspapers on the coffee table, and finally in a corner, the plastic cabinet of her tenure evaluation. She stared at it for a long time. Then she came back to us, standing bunched together in a transfixed group, watching her.

"Mommy," she said, "I want to go for a walk in the park."

The tension broke and everyone smiled. Radha cried. I thumped Jhumki, gently, on the back. Vasilis was more practical. He took the wheels off the back legs of the walker, got two yellow tennis balls from his son, cut holes in them, and affixed them to the walker's legs.

"Better traction for my favorite daughter-in-law!" he said.

And off we all went for a sunny walk in Washington Square Park, still decorated in fall colors. Fat black squirrels, gathering acorns for winter, were too busy to take note of a thin professor watching them with a smile.

E-mail from Dipak Basu to friends and family, Oct 26, 2008

The news just at this moment is good. Jhumki has pulled out of a major crisis which required three days of hospitalization last week.

She returned to New York from California last week and a complication with her cancer and medications required her to be rushed to Memorial Hospital on Monday. After two frightening days, she began to recover and came home on Wednesday to an apartment equipped with things like walker, I-V, hospital bed, oxygen, home nursing, etc. Since then she has steadily improved to the extent that yesterday she walked through the galleries of the Museum of Modern Design, and saw a movie with Alexander. We are all slated for a performance of American Ballet Theater today.

The old witty, confident irreverent, intellectual, considerate Jhumki is back after weeks of suffering. It is a blessing to savor every moment with her. Just before checking out of Memorial Hospital our Jhumki discoursed to her team of attending doctors on the deficiencies of the blended french toast she was served!

We never forget she is desperately ill, and the cancer has impaired her liver. With returning strength, another treatment regimen just may be possible—we will know about this after blood tests and consultation with Dr Hudis. In the meantime every moment she is out, happy and about is precious. We hope it goes on for a long time. We have rented an apartment in Greenwich Village, six blocks from J&A's apartment. Until now the Kumars have unstintedly given us their love and the warmth of their home. We could not have focused so completely on Jhumki without them.

Thank you so much for your good wishes and words of encouragement. When one's planning horizon is down to days and hours, one has a totally different perspective on life, concentrating simply on living the present.

This message was read by many people who were expecting the worst, and was forwarded on to many others. Alexander posted it on Jhumki's CarePage. Messages of delight and encouragement flooded in.

Jhumki was horrified when she became aware of her unfriendly behavior under the influence of drugs, and tried to respond to every message and to contact everyone she cared for.

"I think it was three, four days after I picked them up at JFK, when I got that phone call," Ted Diament remembered. "I think it was from the hospital. The voice said, 'Ted?' and I said, 'Who is this?' and she said, 'It's Jhumki.' And it really was! It was really shocking to hear her. I can tell you it had at least been a month since I had heard her voice that strong. And to hear that, remembering my last encounter with her in the car, it was just astounding.

"I don't recall if it was that evening or the next, when she was already at home. Jhumki wanted to go out to eat. So out we went. I remember looking at Radha. I looked at Radha and I said, 'She wants to go out to eat!'

"We walked very slowly. But we walked. We went to a Spanish restaurant and we had a meal, Alexander, Jhumki, and me. I think it was the nicest meal I ever had. It was a miraculous thing to see her really revitalized, obviously still weakened, but now completely lucid and enjoying her dinner, at a juncture when we all thought she was gone."

"Jhumki called and we chatted a bit," her cousin Preetham wrote. "It almost brought tears to my eyes to hear the old Jhumki again. I did not think I would get that opportunity to engage with that voice, that intelligence and wit. We talked for a little bit about stuff, including the last few weeks. It is hard to rationalize that Jhumki was the one I spoke to today. Anyway, who cares? I am simply happy that we have this Jhumki back."

Radha and I rented an apartment close to the kids. That way we would be nearby without intruding. The recovery had begun. The renaissance was happening. In the next days we established a pattern. After Alexander left for work in the mornings, Jhumki and I would walk three blocks to Think Coffee. Think, a Greenwich Village institution, has great coffee and signature grilled-cheese sandwiches. It is inexpensive, has good wine, and funky music. Over a bowl—it was too big to be called a mug—of Spanish latte one morning at Think, I caught Jhumki up on news. She was emerging from the pure shock of her ordeal and beginning to analyze what had happened.

"So, Baba, it wasn't the cancer or the chemo?"

"No, Jhomi. At least, mostly no. It was those medicines you took for side effects. Especially the Haldol. At Memorial Hospital, Dr. Modi gave you something intravenously to flush all the meds out. It reduced the high ammonia that made you behave strangely. The ammonia levels rose because of liver insufficiency. You are off everything now except the fentanyl patch for pain and lactulose for ammonia."

Having no trouble keeping up with the medical jargon, Jhumki studied me carefully as I said all this. What bothered her immensely, she said, were her unstable behavior and loss of control over herself. Then she looked at her hands.

"Baba, my fingers are straight again."

"Yes, sweetie. Remember the piano at Mem Hospital? Your fingers were stiff because of ammonia too. The tension was making you cringe, cramp up. Your frown's gone. And your hair's coming back nicely. Yay!"

We talked some more while she downed an apple muffin, a chocolate croissant, and the bowl of latte. That afternoon, she walked five blocks to the NYU gym with her mother. It was impossible to imagine seventy-two hours ago, she had been comatose and dying. The gym attendant, whom she knew, greeted her warmly, complimented her hairstyle, and told her it was wonderful to have her back. This pleased her immensely.

Jhumki trudged slowly and steadily on a treadmill for a half hour while Mommy and the young attendant watched her in awe. She came home grinning from ear to ear.

47. A NOVEMBER TO REMEMBER

"Baba, what shall I *do*?"

Jhumki and I were strolling slowly around Washington Square Park, this time without the walker. I answered this very carefully; instinctively aware it was not a rhetorical question.

"What would *you* like to do, Jhomi?"

"What *can* I do?" she countered with some truculence. We were answering questions with questions. Not a good trend.

I thought for a bit.

"Well, Jhomi, you might do the things you couldn't because you were sick. You're getting better, and . . ."

She blinked and I stopped. Her chin went up as she looked at me with brows crinkled.

"I'm getting better?"

"Of course you are, Jhomi," I said with no hesitation, surprising her. "Without the awful narcotics you'll get better than you were in September and October. Will you get fully well? You know I won't say any such thing. Look at you! I can't imagine how ill you were just this Tuesday."

I leaned over to give her a hug, but she freed herself impatiently and resumed walking.

"So what should I *do*?"

Progress! Now then, far be it from a prudent Baba to tell a disturbed Jhomi what she should or shouldn't do.

"You *could* go back to teaching, you know. Write a paper..."

"I can?"

"Those two I'm confident you can."

"But, Baba, I tried typing on my laptop. My fingers don't stretch, and I make tons of mistakes."

"Oh, *foof!* I'll type for you. Not a problem. You think about the paper."

She digested this while I looked at her hopefully. We couldn't lose the new Jhumki to despondency.

"And you two need a vacation," I pressed on. "Go to a warm beach with Alexander. Maybe even go and see Gia-gia in Greece. And I'm so excited about the book you've been talking about writing. I'd love to help with that too. I have nothing much to do, you know."

We made a turn at a corner of the park while she looked into space, thinking.

"Don't decide now," I urged. "Think about it."

Later I got into a spot of bother with my wife.

"Can't you see she's weak and needs rest? Did you *have* to start her off writing papers? And teaching! The baby can barely walk!"

Mommy was, of course, forgetting in her mommyness, that she had once been a Jhomi herself. On many occasions the following dialogue has happened in the Basu household:

"Jhomi, you can't do that. It's too dangerous/difficult/ complicated."

"Mommy, didn't you come to the USA alone with just eight dollars without knowing a soul? And didn't you barricade yourself in that sleazy hotel in downtown L.A. on your first night, and ..."

"Yes, but ..."

You get the picture.

૭๑

Three days later Jhumki unlocked the door of her office and walked in. I entered behind her, put down her backpack, and looked around.

Jhumki's office was a patchwork of originality. It had rows of books with intriguing titles—*Genius: The Life and Science of*

Richard Feynman, Existential Psychotherapy, The USSR Olympiad Problem Book, The Trouble with Testosterone. There were wall posters and rows of clearly labeled binders, shelves with videotapes stacked high beside mini-camcorders and tripods. There were three desktop computers for research by her doctoral students.

I pulled out a chair, sat down, fired up her laptop, opened a fresh document, and looked at her.

There was a pause.

After a while Jhumki spoke ruminatively.

"Baba, I've been thinking."

I paid attention.

"I think the best way to start is by finishing a chapter I've promised for a book that Angie's editing."

I agreed it was good idea and went through an absolutely mind-bending experience.

Jhumki dictated. I typed. While she dictated, she pulled out papers, consulted notes, watched videos, and referred to books— all of this without a pause in her dictation to me. Her primary train of thought—input to me—was collected and coalesced on the fly from multiple multimedia multi-locational sources. She knew precisely which data point was where. There was never a break in her dictation while she looked for information or even thought. It was astounding.

And so it went for a whole week, by which time we got to subchapter 6.5 of Angie's book, and Jhumki was strong enough to get to her office with her backpack by herself, and flexible enough to hit the keyboard like the old days.

On November 5, Jhumki and I collected our brews at Think Coffee and walked to a big NYU housing complex located between 3rd and Bleecker Streets. There was a long line of people in the foyer of the building. Several in the queue noticed Jhumki and came over.

"Wow, we thought you were in California."

"Jhumki! You look real nice."

"Hey, your hair's all grown back. It's so cool!"

A security guard she knew shook her hand. Brent, her colleague Fabienne's husband, gave her a hug. As a matter of fact, she got a lot of hugs that morning. When she reached the end of the line, Jhumki read her paper carefully and disappeared into a kiosk. A few minutes later she came out looking smug.

"Hey, I voted!" she said excitedly.

That night she stayed up until Barack Obama came onstage with Michelle, Malia, and Sasha to deliver his acceptance speech in Chicago's Grant Park. Content after watching the speech on TV, she went to sleep.

On May 5, 2012, in New York, at the third annual Sci-Ed Innovators Expo and Symposium sponsored by the Jhumki Basu Foundation, her mother read out a short message to hundreds of assembled school kids and teachers.

> *I am sorry I could not be present to keynote the event. The President and I express our deep appreciation of the work of Sci-Ed Innovators.*
> *Sincerely,*
> *Michelle Obama.*

Jhumki restarted working with her grad students and visiting outlying schools where she had research programs. One of us always went with her and happily spent on taxis and limos to make her feel comfortable.

She developed a book proposal and sent it to publishers.

And then, to everyone's astonishment, her scan results and blood markers began to move in the right direction.

E-mail from Dipak Basu to friends and family, Nov 3, 2008
Re: Urgent Care Party!

Jhomi continues to amaze. FYI I'm sitting in the NYU gym while she jogs(!) on a treadmill. Though she's getting stronger, Jhomi's liver numbers are still high, and a crash might come at any time. Recently she has been suffering from tummy pain and distension. Hudis advised her yesterday to get an ultrasound checkup for albumin-induced fluid retention.

Kritika, Eric and James had come over and the seven of us headed to urgent care at Memorial Hospital. She chatted with her friends during ultrasound and X-ray. There was music and much laughter. The tests came out negative and Mommy and Jhomi said bye to everyone and went to a performance of American Ballet Theater.

As we see her fighting back the demons, we feel simultaneously proud and helpless and hopeful and apprehensive.

She is meeting with her Physics Dept collaborator tomorrow. She will finish chapter contribution work today and start on her new textbook.

To this, Jhumki's mother responded:

Our spunky Jhomi and I changed shirts in the lobby of urgent care, took a quick ride to the theater, and saw a scintillating season finale performance of American Ballet Theater. One can live life in the shadow of death, or like Jhomi live life to the fullest!

Every happy moment with her is cherished and special.

"You are the best mommy in the whole wide world," Jhumki to her mother after the ballet performance. "Never ever think that you have not done enough."

Radha treasures this moment as one of her best memories

of Jhumki. The testimonial about the best mommy in the world, from a Jhumki who took pride in her non-mushy persona, was straight from the heart. It reflected profound gratitude for a lifetime of love, care, and wisdom.

From Jhumki's CarePage, Nov 16, 2008

Joelle and Alison visited last week and spent long hours sitting with me, walking around and making me feel calm and loved. Julie, Jenn and Emily came this weekend just to see me and we met Stephanie and organizer Jenny in a teahouse and then a coffee place. It was so calming and fun to be with my Stanford friends, the most I've laughed and smiled in months. I'm very grateful for these girlfriends who are so sensitive and caring.

Next week we're going upstate to visit friends, another relaxing experience where we get to take honey out of Jeremy's honeycombs. And then we're daring to think about cooking for Thanksgiving (Eric, Kritika, James and I, all of whom were with me at urgent care) and then perhaps getting away to Florida for the four-day weekend.

As many of you whom I've spoken with know, my mind feels much more clear being off all the medication, and I'm finding my feet literally every day. I just finished the chapter outline for a book and have been doing research with my fantastic doctoral students at SDL. I saw Nancy Gannon's beautiful baby Tillie yesterday and got to spend a quiet evening with her as well.

This weekend was a "non-medical" one: a break from decisions and tests and anxiety, and it made me realize how stressed I have been for weeks and weeks. Just some peace and quiet have let me start a book of fiction that Joelle left me, see people, and cry a little less.

Sending lots love, Jhumki

"The thing I will always take away with me," Joelle Mourad remembered about the visit, "is that when we were about to go she turned to me and said, 'Joelle, what am I going to do when you leave?'

"That I was able to be someone she could be really honest and genuine with, talk about how she was feeling completely openly, and that I could support her at that point in her struggle, meant *so* much to me. That trip was an absolute gift and a magical time."

"She needed you guys very much," I told Joelle. "We were there, always there, Alexander, Radha, and I, trying to keep the disease at bay. She needed to forget it and talk about important and unimportant things, fun things, with friends that she loved.
"

48. DEEP IN DECEMBER

During the darkest hours of September and October, in the hushed twilit corridors of Memorial Hospital, I had tried to count the days.

Will she see tomorrow? I wondered.

Will she see Election Day?

Will she celebrate her thirty-first birthday?

Will she go with Alexander for a beach vacation?

Will she teach again?

Will she go to Greece for Christmas?

Will we ring in the New Year together?

Will she teach class in spring?

In answer to each question I told myself, she is here. Now. With us. Lovable and Jhomi. Tomorrow might come. Be happy with that.

We looked forward only to the next marker of life. We lived in the moment. If we got through today, it was thank you, God. If we got through the next day, it was thank you again, God. Perhaps another day, God? Long-term planning was twenty-four hours.

On November 19, Jhumki turned thirty-one.

Her health was plateauing after three weeks of amazing improvement. She was tiring quickly. Neuropathy was back. She was developing a painful condition called ascetis, caused by faulty albumin management by the liver.

In spite of her ailments, Jhumki walked over with Alexander to our Bleecker Street apartment for lunch on her birthday. She could eat only a few things, and out of those Radha cooked her three favorite dishes: non-spicy *masala dosa, dahi vada,* and *kesari*[21], which she enjoyed. We talked about Joelle and Alison's visit and the Stanford friends who were coming in a group the following weekend. Alexander took her home in a cab to rest up for a birthday dinner at Otto Enoteca with friends. She went there but was too unwell to stay long.

Just before Thanksgiving, Jhumki decided to utilize a gift certificate from her wedding for a stay at Mohonk Mountain House, a resort in the Hudson River Valley. She drove out with her husband and walked around a bit at Mohonk but was generally quite indisposed. The drive back was gruelling. Radha and I were waiting in their apartment when Alexander called from their car.

"She is throwing up," he said to me. "I had to stop three times on the highway just to let her settle down. She's a little dizzy. We are close. Can you meet us at the curb and help her to the apartment while I garage the car?"

I met them at the curb. Jhumki, deathly white and unsteady, got out of the car. I held on to her, and walked her and a suitcase into the lobby.

The elevator arrived. I held her with one hand, pulled open the elevator door with the other, nudging the suitcase along with a foot. As I held the heavy door open with my other foot, Jhumki pushed me away and shook off my hand. I looked around, bewildered. She had moved back into the lobby, and behind me was a young woman, very pregnant, with a child in a stroller. They had appeared out of nowhere. In my exaggerated pose, I

[21] Veggie crepes, yogurt dumplings, and saffron dessert.

was blocking their entry to the elevator.

Jhumki said, "Baba, move!" and, to the mother, "Go ahead, please."

I moved. The lady and the stroller got in, then Jhumki, then the suitcase, and finally me. We emerged on the third floor and were walking along the corridor when she said to me, "Baba, you must *always* hold the door open for a pregnant lady." Then she went to her room and collapsed on the bed.

I will never forget that moment. However distressed she might be, Jhumki never forgot others in need of help.

Through all the anguish Jhumki was still working away at home and at NYU, and she was going to high schools to meet teachers and kids and collect research data. Just after her birthday she sat us down for a talk.

"Mommy, Baba, I think I'm being taken care of too much," she stated, waving aside protestations. "You guys can't put your lives on hold forever. Alexander and I are going to Florida. You need a break too."

We considered.

"Our house does need attention," Radha said slowly. "And Mishti."

"There you go!" Jhumki said.

"And Jhomi," I added, "at Anudip there are several things I need to resolve."

"So it's all settled. We go to the Florida Keys. Mommy goes to California. Baba goes to India."

"Yes, but what about . . ." I began.

But Jhumki had decided. It was a done deal.

E-mail from Alexander to Jhumki's parents, Nov 29, 2008

Casa Morada is an oasis of relaxation! Beautiful, quiet, serene, ultra private and stylish. The day starts with Yoga practice, followed by a super fresh breakfast on the veranda overlooking the bay. During the day we have been relaxing in the quiet island being served delicious drinks. Yesterday we packed lunch and went on a long sea kayak ride around the bay mangrove islands. Saw a bunch of birds: pelicans, herons, egrets, etc. This morning I did two dives: a wreck and a reef dive. Both were great. Jhumki did the Yoga class and had a massage. Later we'll have dinner and then sit for some live acoustic music by the beach. Tomorrow after Yoga and breakfast we will drive to the dolphin research institute for a shallow water dolphin encounter. We are both looking forward to it. Monday we'll do some more relaxing and head to the airport a little after noon.

Alexander returned from Florida with a wife who had relapsed considerably. Radha was anxiously waiting for them in New York. On December 4th, Jhumki was readmitted to Memorial Hospital. At about the same time, while boarding my flight in Kolkata, I received an e-mail from Radha saying, "Dreaded Devastating December is here. I'm petrified."

"Hi, Baba," Jhumki said quietly when I walked into her hospital room straight from Kennedy Airport. And not much else. She was sleepy and tired. I left her with Radha and Alexander, and took my bags to our apartment.

All our attention now concentrated on managing our daughter's pain. Radha took on the role of her pain manager. Radha had e-mailed Jhumki in Florida, "One fact that is believed with great certainty by all the people I've spoken with: *pain can and should be managed.* There is nothing therapeutic about pain and it needs as much attention as the cancer and you can be made comfortable, and yet be functional and non-drowsy."

When Jhumki's initial bout of chemotherapy ended in 2002, she had told her mother, "Mommy, the way you approach things, if you can do that for my cancer then I'll be okay. We will take care of it, and it will get solved."

"She had that complete faith in me," Radha lamented later.

"And I let her down. The thing that I regret most is that she depended on me to *save* her. She never believed she was going to die. As the end neared, she still fervently believed 'Mommy will somehow find a way. She always does.' That's the most painful thing for me. It still haunts me that I couldn't save her."

From a posting on Jhumki's CarePage, Dec 13, 2008

Dear Family and Friends,

Upon our return to NY from Florida on December 1, Jhumki spent her first day back at the School for Democracy and Leadership. It was a tough day, with a gradual weakening and returning signs of the confusion she experienced in Sept/Oct. A blood test showed marked deterioration in her liver function. At her doctor's recommendation, we admitted her to Memorial Hospital on the evening of December 4.

By last Tuesday, December 9, while most of her liver function measures were continuing to deteriorate, her confusion subsided and Jhumki expressed the desire to leave the hospital to teach her last two NYU classes of the semester, administer a research survey, and interview students at SDL. Through her sheer determination we managed to get her released and she made it to the student final project presentations of her Tuesday Teaching Methods class.

She spent Tuesday night at home but, sadly, by Wednesday her nausea had become unmanageable and we were unable to take care of her using medications at home. She was readmitted on that evening and has been in the hospital since.

The doctors tell us that her cancer is advancing fast, and that it cannot be controlled any more. She's spending a lot of the time sleeping and is drowsy when awake. She is not able to converse on the phone or to read e-mail. The I-V medications have controlled her nausea. Gratefully, she's also not reporting feeling pain, which is an improvement over the past two months. We are trying to provide as much comfort and relief as possible. She is in a spacious private room in the VIP floor at Memorial and is being seen by some of the best medical teams in the world. One of her parents or I are always by her side.

Jhumki has a remarkable strength and will, and was able to beat all the odds in October and November. I'm hoping that she can fight her way out of the hospital again, and gain some more time to do the things she likes, but we have to face the dire warnings of her extended medical team here at Sloan-Kettering, that a critical event can occur at any point in time.

She's still fighting, always the fighter.

A few minutes ago, she went on a sprint walk of the hospital corridor with us trying keep up with her I-V stand!

Love,

Alexander.

49. BE AT PEACE, JHUMKI LOVE

Surrounded by close family and dear friends, our angel left us with a smile on her peaceful face. She was pain-free and content. Outside Memorial Hospital's nineteenth floor window, huge snowflakes were floating down on New York's skyscrapers. It was 3:30 pm on Tuesday December 16.

Jhumki clearly told us long ago this was not to be a tragic event (her words).

Alexander had put up pictures and mementos from her travels and from their wedding in her hospital room. We sang her favorite songs from "Dona Nobis Pacem" to "Country Road, Take Me Home." We sat around her bed and talked about everything from her childhood days to the present. She was able to respond by pressing our hands almost until the very end.

To her students Jhumki was a fount of inspiration and compassion, to her colleagues an original researcher and teacher, to her friends a witty, irreverent person. To Alexander she strove to be the perfect life partner. To us she was our baby. It was heart-wrenching that Alexander had just told her how much he loved her and her mother was holding her hands and singing her favorite baby song, "Skinny ma rinky do, I love you," when she breathed her last. We will treasure that exquisite contented smile on her peaceful face.

Tearfully,

Radha and Dipak Basu

50. SO MUCH LEFT TO DO

One of the instructions Jhumki left behind was that a letter from her be read at her memorial ceremony. It was read at Brooklyn's Greenwood Cemetery, where she was cremated on December 18, 2008, and at a memorial event held at Castilleja School on January 24, 2009. On both occasions, Kritika did the honors for her dearest friend, with emotion trembling in her voice, while hundreds of assembled students and colleagues and well-wishers listened, remembered, and wiped their eyes.

I have asked Kritika to read my thoughts to you because she combines clarity of thinking with knowing me well.

I suspect that many of you will talk today of how I have lived my life richly and made the most of my time alive. This is partially appropriate to say because it is true—I've tried my best to take advantage of opportunity and take action on what I believe. This attitude has mostly been possible because I was raised with every sort of privilege, education, and support, and had spectacular role models in my family and mentors. I have lived in a world that has told me constantly that I can pursue anything I desire.

But I want to be clear that the fact that I have lived my time richly does not compensate for dying at this point in my life and, therefore, has not been significant consolation to me. I would have done it whether or not I had cancer. Some people develop a "new attitude on living" because of cancer. I have not. I do not think of living well and living long as dichotomies. I want both. At services, people often talk of the person who died finding peace. I have not. I am not ready to die.

I have a lot of living left to do, and I want to tell you

about it. I would like to have a family. I like kids a lot and have thought a great deal about raising them. I have collected activities to do with kids that range from "philosophical" to "scientific." I have bought children's books that I think are most engaging and appropriate. And I have made all sorts of plans. I have plenty of places left to travel, particularly places with primates, elephants, birds—places with a rich biological of life, where you can marvel at the diversity produced by evolution. There are kids left to teach—I have missed being in a high-school classroom, but the challenges and time commitments of treatment have made it impossible to envision returning. I have teachers left to plan with, articles left to publish, books left to write. I want to take more dance lessons, influence educational policy through a position in government, learn to balance handstand in the center of the room, finish a marathon (not just a triathlon), have a lifetime of 6-monthly reunions with my high school/college friends. There's a dog to take running, a house in which to start a garden. I'd like to continue arguing with my doctor, get a medical degree and work for Doctors Without Borders. And then, of course, there are all the things I haven't even imagined doing that won't get done.

Alexander and I have a whole life left to live together. Of course, as I said, there is the question of having family. Also there is Alexander's sister in Jerusalem to whom I wished to be nearby. I wanted our family to spend time living in India. Alexander and I have many silly songs left to sing to each other, nights left to snuggle, Saturdays left for him to convince me that life isn't just about work but about playing around, sleeping in, and eating well.

It's easy to attribute feelings of peace to someone because we wish it for them. It's easy to be satisfied because it's too hard to admit that the work is not done, that it is not sufficient. I feel bad making your burden heavier and asking for more. I know my doctors worked so hard and have tried their hardest to keep me alive. My friends and family have moved heaven and earth to keep me comfortable and happy.

But I will still say to you honestly that it isn't enough. It isn't enough for me and for people who have had far less than me the world over. There is so much work and living to be done. I have tried to stay grounded in reality and face the world squarely throughout the time that I have had metastatic cancer. So I am trying my best right now to do the same, to tell you that I am not in any way ready to die.

There is so much more left to do.

51. THE LEGACY

The aura remains.

The loss endures.

Jhumki lives on.

"Like a flower, the petals of her life keep unfolding," writes Maria Rivera Maulucci. "How beautiful they are!"

In late 2011, Chris Emdin described to me the lasting impact of Jhumki's accomplishments.

"Her work uses science to present a more robust human being to the world. For a long time, people of color have been told that science is the most difficult thing and they cannot do well in it. So when, with the use of this amazing tool of inclusive teaching, minority kids see themselves as scientists, then we automatically break the mold of *all the other things* they are told they cannot do. And that, simply, is how Critical Science Agency, fueled by Democratic Pedagogy, works.

"If a student believes, 'I can read the science section of the *New York Times* and understand it,' or 'I can have a conversation with folks about science subject matters,' or 'I can do a science project and people think it's brilliant,' then he or she thinks, 'Why can't I do anything else?' Everything else becomes small potatoes! Attendance rates in other classes increase. Kids begin to ask, 'What's going on in my neighborhood?'

"That's the beauty of it!

"The focus on youth, the empowerment of youth, the voice of youth from those hard, bitter, urban streets. Looking at them as people who have much to give and to share. Any pedagogue who is conducting research thus empowers youth to be co-researchers. That's Jhumki's work."

It was Radha who proposed the quirky term, "Sci-Ed Innovators"

in 2009, to a Google group of Jhumki's well-wishers while discussing ways to continue her legacy. And a strange thing happened: the term stuck and spiraled from an idea to a program to a movement. It was fired by Jhumki's vision and propelled by the foundation created in her memory. Much like those massing behind the French tricolor in "Do You Hear the People Sing?" from the stage production of Les Misérables, people stepped forward in growing numbers to hold aloft Jhumki's torch. Leaders of NYU and of the New York City Department of Education, researchers on the way science is taught in schools, and, most importantly, science teachers of inner-city America who seek social justice for their students, have joined the movement.

Sci-Ed Innovators has been selected to play a major role in President Obama's program called 100Kin10, to develop a hundred thousand STEM teachers in the coming ten years.

Annual events in memory of their fallen alumna have been instituted at NYU, Castilleja, and Stanford. New York schools and NARST have established science scholarships in her name.

The modern, globally-linked Jhumki Basu Science Education and Research Center, envisaged six years ago by our daughter, is rapidly becoming a reality at NYU. Local, national, and international Science Education programs of the university and the community will be concentrated there.

The Sci-Ed Fellowship Program for immersion of science teachers in democratic pedagogy is in its third year. Fortunately for Radha and me, who are not educators, several graduates of the annual fellowship have stepped up to manage the program. Some of the fellows were students of Jhumki or were her colleagues, but most did not know her.

Kayla Rubin teaches at the Bronx School of Science Inquiry and Investigation. I asked her how the fellowship program has helped her.

"It inspires me to try new things in the classroom," Kayla replied. "Every day is an opportunity to try something new, things that I have never done before. I am learning right along with my kids. There is an amazing bond created between student and teacher when they learn something together."

Kayla feels the Sci-Ed Fellowship Program, for which she raises funds and develops partnerships, has led to a remarkable network and support system among science teachers who understand the struggles and high points that each teacher experiences daily. Most of them have no such support at their own schools.

While talking to the fellows, I wondered whether all this democracy in the classroom might lead to chaos.

"It *is* chaos!" Marc Sole, who set up the fellowship program's collaboration wikispace, agreed. "But it's *constructive* chaos if done right."

Marc, a science teacher from the New Design High School in Manhattan, went on to explain how he gets it done right. "The right way to do it is to come up with a democratic project. This year in my class we looked at bacteria. I gave the students some constraints, like two petri dishes and Q-tips. Whatever they wanted to test for bacteria was up to them. Then it's all about leveraging their motivation. The kids say, 'I want to see which bathroom has more bacteria' and want to compare bacteria in girls' versus boys' bathrooms. I don't have to worry about them misbehaving because they are enjoying doing something they normally wouldn't do!"

"Through Jhumki's influence I am always thinking about what students take away with them in their toolbox of life," says Anna Poole, a teacher at the Bronx High School of Science, and a leader of the Sci-Ed Fellowship program. "How can they contribute? What do they bring to class for it to be a richer experience? I am learning how to implement these ideas through the Sci-Ed program."

Anna explained how others are adopting Jhumki's method for creating change as the Sci-Ed Fellows movement accelerates. "It's hard, but I am convinced if Jhumki could do it, why can't we all do a little bit of it? Jhumki was an extraordinary person. She had energy resources and emotional resources that not everyone has. But we all have *some* of it and can start out by doing it one day a week that is really interactive. And then it becomes apparent that the more democratic teaching one puts into one's curriculum, the easier it becomes."

Anna sees this as she runs workshops for the fellows. Teachers are encouraged to take baby steps in democratic science teaching, and told that the more they practice, the simpler it will become.

"The light-bulbs went off," Anna concluded, "when fellows realized for themselves that they *and* their students would get the best experience out of it. It's not easy. But it's totally worth it. It's at those moments when you feel, as Jhumki told us in our class that night, teaching is a noble career."

What about Jhumki's kids from SDL?

We have already met Donya, Neil, and Gedison.

For Jhumki's memorial event, Mubinya Casey, petite and artistic, presented Radha and me with an oil canvas bearing Jhumki's portrait. She was interested in art early in her life, and at SDL Jhumki helped her get admission to Parsons and Cooper Union to pursue art. After high school, Mubinya enrolled at Hunter College in Manhattan. She is looking forward to running her own art gallery.

Ashtin Charles, a gangly, bespectacled young man with a self-effacing sense of humor and a graduate of Brown University, was unusually (for Crown Heights) focused on excellence in studies from the beginning. Jhumki made him believe he could get into Brown and obtain financial support. There he studied computer science, Japanese, and visual arts, a combination arising from a childhood interest in *anime*. He hopes to tie the three subjects into a graphic-design career creating animation for Japanese video games. Ashtin works as a page on the sets of CBS News and has met Jaime Foxx, Queen Latifah, and Denzel Washington.

Poet-extraordinaire Jordan Franklin, whom Nancy Gannon remembered as a nervous and excruciatingly shy child, has graduated from Brooklyn College. She is looking forward to a earning a master's degree in creative writing. Her output is prolific, and she has written for magazines like *Rolling Stone*.

The list goes on.

Recognizing the durable legacy that she left behind, the Alumni Council of Teachers College, Columbia University will posthumously confer its Early Career Award on Dr. Jhumki Basu on April 13, 2013, during the university's 125th anniversary celebrations. Radha and I, with several well-wishers, will be present to receive the award on her behalf and cheer her on.

Who was the most influential person in Jhumki's life?

For this question I went to the source. Mother knows best.

""The role model for her was Shanti," Radha said. "That I am convinced of. At Carmel Convent, at the memorial for their slain teacher, Jhumki was extremely emotional. All the girls were in tears. Many students and alumni spontaneously told us how Mrs. Chary influenced their lives. One said, 'I hated science, and she made me love it. I am now a physicist.'

"Jhumki came out of the memorial and told me, 'Mommy, teachers change people's lives.' And *that,* I am certain, is the point at which Jhumki became the passionate, dedicated, extraordinary teacher about whom you are writing."

Twenty days after she passed away, while checking her e-mail, Alexander found a message from SensePublishers informing Jhumki that her proposal for a democratic science teaching textbook had been accepted for publication.

Two years after, Jhumki's co-authors fulfilled the promise they made by her deathbed when SensePublishers released *Democratic Science Teaching: Building the Expertise to Empower Low-Income Minority Youth in Science,* edited by Sreyashi Jhumki Basu, Angela Calabrese Barton, and Edna Tan.

"It's all there!" Chris Emdin rejoiced. He has made the book required reading for his students. And it is the foundational reference for the Sci-Ed Fellowship Program.

In March 2010, George Schaller delivered the inaugural lecture of the annual Jhumki Basu Memorial Series, *Science and Adventure,* at Stanford University.

George is a very special person. He is the architect of the Arctic National Wildlife Refuge in Alaska and Project Tiger in India. He has conducted the first studies of big cats in Tanzania and Brazil's Pantanal wetlands. He has spent more time studying habits of the giant panda in China and the Caspian leopard in Iran than at his own home in Connecticut.

At Stanford, with vivid pictures and exciting anecdotes, George illustrated fifty adventure-filled years as a global conservationist.

Jhumki would have been thrilled had she been present.

Also that year, NASA, recognizing Jhumki's ardent desire to become an Educator Astronaut, assigned physicist space-walker, Lee Morin, to keynote the first Sci-Ed Innovators Expo and Symposium in New York. Dr. Morin wowed the hundreds of students and teachers, who were assembled to showcase science projects, with beautiful pictures from outer space.

At the following year's event, renowned primatologist, Jane Goodall, sent a stirring message of hope to twelve hundred young science enthusiasts. During her keynote address, she acknowledged Jhumki's contributions to making science relevant to underprivileged youth. "Jhumki and I would have got on well together," said Dr. Jane, our daughter's lifelong hero.

Jhumki once said:

> *My achievements are entirely due to the ecosystem of staff and students with whom I have been privileged to collaborate.*

Jhumki, your ecosystem has become self-sustaining.

52. THREE ACCOLADES

Stars: Ms. Jhumki Remembered

Hey!

I'm not a muse, God, or the freaking President of the United States. I'm just a kid, you know—a college student, or in economic terms a broke, inexperienced undergraduate. I don't have an amazing speech or a fancy five star play to get you all thinking Shakespeare. All I got are my words—my words and my breaking voice, still tender from tonsillitis.

I'm not a song and dance woman. Believe me, if I were to dance right now, something would break. All I can say is that the best performances are from the heart. In this sense, Ms. Jhumki was the best performer I knew. Everything she did, whether it was teaching a class or advising us fledglings, she always did it with a smile and something akin to the five star treatments at Marriott's.

I know it sounds cheesy but Ms. Jhumki was golden like a nova, and just like that phenomena, her happiness and concern were reborn in the guise of a teary-eyed nebula. Sure there were rough spots—little black holes she couldn't avoid, but like the rest of us everyday joes she was only human. Unlike most of us everydayers however, she did some extraordinary things.

Ms. Jhumki, I can't write you the speech you deserve. All I can do is say the words, but rest assured. Wherever you are now, whether it be heaven, a science lab, or in this very room, I'm sending you all the love I can trap in these lines.

At the end of the day, Ms. Jhumki was a nova—one of those huge ones that ripped the cosmos apart with the colors of a blind man's dream and she was one of those lucky few that became a gorgeous nebula.

We are the stars she left behind.

MISSION TO TEACH

Jordan E. Franklin
Writer and Poet
Former Student of Jhumki Basu

To the Basu Family and Alexander,

I was so deeply sorry to hear of Jhumki's death. She was an extraordinary woman—kind, compassionate and brilliant. In her shortened life, she touched so many people. I am among those who feel genuinely blessed to have known her. She was one of my very best students ever and over the years we became friends. I know that there are no words that can console you at this time. But I do hope that the memories of Jhumki and the knowledge of how she was admired will help.

Please know that I will never forget her and that she will live, vibrantly, in all our hearts.

Condoleezza Rice
Secretary of State
United States of America

"My candle burns at both ends.
It will not last the night.
But ah, my foes, and oh, my friends,
It gives a lovely light."

Everything about Jhumki was luminous.
It began with her glowing countenance,
It radiated from her white-hot energy,
And it shone forth from her glowing heart.

Her light denied the darkness.
She didn't fight death, she simply ignored it.
She was a tsunami of good that rolled over cancer;
A force of nature that swept aside everything but what was most
important:
Her students and colleagues, her mission to teach and build.

Jhumki's aura remains, like the afterglow of sunset.
She will be there, in each of our days, as an incandescence to light a
path to our own fulfillment, as she did in her meteoric life.

"My candle burns at both ends.
It will not last the night.
But ah, my foes, and oh, my friends,
It gives a lovely light."

Dr. Peter Bing
Chairman-Emeritus
Stanford University Board of Trustees
(Quoted stanzas from Edna St. Vincent Millay)

THE END

ACKNOWLEDGMENTS

Journalist Maithreyi Nandakumar's labor of love in tirelessly conducting over a hundred interviews, complete with voice recorder, big headphones and furry microphone, imparted in me self-belief to write this book.

My deep appreciation goes to Shamim Chowdhury for transcribing Maithreyi's extensive interviews; to Kathryn Nicole Clapper for meticulously editing the manuscript and offering many suggestions for improvement; to Shaun Robinson for building the book's website; to Penny Sansevieri and her team for getting it out to you.

"Thanks" is an insufficient word for Maithreyi, Cheryl Klein, Kritika Yegnashankaran, Mary Brabeck, Jai Natarajan, John Moir, and Marianne Allison for their critique of the work. Without their reviews this book would be just an encyclopedia.

For inspiration I looked to the wisdom of Angela Calabrese Barton, Maria Rivera Maulucci, Edna Tan, Jeremy Dodd, James Monohan, Nancy Gannon, and Helen Dole. With great compassion, Condoleezza Rice, Kathleen Morrison, Aza Rakhmanova, and Sapar Kulianov showed me what set Jhumki on her way on the perilous streets of Russia. From the acumen of Stanford professor William Durham, I understood how Jhumki's fervent interest in her fellow creatures developed into a model for teaching science.

I shall never understand how Drs. Clifford Hudis, Robert Carlson, Fred Dirbas, and Ruth Oratz, foster in their desperately ill patients a faith in life. I shall never fathom where they find the grace to battle a ruthless killer every day. My admiration for them is boundless.

NYU professors Susan Kirch, Robert Cohen, Allen Mincer, Jason Blonstein, Catherine Milne, Mary Leou, Pamela Fraser-Abder, and Fabienne Doucet, your academic façade belied your affection for your colleague. You guided and cheered her on her life's mission.

I applaud Donya Locke, Neil Clairmont, Jordan Franklin, Gedison Ashby, Ashtin Charles, Mubinya Casey, Rashida Gibbs and others of the first wave of young Americans to rise from the runway that Ms. Jhumki built, and become respected and responsible citizens. They are the embodiment of her mission to teach.

When Jane Goodall agreed to speak at the second Sci-Ed Innovators' Day in 2011, I felt it was true recognition of Jhumki's life's work. Later, when I asked her to write the foreword for this book and she said yes, my joy knew no bounds. I hope to vindicate the faith placed by so gracious and caring a person.

Our friends and extended family—the list is long and loving—are the bedrock on which Radha and I built our lives with Jhumki. With her gone, they care enough to make sure we get through each day, each month, each year.

Paul, Ambika, Sue. You made her laugh when her spirits hit their lowest point. You made her pain bearable. The video clip of us impersonating rapper M.C. Hammer in a hospital room, while ranged around a young educator undergoing chemotherapy, with an ice pack to numb her needle-lacerated arm, and laughing until her sides hurt, makes us weep.

Ranga, you are the brother she never had. From when, as little kids, you watched *Star Trek* together in Saket, she affectionately called you "doofus." At the toughest of times, you compelled her to witticism. At the happiest of times, you were there, naturally.

Alexander, you gave Jhumki the best years of her life. Never can a human being match the care and love you showered on her, the shining worlds you opened for her, the joy you brought her.

Radha and I have rejoiced as one and suffered as one as we watched our brave daughter pass through this world. We are glad we had her. We are sad we had her. We grieve. We remember fondly. Each day we light a lamp and watch the smoke spiral to our Jhomi, bearing tidings of goodness that follow in her wake.